Kimon Riefenstahl

Kimon's Greek Table

How to cook, cherish and reinvent culinary classics

teNeues

26.9.2023.

In greatest gratitude
I dedicate this book to
my mother and father,
Danai and Otto Riefenstahl.

My greatest gift are my recipes of life to give yours the Best Flavours!

HELLO
6

BREAKFAST
10

HONEY
30

GREEK SALADS
34

MEZE
42

OLIVE OIL
100

PASTA & RICE
102

THE GOD OF WINE
114

MAIN COURSES
116

MEAT
120

THE JOURNEY FROM BOAT TO PLATE
144

FISH & SEAFOOD
146

SOUPS
174

DESSERTS
188

COCKTAILS
210

THE LARDER
222

GOODBYE
232

INDEX
236

IMPRINT
240

Hello

I am Kimon. I am no accomplished chef you look up to by the end of this book. I am not someone to aspire to. I am also no tidy portrayal of myself. Instead I am planted in the same reality as the rest of you, with occasional chaos and messiness. I am accessible. I welcome you to the inner workings of my mind. You might assume that, for the publication of a cookery book, I would have required a professional education, revolutionary recipes or celebrity status. I would agree with you, but then we would both be wrong. What I required was true passion, patience and a bunch of great people who made me feel that I could be great too. I needed the confidence to believe that readers out there would want to hear my story. From me.

So what I wanted to achieve with this book was to let the beauty of what I love be what I do.
I love to create meals together, to linger at the table over some wine, to spend extra time to shop for ingredients and absorb the joys of good recipes.

With this book what I want to do is to push your food horizon, encourage you to test new flavours and collect some of your fondest memories yet to come around a table. With this book I do not want to promote a diet and tell you what to eat. Because a diet is not only about what you eat, it is also about what you read, what you buy and who you surround yourself with. A diet is all the things we put into our bodies physically and emotionally. And I want to inspire you, page by page, to be more mindful of the things you select through my chapters and recipes.

Some recipes are authentic Greek ones, but occasionally I love to break traditional food rules, too.
I used to distinguish between healthy food and delicious food until I found out that once you find a way to cook them right they are one and the same thing: recipes that satisfy my nutritional requirements, taste wonderful and stimulate my creativity. I started to be more purist about the products I stir into my pots and pans and more aware of where my food comes from. I would like to see original products flourish and small farmers and cheese or olive oil producers empowered.

This is what I hoped to write into my book the day when I first had the idea of writing a cookery book many years ago. It progressed rather slowly, but I do not believe in rushing things. I knew it might take a year or even 10. I knew if this book was meant to be, it would find its way eventually when the time was right. And even though my ambitions were belittled frequently, the right time came after all. It came with the right people. Friends, colleagues, fellow passionate cooks and family. On this journey those people tested me, disagreed with me and criticised me. And they taught me, supported me and inspired me. But what they did above all was to bring out the best in me. And that made it all worthwhile.
This book is designed around those people. And around what you'll find inside my kitchen: fun, good food and life. As in yours.
Welcome to the inner workings of my mind.

Πρωινό

BREAKFAST

KALIMERA – GOOD MORNING

I'm a breakfast type of guy.

The best breakfast memories cannot be bought from a store, shuffling along with your mind set on your next appointment, grabbing a coffee to go and a Koulouri in a paper bag. Over the years I have collected some of my happiest moments over breakfast. More are yet to come.

When it comes to breakfast, everybody seems to gravitate to a different side of the broad spectrum which boasts phenomenal sweet and savoury options. My tastes wander backwards and forwards during the week, between cooking up hearty scrambled eggs with chilli flakes, or light Greek yoghurt with honey and bee pollen. Some people barely eat anything at all in the early morning hours. To me, this is always a sad sight. Growing up, I spent most of my childhood at my grandparents' house. My grandmother claimed that joy comes in the morning, and that breakfast was the key to creating a bright day for yourself. It is one of those time-tested bits of advice. Coming of age you often realise that those old wives' tales, the simple bits of folk wisdom usually handed down from generation to generation, are quite often right. Or at least they contain some truth. I would always wake up to the tempting smells of my grandma's breakfast preparations crawling into my room from the kitchen downstairs.

Food is memory. Throughout my life, at home and during my travels, I have collected many impressions and through cooking – our common ground – everybody can taste of my discoveries.

If I could choose, I would start off my Monday with a peaceful morning moment with my parents, no television, little music, only surrounded by the sound of peoples' voices and the rustling of my father's newspaper. Sea view, please. On Tuesday, I would choose a hearty feast with friends, yelling a discussion at one another in a populated café in the vibrant Thessaloniki city centre. I would enjoy the sight of the enormous selection of sweet and savoury bits behind the glass counter and greet all sorts of people walking in and out, engaging me in a quick verbal update on the comings and goings. On Wednesday, I would love to see myself sipping a café au lait at a white pavement table in Paris and practise my French when ordering off a menu I barely understand, trying hard to read whether I just proposed to the waitress or ordered a hard-boiled egg. On Thursday, I would select a small number of people I am fond of and practise my cooking. I would dish up the broadest selection of dishes, from yoghurt to cake to scrambled eggs, along with a steaming Greek coffee. I would serve it all on a beautiful table just next to my herb garden with a gorgeous view over the Aegean Sea. There would be an annoying cat between our feet. On Friday, I wish myself to New York City's vibrant breakfast shops with a friend or two, the coffee smell lingering in the air and some smooth jazz tunes in the background. From my seat at the bar counter I would watch the staff swirling around and the barista producing one steaming cup after another. Once I finished breakfast I would be tempted to just continue sitting right on that very spot and exchange my empty coffee cup for a chilled glass of wine and stay straight on until the lunch hour. For Saturday, I wish the whole of my family upon myself. My family is blessed with truly opinionated women, and discussions would get going in the kitchen while everyone is preparing their ingredients, and would continue knee-deep into the meal. We would dissect everyone's social lives. The young kids would learn things they probably aren't supposed to, relaxing the standards of table behaviour. It would be chaotic and loud and wonderful. On Sunday, I would start off easy. I don't have to get dressed but would be free to experiment on my own and for myself. I would just pull some tomatoes from my fridge, fry an egg and mix it all into some great new dish while playing some of my favourite tunes. I would experiment so long that, eventually, I would end up with too much food and be forced to invite some company after all. But most importantly, I get to stay in my pyjamas and for that I am grateful.

Until now I revealed 'Who is at the table?' and 'Where is that table located?' Time to continue to the third and most important question: 'What is on that table?'

Greek Yoghurt with Honey, Nuts & Bee Pollen

serves 1

I prefer it in the morning. It is the first thing I crave waking up. Right in bed to start off my day perfectly. Or to serve as a snack at any time of day. There are an impossible number of variations, but I personally am sure that the Greek style is the smoothest. I am writing down this recipe in order to guide you on which way works best as to what I have discovered after years of experimenting: plain yoghurt is rather tasteless and one could get bored quite easily. It satisfies you alright but you would not crave more or consider having a second helping. Add some honey, some sweetness. I favour just a little, since I dislike it if this sensation gets too dominant. I know people who would leave it at that. Plain yoghurt plus the sweetness. Just yoghurt and honey. I am more creative than that and I relish adding a few other elements to make it a proper recipe for pleasure. Especially nuts. Again it is a matter of taste but, when having a spoonful, I enjoy suddenly finding a harder bit mixed among the yoghurt and honey. It took me quite some time to discover the benefits of the next ingredient and estimate just the right amount to use, but now I could not imagine life without it: bee pollen is a playful and colourful element. It adds some extra excitement to the yoghurt and eventually makes my recipe different. So now I have made you aware of which ingredients need to be stirred into the yoghurt, you simply need to properly stir them in to a smooth unity. I like to take my time and actually enjoy the moment. It could be a quick takeaway though too, if you must. Yoghurt in whatever variation satisfies and nourishes the body and you should always try to include it in your routine, whenever you feel like it, with no limitations on how and when and where. I have given you the best ingredients; the rest is up to you.

FOR THE GREEK YOGHURT

1½ tsp	pistachio kernels
300g	plain Greek yoghurt
2 tsp	honey
1 tsp	walnuts, crushed
1 tsp	bee pollen
1 tbsp	dried cranberries or raisins

1. Use a mortar to grind the pistachios.

2. Spoon the yoghurt into a bowl and beat for 1-2 minutes with an eggwhisk until fluffy. Now transfer the yoghurt into a serving bowl and drizzle with the honey.

3. Lastly, sprinkle with the pistachios, walnuts, bee pollen and cranberries or raisins.

Farm Egg

serves 1

For a successful start to the day, good breakfast decisions are required. Generally I believe that unsuccessful people make decisions based on their current situation while successful people make decisions based on where they want to be. What happens though if your current situation is to be tucked up in a warm bed but you want to be at the breakfast table? Some days it is easy, but other days you cannot even decide whether you need two litres of coffee, a tight hug or two weeks of sleep. On such a morning, it is better to leave the decision-making to somebody else. To me, in that case. Because my Farm Egg recipe allows you to refrain from deciding on whether you want eggs, ham, cheese, spinach, mushrooms or bread. You take them all. I cannot promise that after a nice plate of Farm Egg the rest of the day will be filled with good decisions. But at least you have already made one good decision that day: Farm Egg.

FOR THE FARM EGG

2	handfuls fresh spinach
	lemon juice
	Greek olive oil
40g	fresh mushrooms, finely diced
50g	ham, finely diced
40g	tomatoes, peeled and diced
	fine sea salt and freshly ground black pepper
1	egg
60g	Gouda cheese, finely diced
1 tsp	chives, finely chopped
	Homemade Croutons (see p. 226)

1. Start with the spinach. In a large pot, bring water to the boil and blanch the spinach for approximately 40 seconds. Set aside and drizzle with lemon juice and olive oil.

2. In a small pot, heat the olive oil and sauté the mushrooms until nicely browned. Stir in the ham and tomatoes. Season with a pinch of salt and stir the ingredients for 1 minute.

3. Meanwhile, heat water in a separate pot. Put the egg into the boiling water and cook for 5 minutes until hard-boiled. Remove the egg with a slotted spoon and peel off the shell.

4. Start arranging the plate for the farm egg from the outside in. Arrange the cheese in a circle on the plate but leave free space in the centre. With a spoon arrange the ham, mushrooms and tomatoes on top of the cheese. Sprinkle chives in the centre of the plate and place the boiled egg on top. Season the egg with a pinch of salt.

5. Lastly, spread the spinach all around the egg, then place the crispy croutons, evenly spaced, on top of the spinach and serve.

Augofetes – Greek Toast

serves 2

FOR THE AUGOFETES

4	eggs
250ml	milk
	orange zest from ½ orange
30g	brown sugar
1 tsp	baking powder
1	vanilla stick, extract
1	pinch of salt
6	slices white bread, cut into strips the width of 1–2 fingers
	sunflower oil, for frying

TO SERVE

	honey, to taste or
3 tsp	ground cinnamon and
100g	caster sugar

1. In a bowl, whisk together the eggs, milk and orange zest. Stir in the brown sugar, baking powder, vanilla extract and pinch of salt. Soak the bread strips in the liquid for 5–10 minutes.

2. For the cinnamon-sugar (if using), mix the cinnamon with caster sugar and stir with a fork. Set aside.

3. In a frying pan, heat the sunflower oil over medium heat. Brown the soaked strips of bread on both sides until golden and then remove them.

4. Either drizzle the bread with the honey or coat it with the sweet cinnamon-sugar blend. Serve either option warm.

Spicy Scrambled Eggs with Feta Cheese

serves 2

I woke up to the cockerel's crow and thought about my breakfast eggs. On that morning I found the chicken coop deserted except for the cockerel by the fence: 'The ladies are inside on strike.' He nodded towards the coop: 'They have joined the feminist movement and are fighting for equal working conditions. They will be on strike until they are allowed to perform the cockerel's duties! But I have always done the wake-up crow! Hens lay eggs, cockerels wake the humans!' Confused, I went to see the ladies. 'Be seated. We wish to renegotiate terms.' Giselle, the chairchick of the coop council, read out their demands. She finished and I lowered my voice: 'But ladies, don't you know that that it is not actually the cock's crow that wakes up humans?' The chickens craned their necks towards me. 'Only the smell of scrambled eggs can do that!' I looked at them meaningfully. 'I am willing to offer you an opportunity to produce eggs in order to wake up the humans: a stable, sustainable workplace.' The proposal was discussed. 'We want extras!' I scratched my chin. 'I can add some cherry tomatoes. Even feta cheese.' 'Chilli?' 'Agreed.' Giselle printed out the new contract, I signed, and left with my breakfast eggs. The next morning, I woke up at around noon. 'May I speak to the cockerel?' I asked when I reached the coop. The hens gave me an innocent look. 'The cockerel is on a mute-strike. He is inside, trying to lay an egg.'

FOR THE SCRAMBLED EGGS

6	eggs
	fine sea salt and freshly ground black pepper
10	cherry tomatoes, halved
	Greek olive oil, for frying
1	spring onion, white part, finely chopped
1 tsp	fresh dill, finely chopped
100g	feta cheese
	dried red chilli flakes

1. Crack the eggs into a bowl and use a whisk to beat them until foamy. Season with one pinch of salt and pepper. Sprinkle the halved cherry tomatoes with salt.

2. Heat a generous amount of olive oil in a pan over medium heat. Sauté the cherry tomatoes and spring onion until they have softened. Now add the eggs to the pan without stirring for several seconds. Then stir thoroughly with a wooden spoon, and interrupt again for a few seconds. Repeat until the eggs are softly set and slightly runny in places. Add in dill, then crumble in the feta cheese before giving it all a final good stir.

3. Sprinkle the golden scrambled eggs with chilli flakes as preferred and serve with salt and black pepper on the side.

Original Thessaloniki Koulouri

serves 8

Greeks are classy men, and the ones from the city of Thessaloniki pursue a well-rounded lifestyle: they indulge in well-rounded events and round-table dinners with several rounds of drinks. Naturally, they follow a well-rounded diet, which makes my perfect nutrient-packed snack the traditional circular bread named Koulouri Thessalonikis! Time for a story-go-round: the Koulouri is appreciated for its nutritional value, simplicity of taste and ease of preparation. The origins of the classic Thessaloniki Koulouri lie in the history of the city, beginning in the period of the Byzantine Empire. It was sold early in the morning by street vendors with baskets on their heads. As the centuries went on, it gained popularity all around Greece and in Thessaloniki, its city of origin. You will still find it on every corner, at public places and monuments. For instance, all around the Rotunda, a monument which got its name from – who would have guessed – its massive round structure. So to round up the story: Thessaloniki's sesame-seed Koulouri has stayed in the Greeks' hearts as one of the most beloved traditional Greek bread products, and its recipe is often kept secret. Nevertheless, I, a well-rounded guy, am willing to step out of the circle and spread it around the globe!

1. For the crust, pour the boiling water into a heat-resistant bowl. Use a whisk to stir in the flour. Add the cold water and the sesame oil to the bowl and, lastly, drizzle in the honey. Once the ingredients are whisked together, transfer the liquid to a baking tin and set aside.

2. Cover the bottom of a deep bowl with sesame seeds. Also set aside before proceeding with the dough.

3. To make the dough, preheat the oven to 200°C and cover a baking tray with baking parchment. Into a large bowl add flour, cold water, yeast, olive oil, tahini or sesame paste, sugar and salt. Use an electric mixer on medium speed to combine the ingredients for 3–4 minutes, then switch to high speed and continue mixing for another 5–6 minutes, until the texture is smooth.

4. Cut the dough into chunks weighing about 100g each. Use your hands to shape each of the chunks into rolls approximately 30cm long and shape these into rings.

5. Now coat the Koulouri rings: Dip each of the rings in the crust mixture, then both sides into the sesame seeds. Transfer the Koulouri to the baking tray and allow them to bake in the oven for 10–15 minutes.

6. Once baked, the Koulouri rings take on a light brown colour and crispy texture. Let them cool for 10 minutes before serving. Enjoy plain with coffee or warm with cream cheese.

FOR THE CRUST

150ml	boiling water
20g	plain flour
150ml	cold water
20g	sesame oil
30g	honey
4	handfuls sesame seeds

FOR THE DOUGH

720g	plain flour
420ml	cold water
20g	fresh yeast
30ml	Greek olive oil
60g	Greek tahini or sesame paste
45g	granulated sugar
15g	fine sea salt

Marble Cake

serves 4

Greece remains trapped in a labyrinth of rugged paths, searching for a way out. Some passageways seem unending, the journey is full of countless wrong turns and sometimes, when the exit appears to be near, the country finds itself back at the very spot where it started. The world sees a shadow over Greece, a shadow cast by the high hedges of the maze and a place that in many ways is lost. Yet I live here, and when I step out in the morning, the sunshine falls onto my face and the beauty of nature seems to drip down in thick, sweet drops from every leaf like morning dew. I cannot help but feel that Greece is the sweetest land of all: rich in more ways than it is poor in others. And while I enjoy the warming rays tickling my face, I know well that I will applaud you, my homeland, in the bright times, and I will sit with you in the dark times, and I accept you as a blend of both: a dark batter and a light batter. But no matter how often the world believed you were turning completely dark, I stand here and watch you begin again at every sunrise, lighting up a new, flawless morning.

FOR THE CAKE

	butter for greasing
250g	butter, softened
250g	granulated sugar
300g	plain flour
5	medium eggs
5g	baking powder
1	pinch of vanilla sugar
	cocoa powder
	dark chocolate curls, to decorate

FOR THE COATING

1	egg yolk

DISH

Baking dish: rectangular 25 x 10 cm

1. Preheat the oven to 180°C and grease the loaf tin.

2. For the batter, combine the butter, sugar, flour, eggs, baking powder and vanilla sugar in a mixing bowl. Beat slowly with an electric mixer to combine, then at medium speed for about 2 minutes until you have a smooth batter.

3. Transfer half of the batter to the prepared baking tin and set aside. Stir the cocoa powder into the reserved batter until it takes on a deep chocolatey colour. Pour the mixture into the baking tin on top of the vanilla layer. Using a knife, swirl the cocoa batter into the vanilla batter to create a marble effect.

4. Before baking the cake in the oven, use a fork to beat the egg yolk in a separate bowl until foamy. With a brush, gently dab the surface of the cake with the mixture, which will result in a shiny surface once baked. Bake in the oven for approximately 40 minutes. When cool, sprinkle the top with dark chocolate curls.

Traditional Village Spinach & Cheese Pie

8 pieces

'So, exactly what is it that I need for a pie to taste as good as yours?' 'A lifetime of experience', and the tiny lady's face lit up with a proud smile as her aged hands moved with an incredible speed, kneading the dough. 'You could have had a career as pie-maker!' 'I did!' She laughed a croaky laugh. 'Along with a career as a leading politician, teacher, gentle paramedic and the many other professions required in this house when raising a family. But indeed, pie-maker was my most recognised position.' She laughed again. We continued making the pie and I thought about the many opportunities the women of new generations have, being able to travel abroad, receive a formal education, free to live the lives they choose. 'I was born in this small village, learnt young how to maintain a home … I barely ever left the place, got married, had my children and raised them in this house. Then my grandchildren came and before I knew it I had grown old and wrinkly', she laughed again. I paid her a regretful glance. 'I guess women should consider themselves lucky. Such a life has become quite rare. You know what I mean, having spent your life in this house, devoting it to your children and finding yourself grow old just like that …' She looked at me, thinking intensely: 'How right you are!' Her face lit up: 'Sometimes I forget how lucky I am! For it is a privilege denied to many.'

TIPS FOR THE FLOUR

The flour will determine the taste of the crust. Durum wheat flour is ideal, but alternatively I suggest Thebes flour with cornmeal or lemon flour for ease of kneading.

You may also make a 1:3 flour mix with rye, barley, oats, corn or wholemeal flour depending on the preferred flavour.

TIPS FOR CRISPNESS

Mix the flour with olive oil and rub it between your hands, drizzle with water and leave to stand.
The longer you leave it to stand, the crispier the texture will be once baked.
When layering the sheets, press each one gently to allow heat to escape once filled.

FOR THE FILLING

1kg	spinach, cleaned, drained and chopped
1	onion, grated or finely chopped
5	leeks, thinly sliced
10	spring onions with leaves, thinly sliced
	fine sea salt and freshly ground pepper
1	bunch fresh dill, chopped
220g	trachana (fermented grains and yoghurt)
450g	feta cheese, crumbled
2	eggs
200ml	condensed milk
220ml	Greek olive oil
70ml	water
	Greek olive oil, for greasing

FOR THE DOUGH

1	packet of filo pastry or 6 sheets of homemade filo pastry
110ml	Greek olive oil

DISH

Large baking dish: square 40 x 42cm
round 36cm diameter

1. Start with the filling. Use a mortar to grind the spinach leaves in a bowl until mushy. Add in the fresh onion, leek, spring onions and their leaves. Season with a pinch of salt and pepper. By hand, combine the ingredients and rub them between your palms for about 1–2 minutes. Add in the dill. Now mix in the trachana and feta cheese and again combine the ingredients by hand.

2. Crack the eggs into a small bowl and mix in the condensed milk and the olive oil. Reserve half the mixture and set aside. Pour the rest into the vegetable mixture and give it all a gentle toss to combine.

3. Drizzle approximately 50ml water into the reserved liquid to dilute the mixture a little. Brush a generous amount of olive oil onto the bottom of the large baking dish until thoroughly greased.

4. Continue by layering the pie. Place firstly a sheet of filo pastry into the dish and gently press it into the sides with your fingertips. The sides may overlap the edges of the dish. Moisten the pastry by spraying or brushing a small amount of the diluted egg mixture all over the surface of the pastry.

5. Proceed with the second layer by placing another two sheets of pastry on top. Sprinkle with some olive oil in between as well as on top of the sheets. Again moisten with the diluted egg mixture and finally spoon the filling on top.

6. Cover with another layer of three sheets of pastry. They should be adjusted to the size of the dish and not overlap its edges. Layer the overlapping sheets over the surface and moisten with the remaining egg mixture. Preheat the oven to 180°C.

7. With the tip of a knife, mark the pie into pieces and drizzle with olive oil. Transfer the baking dish into the oven and bake for 60 minutes, until crispy. Cut into pieces and serve hot.

8. Optional serving suggestion: for a more intense flavour, season the pie with fresh mint, parsley, myrrh, wild mountain Angelica or stamnagathi if desired.

HONEY

If humans were raised like bees, we would make life blossom every day.

If I was raised like a bee, I would have probably grown up in the area of Sithonia. In Nikiti, a small town close to my home, because it hosts more than 85,000 bee hives and has one of the biggest bee populations in Europe. I did grow up in this area, but that is about the only thing I have in common with a bee. On a warm summer morning when I enjoy my breakfast on the terrace, I admittedly find their buzzing presence quite irritating. But what would some of our breakfast dishes taste like if we did not have honey to sweeten them with? What would we stir into our milk and teas to cure our sore throats if it was not for honey? Apart from honey, the bees gift us bee pollen, propolis and royal jelly. No human could ever reproduce any of these health-boosting products; neither can we reproduce anything else that bees do. Because bees have unravelled the mystery of how to make life sweet: they make it blossom every day.

If humans were raised like bees, we would be the most honourable creatures on the planet. Not for labouring hard, but for labouring hard for others. We would share the results of our work without expecting or getting anything in return. If humans were raised like bees we would not feel that our daily acts and efforts do not make a difference and get discouraged from carrying out our duties. If humans were raised like bees we would cherish the fact that even the most minimal product of each one of us contributes to a great result. We would never be on our own. If we were raised like bees we would work together as a team, each of us committed to preserve the home, the family and nature. We would instinctively know that life is sweeter when shared. And no matter how far we would fly out, we would always come home. Everybody would look the same, we would sip life's sweet nectar and preserve the planet. Every day. Without limits and without impossibilities. Scientifically it is impossible for a bumble bee to fly. But the bumble bee doesn't know it can't — so it goes on flying anyway. Couldn't we?

Χωριάτικη σαλάτα

GREEK SALADS

GREEK SALADS

There are plenty of salad recipes out there but I love only Greek Salad. I love the Traditional one, as it is pure yet not flawless. I love the Bohemian one, as it is substantial yet not excessive. I love the Gastronomic one, as it is beautiful yet not indestructible.

Greek Salad is pure, substantial and beautiful; just as nature is pure, substantial and beautiful.

I love my daily walks through my vegetable garden, my daily sea view over emerald waters, my daily full plate of ripe tomatoes, cucumbers, and the intense green of the thick olive oil. Day after day I have a full plate of this colourful, rich salad on my table. Once the bottom of the plate is reached, I soak pieces of bread in the salty residue of olive oil and tomato juice and swipe up the last fragments of feta. Day after day, I love the comfort of knowing that I will be able to absorb the same joys again tomorrow. The salad is also my daily gentle reminder that nature is pure, substantial and beautiful yet not flawless, not excessive nor indestructible. A reminder that one day there will not be another full plate on my table. That one day, the last drop of oil has been absorbed.

Traditional Greek Salad

serves 2

❖

FOR THE SALAD

2	large tomatoes, cut into wedges
	fine sea salt
1	small, red onion, finely sliced
½	cucumber, peeled and roughly chopped
¼	red pepper, sliced
¼	yellow pepper, sliced
	Greek olive oil
1 tbsp	capers
1 tbsp	caper leaves
1	handful of black olives
1 tsp	fresh oregano, finely chopped
100g	feta cheese, crumbled

1. First, drain the tomato wedges by sprinkling them with sea salt and allowing them to sit for 10 minutes.

2. Meanwhile, continue with the rest of the ingredients. In a separate bowl, mix onion, cucumber, red and yellow peppers by hand.

3. Add the drained tomato wedges into the salad. Drizzle olive oil on top as preferred. Add capers, caper leaves and olives and give it all a very gentle toss to mix.

4. Lastly, sprinkle with oregano and crumble the feta cheese on top. Serve the colourful salad with toasted white bread.

Bohemian Greek Salad

serves 2

FOR THE SALAD

1	cucumber, peeled
1	red onion, finely chopped
1	green pepper, cut into strips
1	spring onion, finely chopped
1	handful of black olives, pitted and halved
1 tsp	capers
	Greek olive oil
2 tsp	white balsamic vinegar
	fine sea salt
	fresh basil, finely chopped
10	cherry tomatoes, halved
	Katiki Domokou curd cheese

1. Firstly, use a spiraliser or julienne cutter to grate the cucumber into spiral strings and toss them into a serving bowl.

2. Add onion, green pepper, spring onion, olives and capers into the bowl. Shower all with olive oil as preferred and, lastly, sprinkle with 1 teaspoon white balsamic vinegar. Season with salt, then set aside.

3. In a kitchen bowl, thoroughly mix little olive oil with basil, 1 teaspoon white balsamico and salt, then toss in the halved cherry tomatoes. Mix by hand until the tomato halves are fully covered with the marinade. Add them to the rest of the salad.

4. Lastly, spoon the creamy curd cheese on top of the Bohemian Greek Salad and serve with toasted white bread.

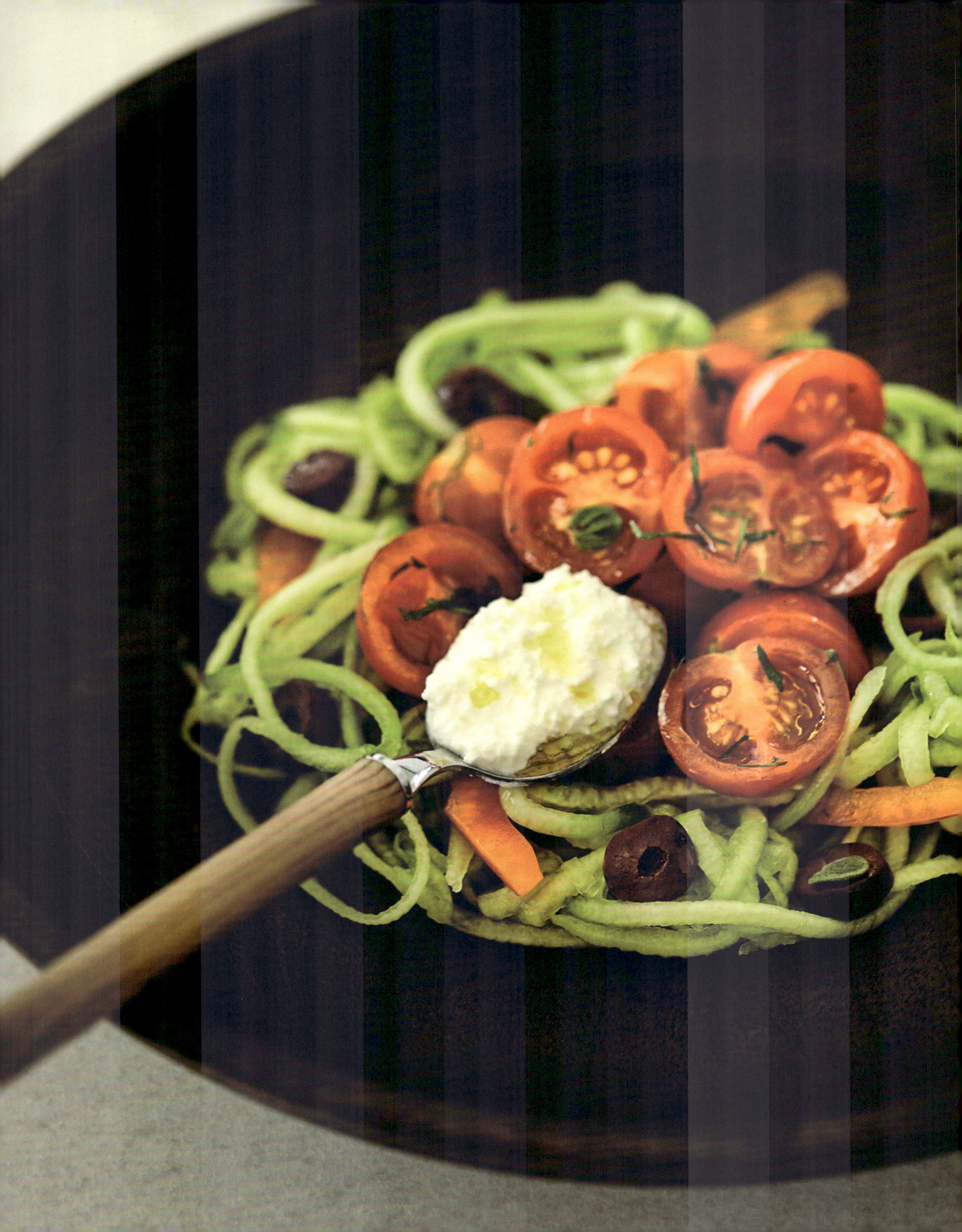

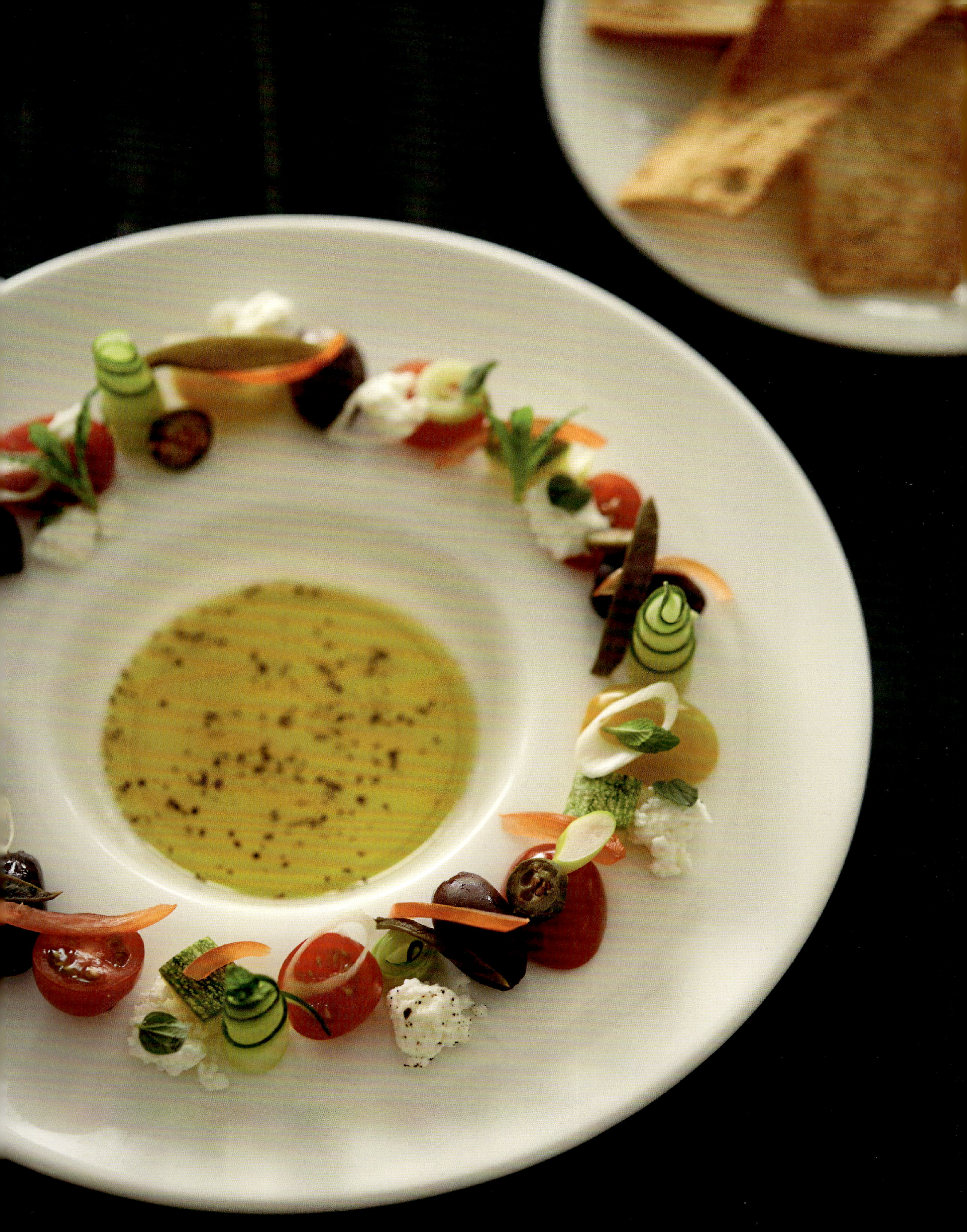

Gastronomic Greek Salad

serves 2

DISH

Bowl with a wide rim

FOR THE SALAD

1	handful Santorini cherry tomatoes, halved
½	cucumber, unpeeled and thinly sliced
1	red onion, finely sliced
¼	red pepper, sliced
¼	yellow pepper, sliced
100g	feta cheese, diced
4	black olives, pitted and halved
1 tsp	capers
1 tsp	caper leaves
	Greek olive oil
1 tsp	fresh oregano
	fine sea salt

1. First, place the halved cherry tomatoes equally spaced around the rim of the bowl. Roll the cucumber slices artfully into cylinder shapes and place alongside the cherry tomatoes.

2. Arrange the onion, red and yellow peppers, feta cheese, olives, capers and caper leaves in between the cucumbers and tomatoes around the rim.

3. Pour a generous amount of olive oil into the centre of the bowl and sprinkle with oregano and a pinch of sea salt.

4. To eat, gently push the colourful ingredients from the rim into the olive oil and enjoy with toasted white bread.

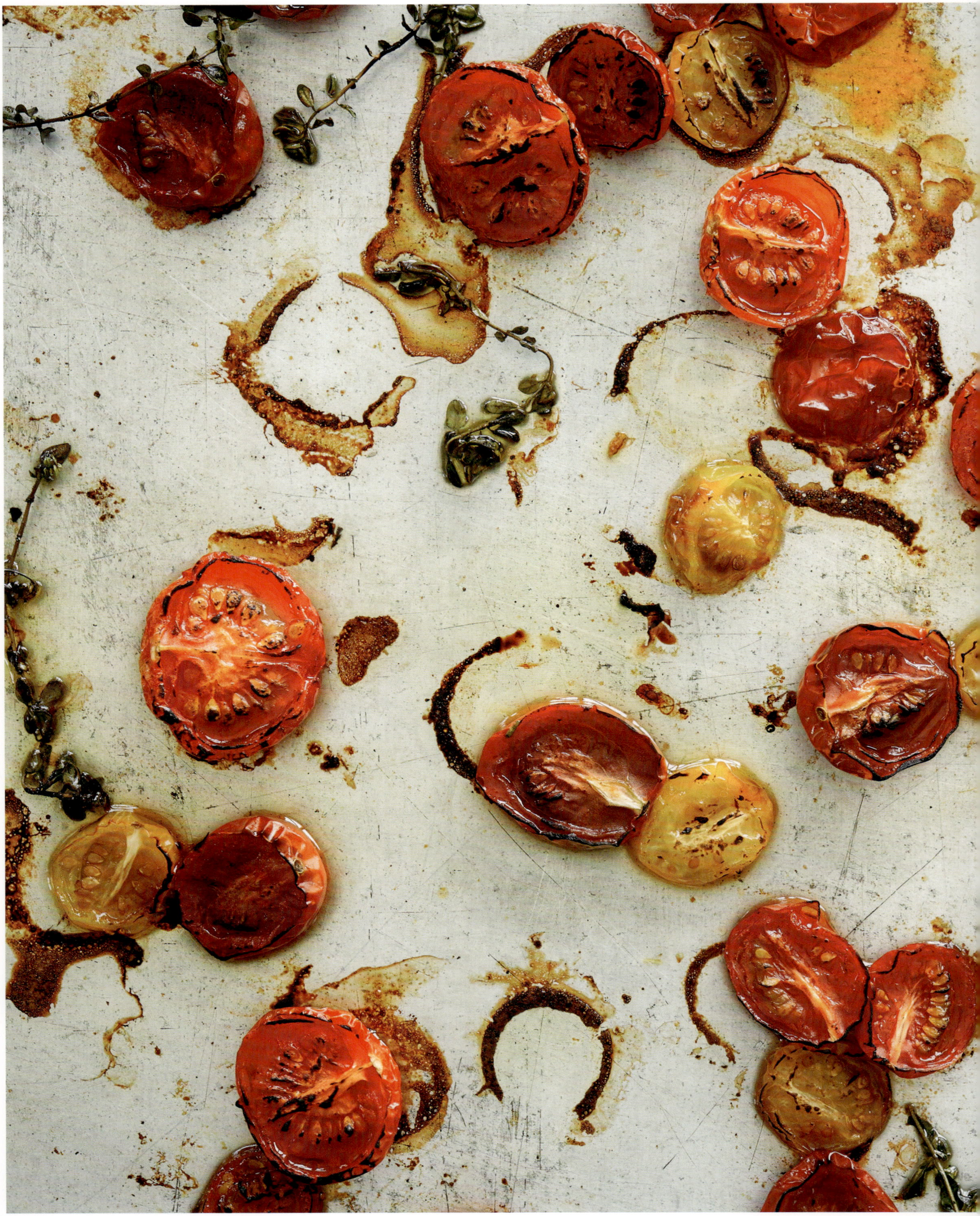

Μεζές

MEZE

MEZE MEANS FRIENDSHIP

Sometimes people sit down for an ordinary get-together at a table and share some dishes and a pleasant time. But sometimes people sit down for a get-together that could never be described as ordinary, on a table that is their favourite place to be. They share small dishes that day, but share friendship every day. That is a meze.

A proper meze must be authentic, fun and rich in small things contributed by everyone gathered around the table. Of the many plates some have to be a variety of light dips. Dips are like quality conversations. Maybe the very first attempt in making one is a little challenging, but then the recipe comes to you naturally. Some are spicy others are sweet, but generally there must be lots of different dips with different flavours, none like the other. All are served and eaten with bread. Bread is a symbol for sharing. Instead of serving your own plate, the atmosphere is nourished by everybody dipping their piece of bread into every bowl, helping themselves and trying every single one of them. Dips make your meze fun.

They are usually followed by few vegetable dishes. Not everybody is a great fan of vegetables but at the same time you would not want to avoid them. Eventually you even enjoy them if prepared the right way. Vegetables are like discussions. They contribute to the meze with their nutrients, they are healthy, interesting and diverse, the small aspects that nourish your body or mind. Every good meze needs a few vegetable dishes to make it interesting.

The next addition to the table is something pure and original, preferably fried calamari or fish. These represent authenticity. Because these dishes need to be served the way they are with all their flaws and details, their dark bits and light bits, loved for their originality, neither decorated nor beautified. If the people at your table are not too picky, flaws will be accepted and beloved the way they come.

Always serve a good portion of a colourful, simple Greek Salad. Fresh and uncomplicated, easy and light, the salad bowl is often the centre of the entire meze.

Not everyone at your table will stay all the way through. Some might leave earlier than expected. Others will temporarily be gone and rejoin the table at another point in time. Some might leave the table unexpectedly perhaps because they enjoyed the meze, but joined somebody else's table, or simply shifted their priority. It might take some courage to accept their sudden departure, but acceptance will finally be better than trying to convince somebody to stay seated. The distance between your chairs will grow wider apart and eventually the picture won't resemble the meze you started with. But as long as you have a few people around the table, who sit close to you, all the way through, tasting all the dishes even if they are not their absolute favourites, then you have what I consider a real meze. A real friendship. And I have.

Original Greek Tzatziki

serves 6

———※———

Tzatziki is the heart of Greek cuisine. It's the ever-present dish in a Greek's life made of all the things we love to eat. Tzatziki is the bouzouki playing a traditional song. It's as Greek as a group of friends dancing the sirtaki. And it's as Greek as ouzo and an important part of our culture's hospitality. The recipe has been passed down the generations just like the plate is passed around the table. Sharing a bowl of Tzatziki is like sharing our greatest passions — passion for food, passion for music and passion for friendship.

FOR THE TZATZIKI

1	cucumber
15g	fine sea salt
1kg	plain Greek yoghurt
2	garlic cloves, grated
1	bunch fresh dill, chopped
¼	bunch fresh mint, chopped
20ml	ouzo
1	pinch of white pepper
100ml	Greek olive oil
	toasted pita bread, to serve

1. Use a coarse grater to grate the unpeeled cucumber. Season with salt and set aside to drain the liquid.

2. Mix the yoghurt with the garlic, dill, mint, ouzo, white pepper and olive oil. Combine thoroughly by hand. Season to taste with salt.

3. Squeeze the grated cucumber with your hands to let all remaining liquid escape. Then stir it into the rest of the ingredients and mix with a wooden spoon until you get a creamy Tzatziki.

4. Serve with toasted pita bread.

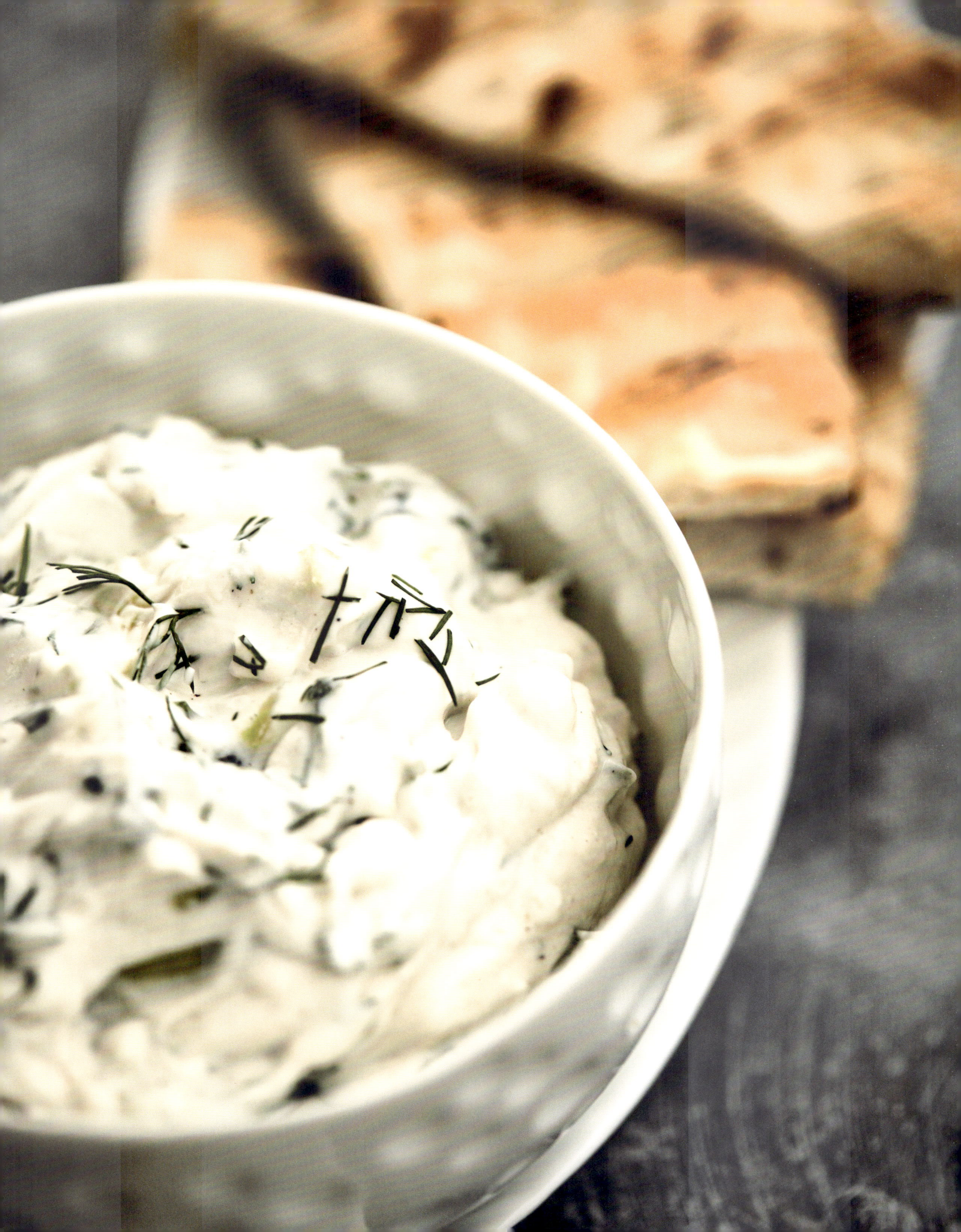

Goat Cheese Coins with Sweet Tomato Marmalade

serves 2

———※———

How often do you encounter a recipe so desirable but also so simple to get to know? I discovered this one while trying to find a way to preserve my cherry tomatoes. I enjoy harvesting tomatoes, which are surprisingly easy to grow, from my own small garden. Even a single plant would bear a crop of juicy fruits throughout the summer months. I have eight. I pick my tomatoes all season long, even on the very hot days of the Greek summer, and I am determined to not let even one of my bite-sized tomatoes go to waste. While picking them, I get excited over what to do with them later, and tomatoes just give you plenty of flexibility. Experimenting over and over again, pairing a homemade sweet marmalade with crispy cheese ended up being one of my absolute favourite starters of all time – simple yet purely delicious.

FOR THE MARMALADE

100ml	water
200g	granulated sugar
200g	cherry tomatoes, halved
2	cinnamon sticks
4	drops lemon juice
20g	unsalted butter

FOR THE GOAT CHEESE COINS

1	large egg
25g	ground almonds
25g	ground pistachios
50g	crushed cornflakes
	water
	plain flour for coating
100g	goat cheese, sliced into coins
	vegetable oil, for deep-frying

1. Start with the marmalade. In a small pot over medium heat, combine the water, sugar, cherry tomato halves and, lastly, add the cinnamon sticks. Bring to the boil and reduce the temperature to low before allowing the marmalade to simmer for 20 minutes. From time to time use a small soup ladle to remove any foam that rises to the top.

2. Flavour with the lemon juice and let the butter dissolve inside the pot. Allow the marmalade to simmer for another 4 minutes before removing from the heat. Discard the cinnamon sticks.

3. Continue with the breading for the goat cheese coins. Crack the egg into a bowl and use a fork to beat it until foamy. In a separate bowl mix the ground almonds and pistachios with the crushed cornflakes.

4. Start breading the goat cheese coins. Have four bowls ready for this process — the first bowl containing water; the second bowl flour; the third bowl the foamy egg; and the fourth bowl the nuts and cornflakes mixture.

5. Bread the goat cheese coins in the above listed order: first, dip them one by one into water, then coat with the flour, next dip them into the egg and, lastly, coat with the nuts and cornflakes.

6. In a small pot heat vegetable oil over high heat. Test whether the oil is hot enough by tossing in a small piece of bread: if it sizzles, the oil is ready. Deep-fry the cheese coins until crispy for about 2 minutes on each side. Remove with a slotted spoon.

7. Serve warm, each coin topped with a dollop of the sweet tomato marmalade.

Spetsofai – Greek Farmer's Stew

serves 4

FOR THE SPETSOFAI

7	green peppers
	Greek olive oil, for frying
	sunflower oil, for frying
3	aubergines, sliced
800g	Greek farmer's sausage, roughly sliced
2	garlic cloves, finely chopped
1	white onion, finely chopped
½	spicy pepper, sliced
1½ tsp	passata
1 tsp	tomato purée
2 tsp	fresh mint, finely chopped
3 tsp	fine sea salt
2 tsp	freshly ground black pepper
	dried red chilli flakes

1. Start with the peppers. In a pan over medium heat, brown the whole peppers in olive oil. Remove from the heat and peel while still warm, then cut into rough chunks. Discard the seeds and stem.

2. In a separate pan, heat sunflower oil over medium heat and sauté the aubergine slices until softened. Remove and pat dry with paper towels. Cut into bite-sized chunks.

3. In a third pan over medium heat, brown the sausages along with garlic and onion in sunflower oil. Stir in the spicy pepper and the passata and tomato purée. Then add the softened aubergine slices and pepper chunks. Leave to simmer for 4–5 minutes, then season with the mint, salt and pepper.

4. Lastly, stir the Spetsofai thoroughly and season with chilli flakes to taste.

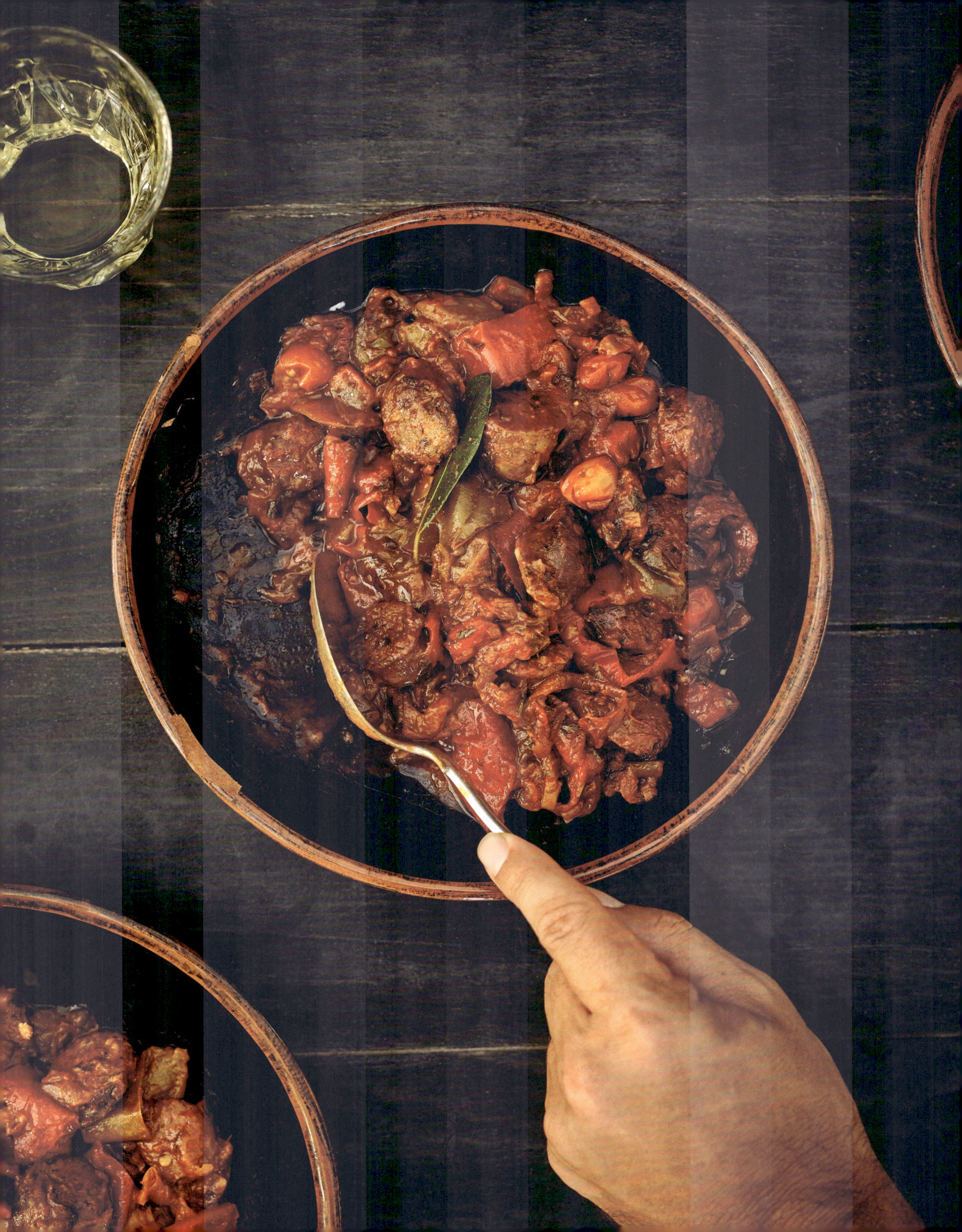

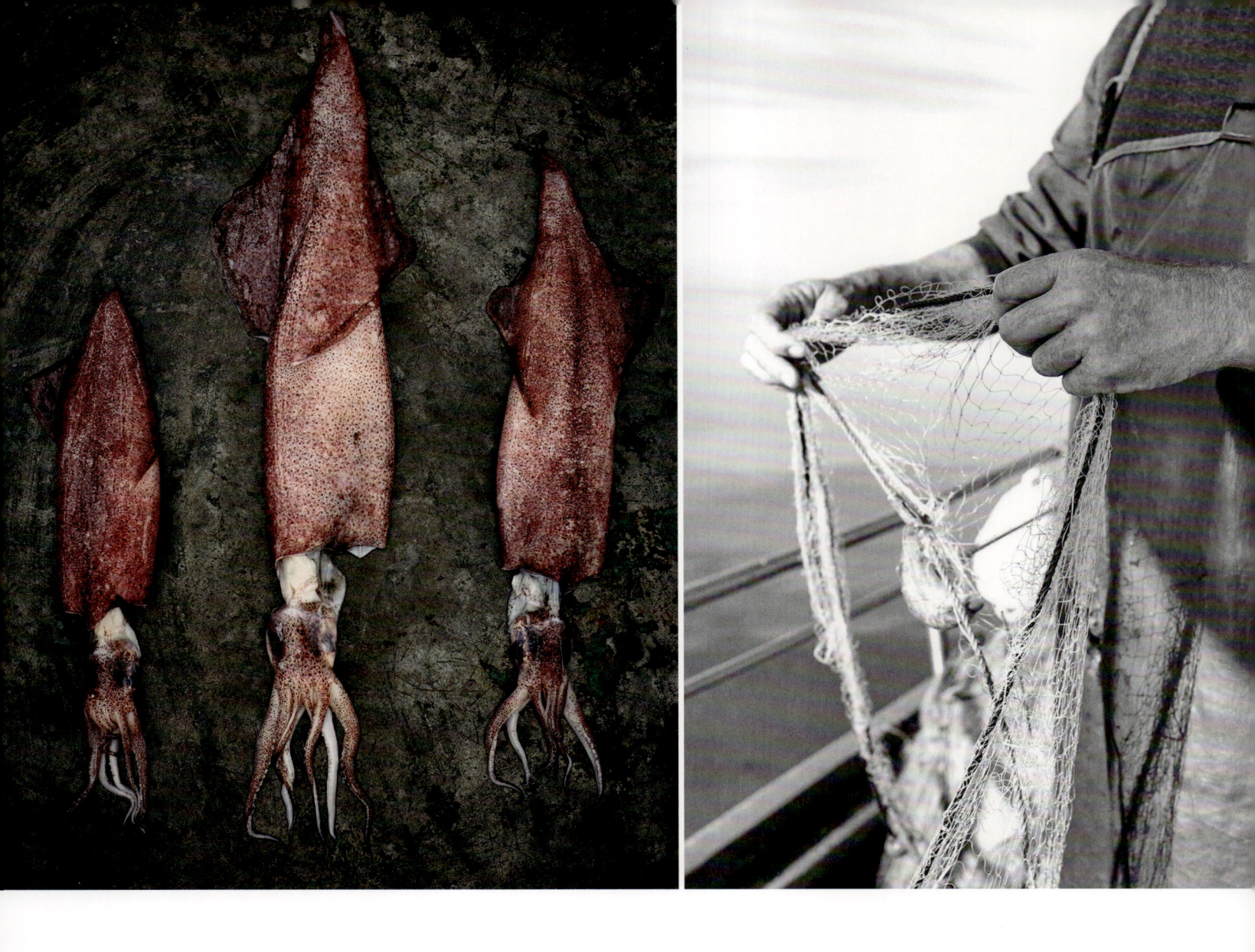

Crispy Deep-fried Calamari

serves 2

The Greeks agree that almost the best moment of life by the sea is when you feel your bare feet touch the soft sand and the clear sea sends a gentle wave onto your toes alongside a cold sensation to tickle through the body. Then again, all Greeks agree, that the other almost-the-best moment is when you then look up towards the horizon and the orange of the sun appears to melt into the sea, adding shades of gold into the otherwise deep blue colour. But all this is nothing compared to the sound of music composed of the percussions of the waves and songs of the seagulls, which to absolutely all Greeks is almost the best moment. But to take a deep breath and smell the clean air as one soaks in the aroma of salt, wind, seaweed and the invigorating freshness of seawater is undoubtedly, for every single Greek I know, the by-far-almost-the-best moment. I agree with this as I lift my fork to my mouth. Like all Greeks do, I humbly shut all my senses to everything around me. And take a first bite.

FOR THE DIP (OPTIONAL)

30g	pine nuts
70g	fresh basil, finely chopped
2	garlic cloves, finely chopped
2 tsp	Parmesan cheese, grated
8 tsp	Greek olive oil
1 tsp	white balsamic vinegar, plus extra to taste
	fine sea salt and freshly ground black pepper

FOR THE CALAMARI

500g	calamari
2 tsp	fine sea salt
	plain flour for coating
	water
	sunflower oil, for deep-frying
	lemon, to serve

1. Make the dip. In a pan over medium heat, roast the pine nuts without any oil.

2. Transfer the basil, garlic, Parmesan cheese and roasted pine nuts to a blender. Blend on high speed for approximately 1 minute before adding the olive oil and balsamic vinegar. Continue blending until you have a smooth dip. Season to taste with salt, pepper and extra balsamic vinegar. Set aside.

3. Now continue with the calamari. Clean the calamari thoroughly under running water. Use a sharp knife to cut the calamari into approximately 1 cm wide rings. Season with salt.

4. Have two bowls ready for the coating, one containing the flour and the other containing water. Coat the sliced calamari firstly in flour, then dip each one into water and set aside.

5. Into a medium-sized frying pan, pour enough sunflower oil to deep-fry the calamari rings, or use a deep fat fryer. Heat the oil to medium-high heat and test if the oil is hot by dipping one of the calamari rings into it. If it sizzles the oil is hot enough. Deep-fry until golden and crispy.

6. Remove the calamari using a slotted spoon and pat dry on paper towels. Serve hot with a squeeze of a lemon and the aromatic dip.

Red Pepper Paste

serves 2

With a spring clean, a house awakes after the winter, almost no different to a hibernating mammal. Clearing dust from the edges of each room is like brushing sleep out of the eye, blinking in the blinding rays of sun streaming through the open windows and yawning at the clean air flooding the parquet. As the light streams through the corridors and crawls up the walls I found spring was the most accomplished architect, for I could tell my house was not the same that day when it took a deep breath at the joy of new life. I meanwhile opened each drawer and found several treasures in them that were forgotten, misplaced or that had just never reminded me that they were there: glass was clinking when I went through a number of old red wine bottles and suddenly I held a small glass container which, too, had slept for quite long in the back of a dark drawer like a ripening vintage wine. I woke it by popping its lid and took a taste of its flowery bouquet, its rich blend of warming spices and a sharp chilli note to tickle my tongue. A little jar of red pepper paste popped open like a spring flower, melted in my mouth like the last bits of snow and just then I realised how dearly I had missed spring, how lovely its taste, and spoonful after spoonful I was eating it all like a hearty breakfast after a long winter's sleep.

FOR THE RED PEPPER PASTE

2 tsp	Greek olive oil, for frying
1	garlic clove, peeled
1kg	red peppers
1 tsp	paprika
1 tsp	dried red chilli flakes
2	pinches of fine sea salt
1	pinch of freshly ground black pepper
2 tsp	balsamic vinegar
100g	feta cheese, crumbled
	toasted white bread, to serve

1. In a pan, heat the olive oil over medium heat. Stir in the garlic and whole red peppers. Sweat the vegetables until softened and flip the peppers occasionally to ensure they brown on all sides.

2. Peel and core the peppers while still warm. Toss the flesh into a blender or food processor along with the sautéed garlic, paprika, olive oil and chilli flakes and mix on medium speed into a uniform paste.

3. Now season the paste with the salt, pepper and vinegar. Lastly, add the crumbled feta before mixing once more on medium speed to combine the ingredients until velvety.

4. Enjoy as a flavourful spread on toasted white bread. Preserve in an airtight jar.

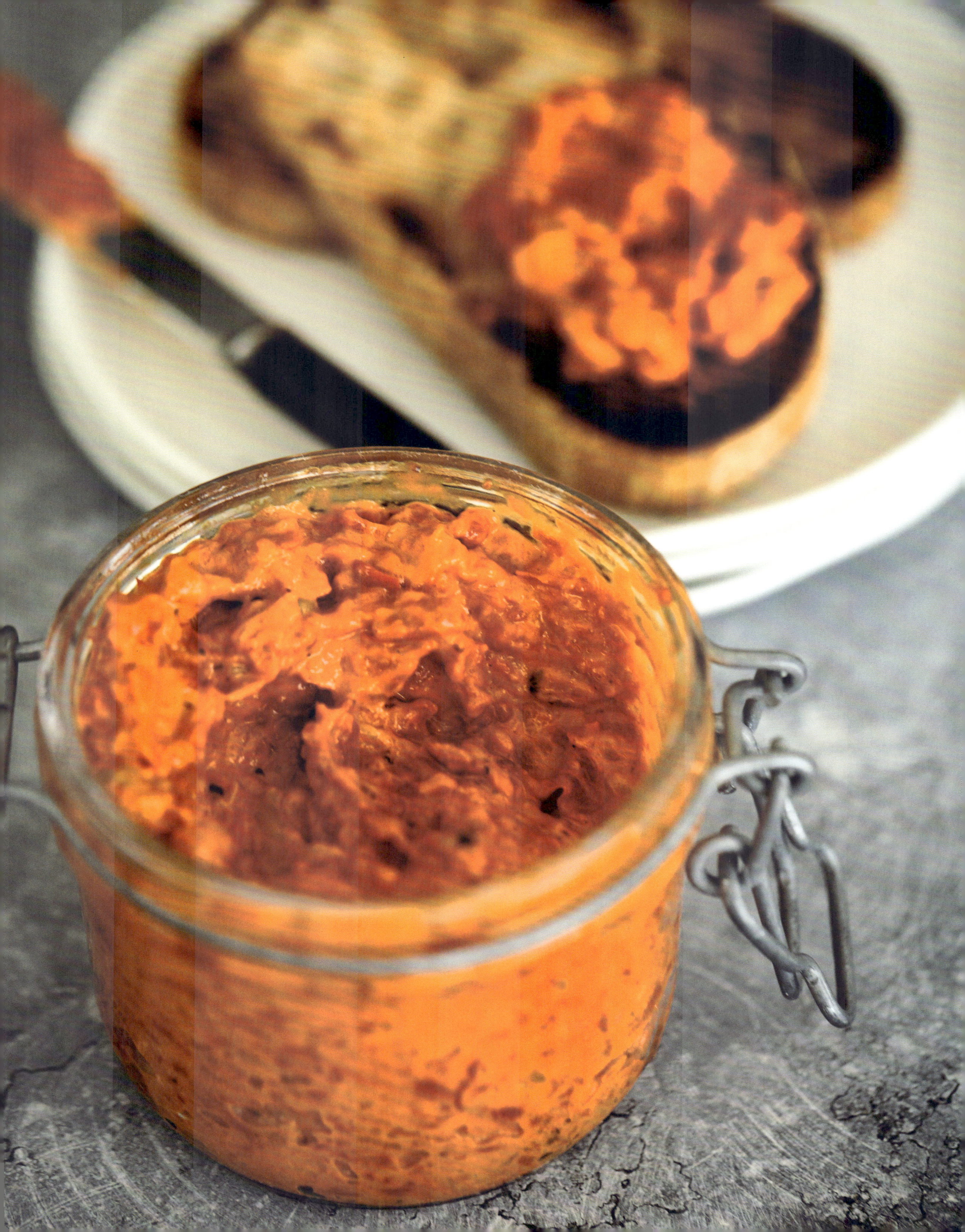

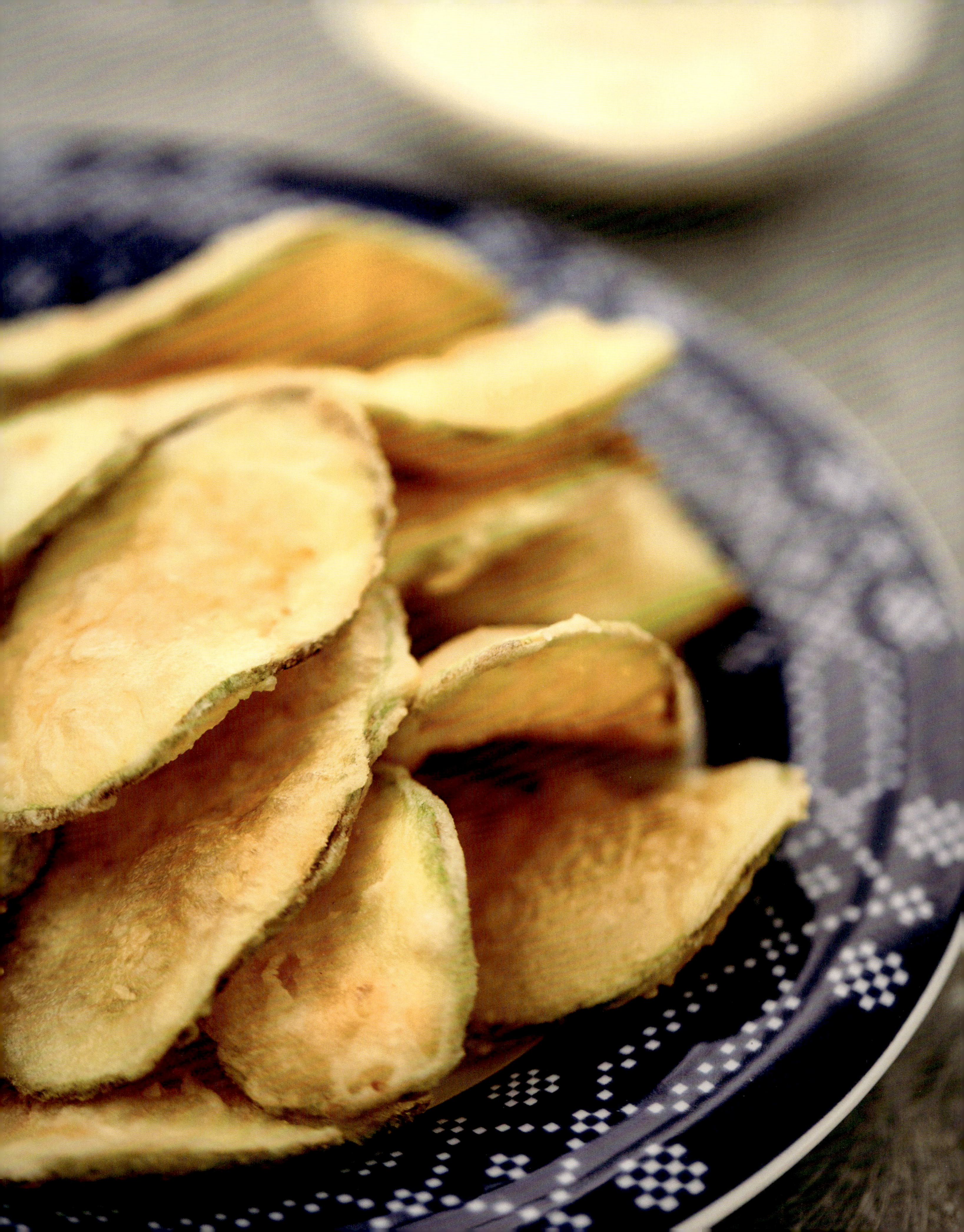

Crispy Courgette Chips

serves 4

'Jesus!', I exclaimed when I saw myself in the mirror. It was only me, but the resemblance was stunning. I had returned from my first trip to the monasteries of Mount Athos: I had grown a full beard and was still wearing the simple robe I wore every day there. In the morning I met with some of the monks who had free time to spare in the garden and chatted about their easy-going lifestyle. Thanks to the simple dress code and complete neglect of styling I saved up to 30 minutes in the bathroom every morning. With no females on the peninsula though who could occupy the mirror for their morning routine, I probably saved up to two hours. Two hours more to embrace some good man talk, to spend the afternoon sitting on a bench with a glass of wine and crunching the crispy courgette chips like mates in front of the TV with a can of beer and a packet of crisps. I rub my belly and take a sip. Men home alone.

FOR THE COURGETTE CHIPS

- 2 medium-sized courgettes
- fine sea salt
- plain flour, for coating
- water
- sunflower oil, for deep-frying
- skordalia (garlic dip), to serve

1. Start by washing the courgettes thoroughly. Remove the stalks and ends and cut into thin slices using a slicer.

2. Place the courgette slices in salted water and set aside for 10–15 minutes.

3. Have two bowls ready for the coating, one containing the flour and the other with water. Coat each slice first with flour and then dip into water just before frying.

4. Into a medium-sized frying pan pour enough sunflower oil to deep-fry the coated courgette chips, or use a deep fat fryer. Heat the oil over medium-high heat and test if the oil is hot by dipping one of the chips inside. If it sizzles the oil is hot enough. Deep-fry the chips until golden and crispy. Serve hot with skordalia as a condiment.

Smoked Mackerel

serves 3

Like calligraphy stretches the white brush over the blue canvas of the sky, the image of a plane makes me feel homesick for places I have never visited, hungry for foods I have never tasted. I cannot step through the doors of an airplane right now, but the most I can do is get a glimpse of that different country through what I call a 'culinary window'. This way I travel to all sorts of places without leaving my spot under the shade of the pine trees, with a sea view ahead, a glass of ouzo and a plate of smoked mackerel in front of me. Exotic ingredients are my compass when satisfying my wanderlust, and in this way a Japanese-style mackerel became one of the souvenirs I collected from a previous not geographical but culinary trip overseas. It matches perfectly well with the ouzo, an exciting blend of cultures, the nostalgia of the familiar with the thirst for the unknown. And who knows, perhaps somewhere out there is a Japanese man, sitting peacefully in his Zen garden, under the shades of a cherry blossom tree eating his mackerel and sipping away on a glass of chilled ouzo. Then both of us would be travelling the world right now, at least a little at a time.

FOR THE MACKEREL

80ml	mirin
270ml	sake
20ml	soy sauce
200ml	water
1	small red onion, thinly sliced
3	mackerel, cleaned and filleted

1. Prepare the marinade. Into a stainless steel or glass bowl, pour the mirin, sake, soy sauce and water. Stir with a fork until combined and whisk in the red onion slices.

2. Drop the mackerel fillets into the bowl. Cover or seal the bowl and marinate for 40 minutes in a cool, dry place.

3. Preheat the smoker. Slowly smoke the fish until it takes on a deliciously moist texture. Enjoy plain with a glass of chilled ouzo or tsipouro.

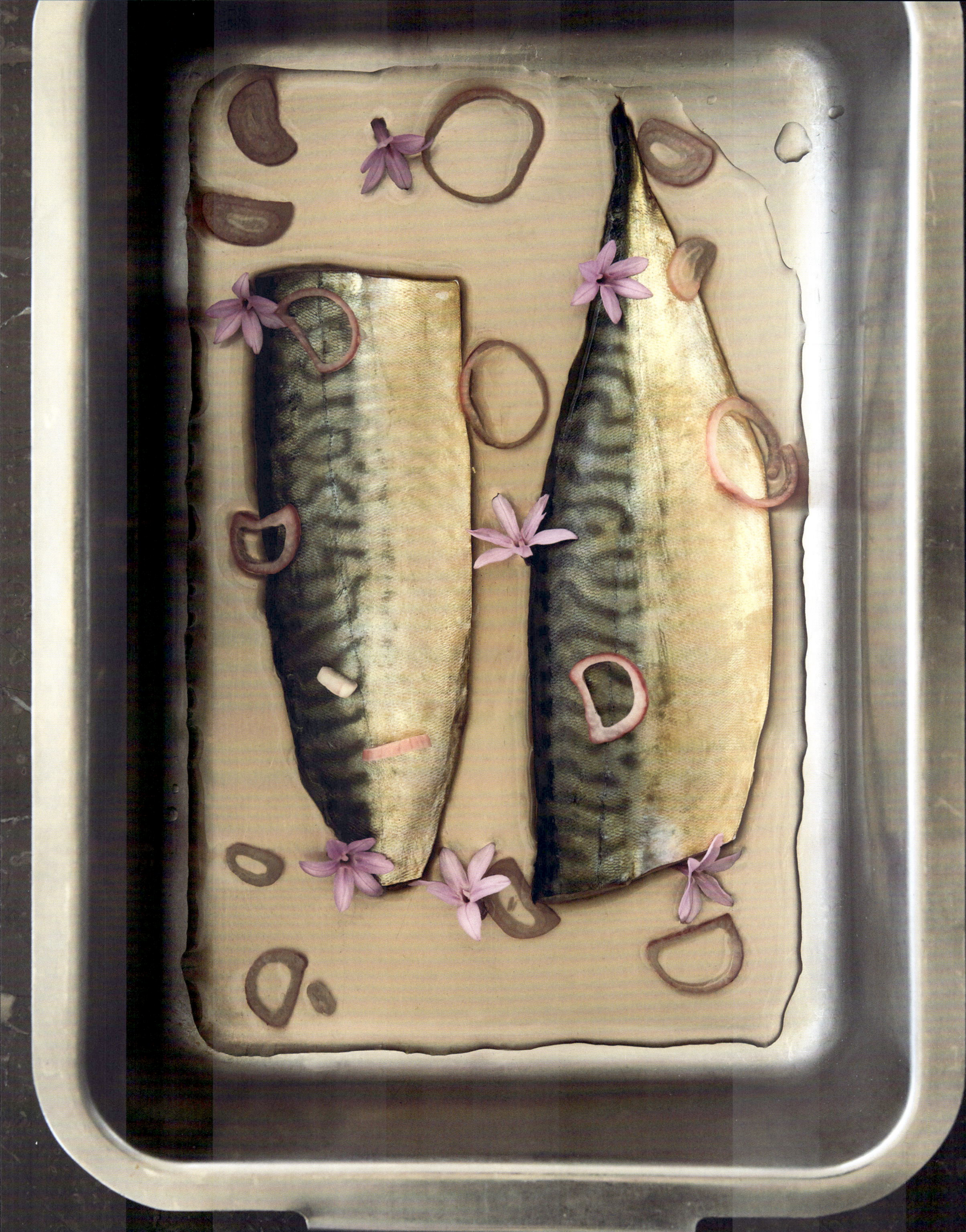

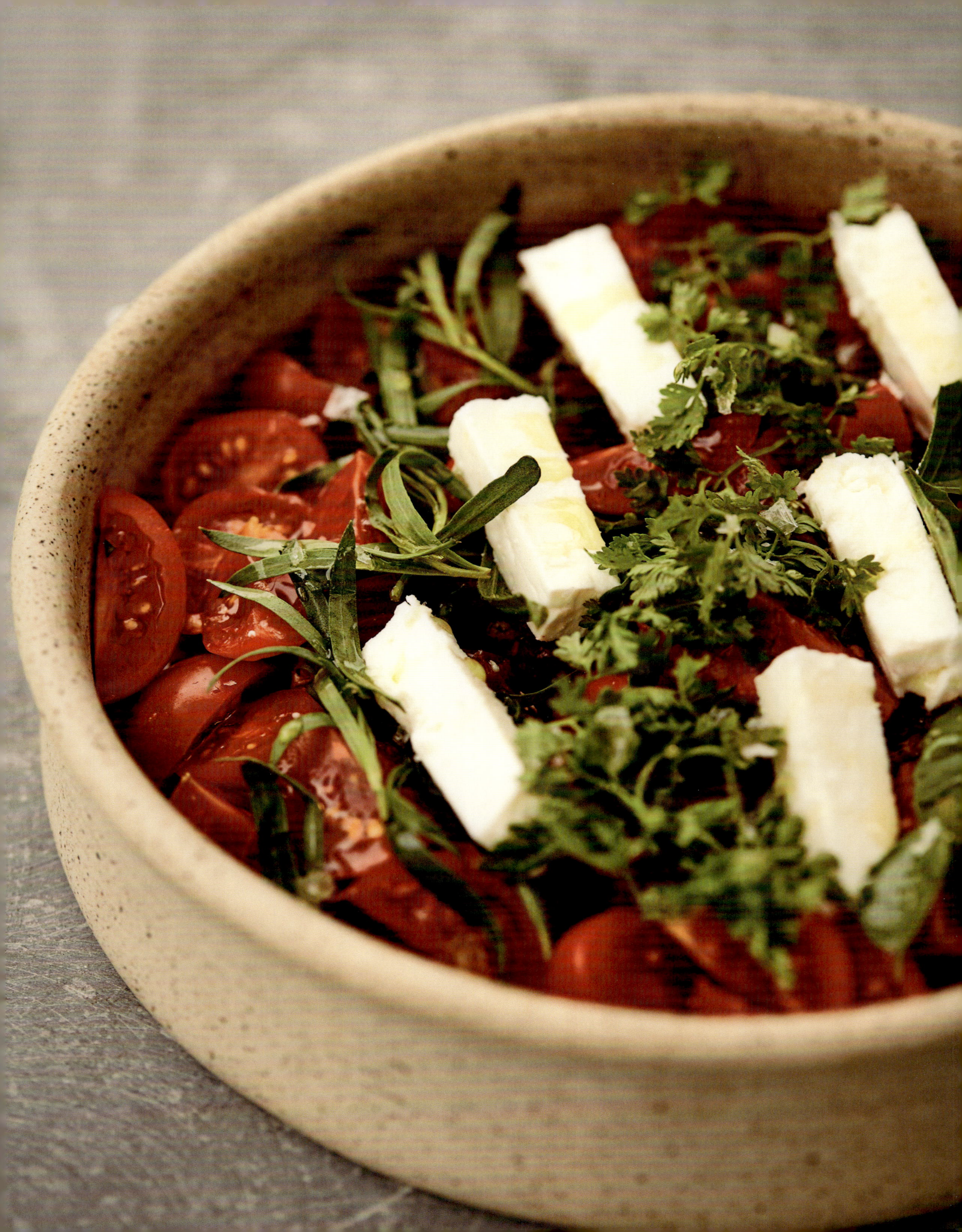

Juicy Cherry Tomatoes with Goat Cheese and Fresh Herbs

serves 2

My friend's tiny restaurant is named after his mother, who ran the place before the family business was passed down to him. I was sitting at one of the old wooden tables when he delivered the salad I ordered, humming along to the old Greek song playing in the background. I knew this salad, along with most things, was directly adopted from his late mother, and the old wooden floor creaked under his steps when he whirled behind the outdated bar to collect two glasses of wine: 'Did you never think of renovating this place?' I glanced at the black and white photographs on the wall. 'Just making it yours instead of maintaining it like your mother's? Or is this what she would have wanted?' 'It is what I wanted one day. I recall how she was polishing a vase, the one right there actually', he pointed at an old-fashioned glass container on one of the unmoved cabinets. 'I announced that I had great plans for this place. I would change it into a modern restaurant with innovative cuisine and kept on describing the place I fantasised about. She smiled and said how she, too, had such plans when she herself took over the restaurant from her own mother. One day she had simply changed her mind.' 'And so did you?' He nodded. 'The day she left you the place', I concluded. 'Yes, the day the place was all I had left of my mother.'

FOR THE CHERRY TOMATOES

20	cherry tomatoes, halved
	white balsamic vinegar
	coarse sea salt
	Greek olive oil
	whole basil leaves
	whole tarragon leaves
	whole coriander leaves
100g	goat cheese, cut into 6 rectangles

1. Put the cherry tomatoes onto a serving plate.

2. Drizzle with balsamic vinegar as preferred and sprinkle with salt. Garnish with olive oil in a light zigzag movement.

3. Cover the tomatoes with the basil, tarragon and coriander leaves and finally place the goat cheese pieces evenly spaced on top.

Stuffed Aubergine with Minced Meat and Feta Cheese

serves 4

Rumour has it that Greeks only love their own cuisine. I can wholeheartedly invalidate this statement, for I personally am very fond of Italian cooking. My Greek friends, though, are not as open-minded for foreign kitchens, so without further ado I chose to simply broaden their culinary horizon by taking them to Bella Italia. A mouth-watering smell of the pizzeria greeted us by the door. 'Buona sera! Benvenuti!' The waiter took our jackets and led us to my usual table with its chequered tablecloth, a candle burning and some Italian tunes in the background: 'I'll have my usual', I gave the waiter a wink and he promised to come back with cutlery. I rubbed my hands and told my friends: 'This is the best Italian restaurant I know, original Italian cuisine! After tasting the dish I ordered, you will be convinced for sure!' There were sceptical looks when the waiter returned to our table. He laid it with forks, knives, small plates, cutting boards and an oven dish, while I started to unpack my groceries of aubergines, Greek olive oil, feta cheese and, and, and … 'Just wait, you will see!' I started preparing the authentic Greek stuffed aubergine. The waiter came back with my order of the 'usual': a small bowl of Italian Napolitana tomato sauce which I spooned onto the aubergines before handing them over to cook in the oven. 'You see!' My friends were closing their eyes in enjoyment, nodding approvingly and claiming it was the best Italian food they had ever eaten. I must admit it, this Stuffed Aubergine with Napolitana Sauce is so good, one could almost think it to be Greek.

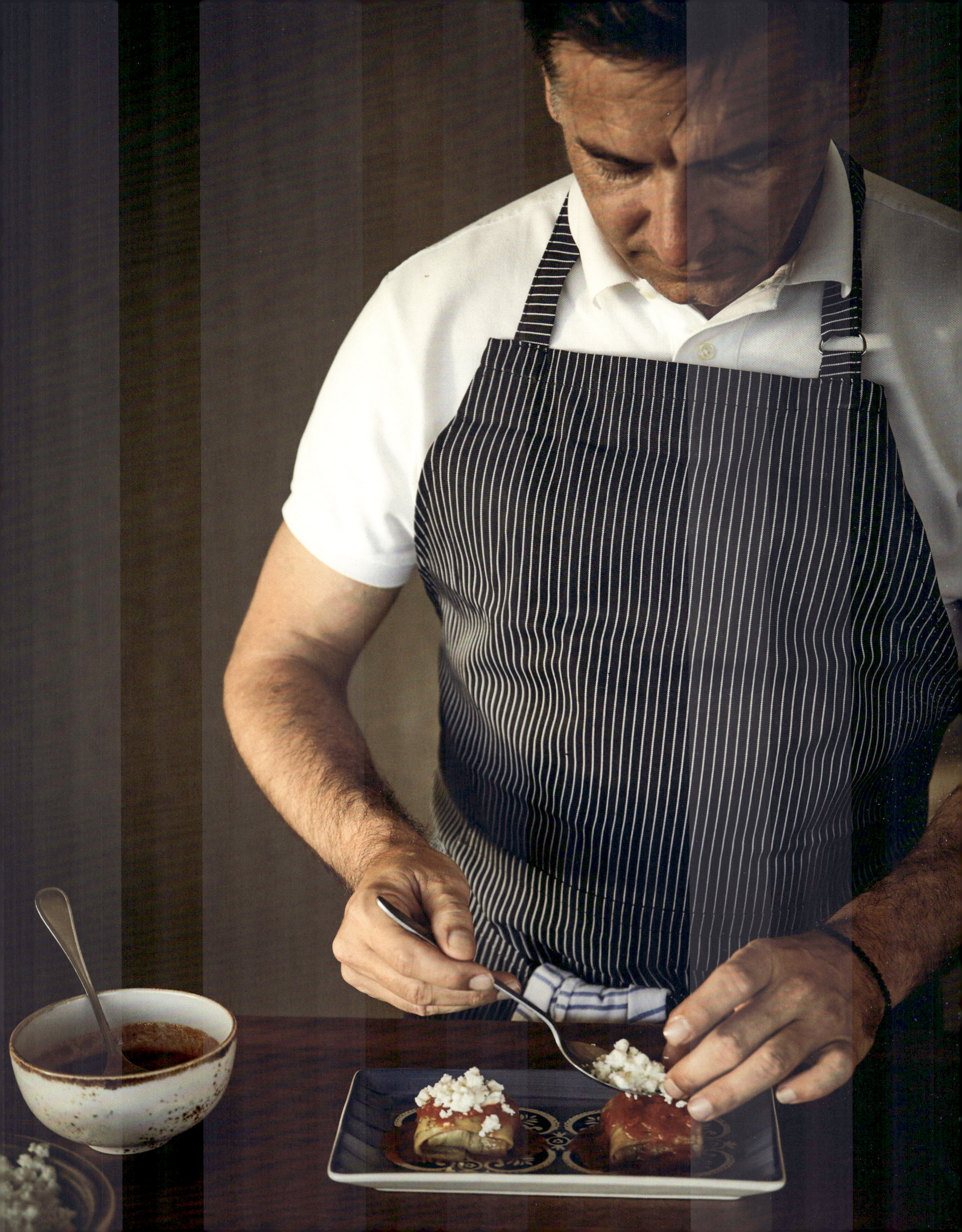

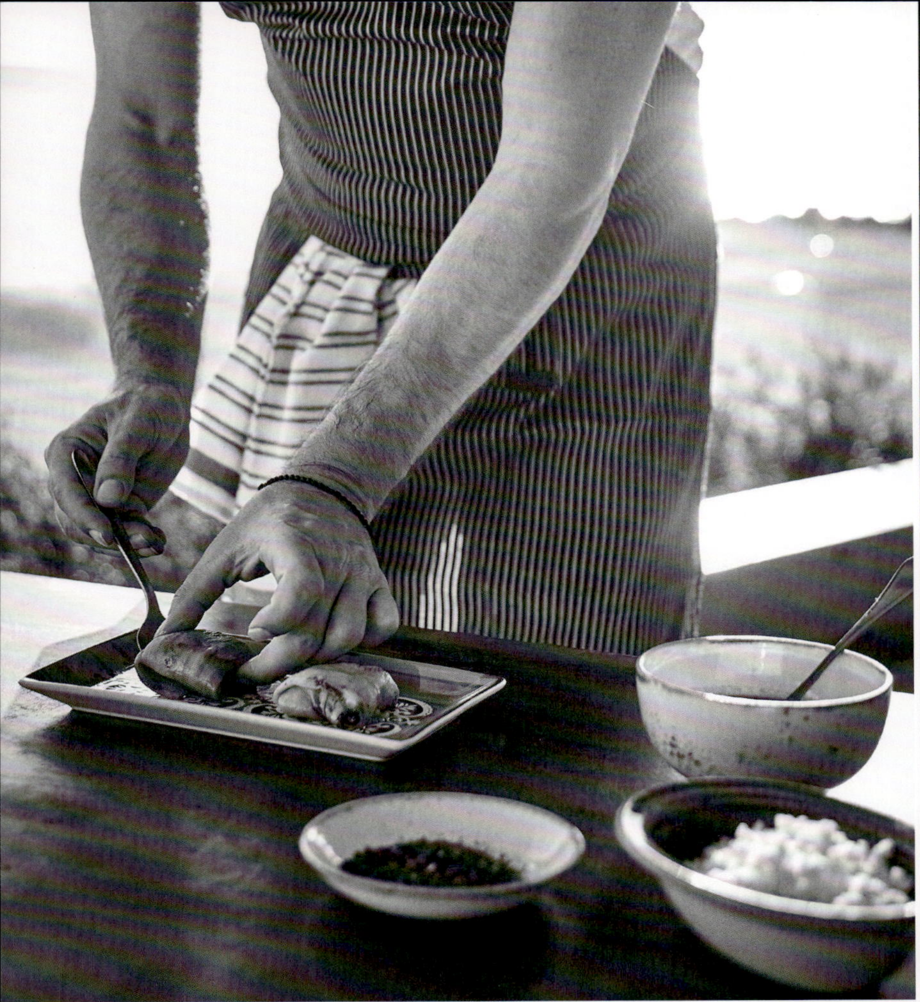
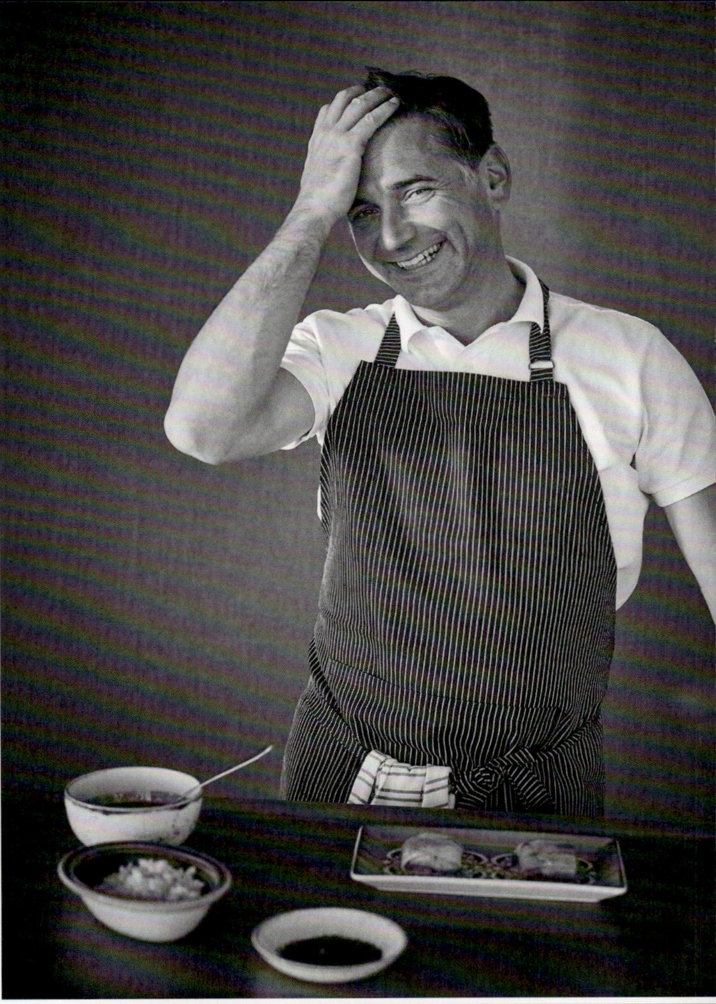
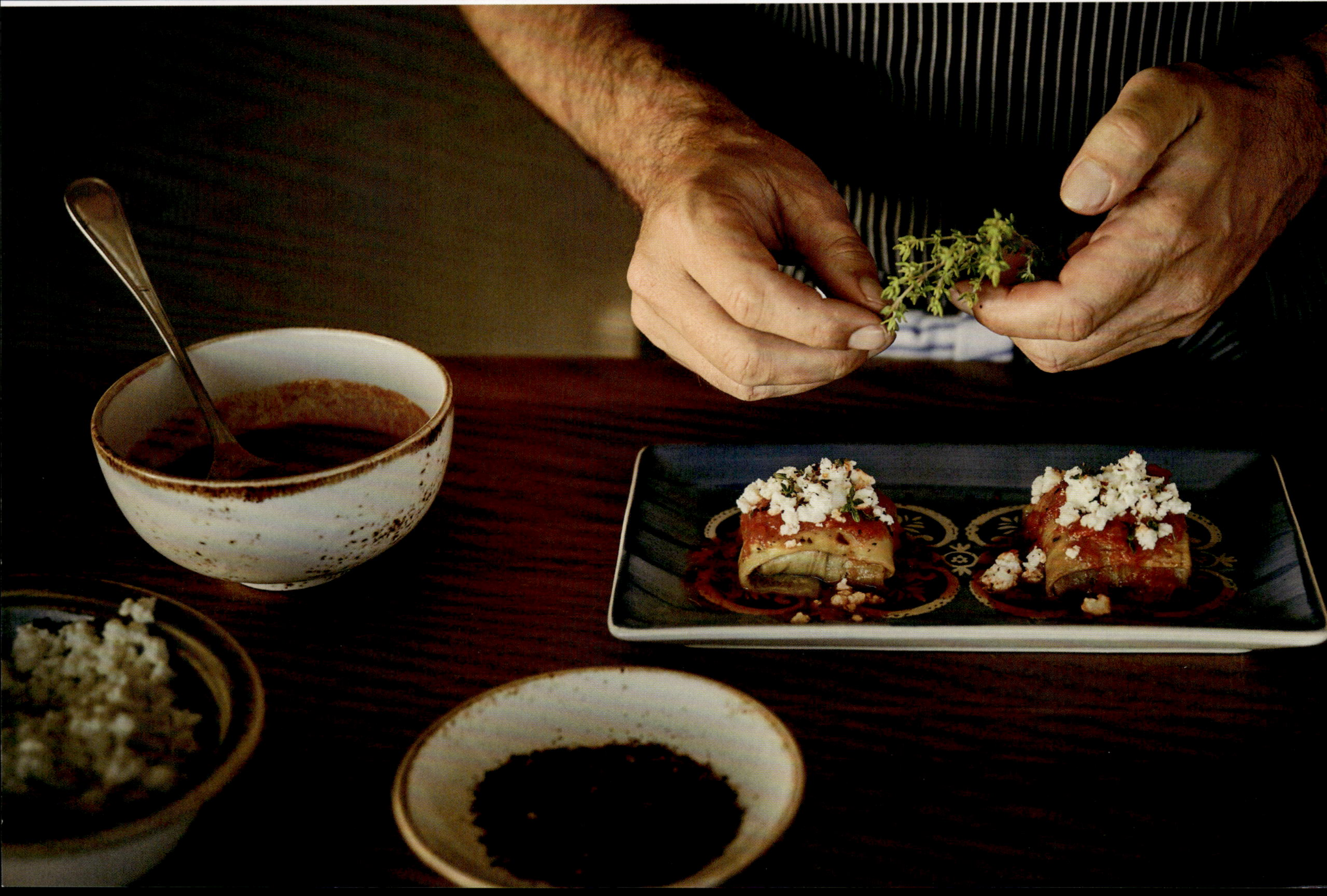

FOR THE STUFFED AUBERGINE

5	aubergines
	sunflower oil, for frying
2	white onions, finely chopped
2	carrots, finely chopped
2–3	sprigs of fresh thyme
½	garlic clove, finely chopped
300g	minced beef
	Greek olive oil, for frying
8	sprigs of fresh oregano, stripped
60ml	red wine
	fine sea salt and freshly ground black pepper
1	handful fresh parsley, chopped
1 tbsp	white balsamic vinegar
300 g	Napolitano sauce
100 g	Greek feta cheese

DISH

small oven dish

1. Preheat the oven to 180°C.

2. Cut the aubergines lengthways into thin slices, approximately 5 mm thick. Fry the slices in the sunflower oil over medium heat for about 1 minute on each side. Remove and pat dry with paper towels. Use a sharp kitchen knife to peel off the skins. Take two slices and arrange one on top of the other, cross-wise. Repeat until all the slices are arranged accordingly.

3. For the stuffing, you require two sauté pans. In one sauté pan heat a little olive oil over medium heat, sauté the onion, carrots, thyme and garlic, reduce the heat and simmer. Meanwhile in the second sauté pan, fry the minced meat in olive oil over high heat. Brown the meat until well fried and break it up with a wooden spoon. Season with the leaves from six of the oregano sprigs and allow it to fry for about 2 minutes before deglazing with the red wine. Season to taste with salt and pepper.

4. After approximately 2 minutes, add the vegetables from the first pan into the meat. Let the ingredients combine for 6–10 minutes before stirring in the chopped parsley. Remove from the heat. Adjust the seasoning if necessary. Flavour with the remaining oregano and mix in the balsamic vinegar.

5. Now spoon the minced meat into the centre of the crossed aubergine slices and fold over to make parcels.

6. Sprinkle a small oven dish with olive oil and transfer the stuffed aubergine parcels onto the dish. Cover each one with 1–2 tbsp of Napolitano sauce and sprinkle with feta cheese. Bake for 15 minutes. Before serving, sprinkle once more with feta cheese.

Three Dips

I chose no more than three dips for this book, hoping that they are enough. Perhaps this is a mistake. Then again, I certainly made more than three mistakes in my life. I broke promises, I broke rules and I broke hearts. I guess this raises the question of what kind of a person I am to admit such horrors. I am a person who sometimes took a risk and invested just to see myself lose. I tried to lead, to teach and failed miserably. I am a person who is afraid, who sheds tears and who seethes with anger. But then again, in many of these situations, there was care behind my fear, happiness behind my tears and sometimes love behind my anger. I am a person who is also willing to follow in order to lead, to learn in order to teach and to fail in order to succeed. I learnt to be more cautious when taking a risk, to let go, and eventually I became a person who achieves. Often I kept promises, I respected rules and perhaps there are a few hearts I mended. Being right, being wrong, being neither, being loved, being despised and being forgotten shaped me into who I am, and if somebody ever asks me what kind of a person I am, the answer to this question takes no more than three words, hoping that I am enough: just a human.

Aubergine & Pomegranate Dip

serves 4

FIRST DIP

6	aubergines
1	garlic clove, chopped
	seeds of 2 pomegranates
½	handful fresh parsley, chopped
3 tsp	walnuts, chopped
50ml	Greek olive oil
4 tsp	white balsamic vinegar
4	pinches of fine sea salt

FOR THE DECORATION

crushed walnuts
pomegranate seeds

1. Preheat the oven to 180°C. Start with the preparation of the aubergines. With the tip of a sharp knife, punch several holes into the aubergines. Place them onto a baking tray and cook in the oven for 45 minutes until softened.

2. Place a sieve inside a plastic bowl. On a cutting board, cut the aubergines in half and use a spoon to scoop out the flesh and collect it in the sieve. Try scooping the flesh with as few seeds as possible. Refrigerate the sieve and bowl for 60 minutes while the liquid drains from the flesh.

3. In a blender, combine the garlic, pomegranate seeds, parsley, walnuts and olive oil. Blend on high speed until smooth.

4. Add in the drained aubergine flesh. Season with the balsamic vinegar and salt and combine all the ingredients by blending them on high speed. Serve in small scoops and decorate with crushed walnuts and pomegranate seeds.

Beetroot Dip

serves 2

SECOND DIP

5 tsp	Greek olive oil
7	pinches of fine sea salt
5	raw beetroot, stripped of leaves
700g	plain Greek yoghurt
150g	walnuts, crushed
1	garlic clove, grated
2½ tsp	strawberry jam
1 tsp	raisins
2½ tsp	white balsamic vinegar
1	pinch of freshly ground black pepper

FOR THE DECORATION

½ tbsp	raisins
	crushed walnuts
	dill

1. Preheat the oven to 180°C. Cut five pieces of kitchen foil approximately 40 x 20 cm. Sprinkle the foil generously with olive oil and salt. Now place each beetroot in the centre of a piece of foil and wrap into small parcels. Ensure that the end is closed tightly but allow some air in the base. Bake them in the oven for 90 minutes. Towards the end, check softness by inserting a toothpick.

2. Once the beetroots are cooked, carefully undo the parcels. Let cool a little, then peel the vegetables while still warm. Grate four of them through a coarse grater and set the remaining one aside for decoration. Drain the grated beetroot and add to a serving bowl.

3. Add the yoghurt, walnuts, garlic, strawberry jam, raisins, balsamic vinegar and olive oil and season with salt and pepper. Mix all the ingredients thoroughly by hand.

4. Finely chop the last beetroot. Decorate the dip with the beetroot, raisins, walnuts and dill.

Giant Bean Dip

serves 4

THIRD DIP

250g	dried butter beans
100g	sun-dried tomatoes
500ml	water
	Greek olive oil, for frying
1	garlic clove, chopped
1	white onion, sliced
2	sprigs of fresh thyme
1	pinch of fine sea salt
1	carrot, sliced
1	red pepper, chopped
250ml	red wine
5	celery leaves
	fine sea salt and freshly ground pepper
	juice of 1½ lemons
1-2 tsp	dried red chilli flakes (optional)

FOR THE DECORATION

carrot, thinly sliced
radish, thinly sliced
dill

The previous day:

1. Let the butter beans soak in salted water overnight.

The following day:

2. In a pot, bring water to the boil. Remove the soaked beans with a slotted spoon and transfer them into the boiling water. Cook them for 2–2½ hours until softened.

3. Soak the sun-dried tomatoes in 500ml water for 30 minutes. Reserve the sun-dried tomatoes and the tomato water separately.

4. Preheat the oven to 170°C. In a medium-sized pot heat the olive oil over medium heat and sauté the garlic, onion and thyme. Season with a pinch of salt and simmer for approximately 3 minutes. Stir in the carrot and pepper, then continue to sauté for approximately 6–8 minutes until translucent. Add in the softened beans and sun-dried tomatoes. Allow the ingredients to combine before deglazing with the red wine. Finally add 400ml of the reserved tomato water, bring to the boil and cook for 10 minutes.

5. Put the ingredients into an oven-proof pan and transfer to the oven. Allow to cook for 15 minutes until golden, then use a slotted spoon to drain the vegetables and spoon them into a blender. Add the celery leaves and season with 4 pinches of salt, pepper, lemon juice and red chilli flakes if desired.

6. Blend the purée on high speed. Add the remaining 100ml of tomato water if more fluid is required and blend until velvety. Serve warm in scoops and decorate with slices of carrots, radish and dill.

Grilled Feta Cheese

serves 2

———✹———

'You can't rush feta', the producer explained.
He offered me a single white cube on a wooden plate: 'The flavours have to develop over time. Take a piece and I will tell you all there is to know about feta.' 'I would love to but I don't have time, I really just want to buy a few grams.' I stretched out my fingers for the cheese but instantly he removed it from my reach.' How regretful. Like I said, you can't rush feta.' He turned his back on me and was about to walk away. 'Fine!' I yelled after him. He grinned a mischievous smile when I took the soft cube between my fingers.
With the first bite my taste buds demand the flavour of a fresh tomato and crisp cucumber. 'For an original feta, goat's and sheep's milk is heated, mixed with rennet, drained, salted and aged. The skinless cheese needs no compression, no bizarre ingredients, and neither is multiple-year ageing required …' The producer fell into a lengthy monologue before he concluded: 'When I make feta, every factor becomes extremely influential on the final flavour. I am sure you are interested in the factors that affect feta …' I hesitated but he stretched out the wooden plate once more. 'Another piece?'
The feta's pleasant smoothness blends with the spice of Mediterranean cuisine on my tongue, while the producer keeps blabbering on: '… So lastly, the type of flora the animals consume can have an excessive impact on texture and flavour.' He said finally. I shifted in my chair for, in the meantime, I had taken a seat. 'The method has never changed, we have produced feta in this country in the same way always, ever since after the war. I am sure you are interested in the history of feta?' 'I really must go, I don't have …' He stretched out the wooden plate once more. 'Not even interested in another piece? You can't rush feta.' The soft piece tasted salty when it melted in my mouth, like a hint of the Aegean.
'Naturally, I meant the Trojan War. The first cheesemaker had a good eye for production', he winks. 'The first feta producer mentioned was the Cyclops Polyphemus in Homer's *The Odyssey*. Odysseus, the hero of the story, tried to steal his cheeses and his crew devoured most of his stock when the giant surprised them in the cave … I am sure you know *The Odyssey*? No?' He took a heavy book from the dusty shelf and opened the first page. 'Please, have another piece … You can't rush feta.'

FOR THE FETA

100g	feta cheese, whole piece
½	tomato, sliced
	Greek olive oil
	fine sea salt
1	spring onion, chopped
⅓	chilli, finely sliced
	zest of ½ lemon
1	pinch of chopped fresh parsley
1	pinch of chopped fresh oregano

1. Preheat the grill, or the oven to 180°C

2. Use paper towels to pat the piece of feta cheese dry and place it onto a sheet of kitchen foil. Add the tomato slices on top of the feta, drizzle with a generous amount of olive oil and sprinkle with salt.

3. Now top with another layer of spring onion and chilli. Season with the lemon zest, parsley and oregano.

4. Tightly fold the foil over the cheese.

5. Now grill the feta cheese for approximately 5 minutes on both sides, or alternatively roast in the oven for a total of 12 minutes. Enjoy hot with white bread.

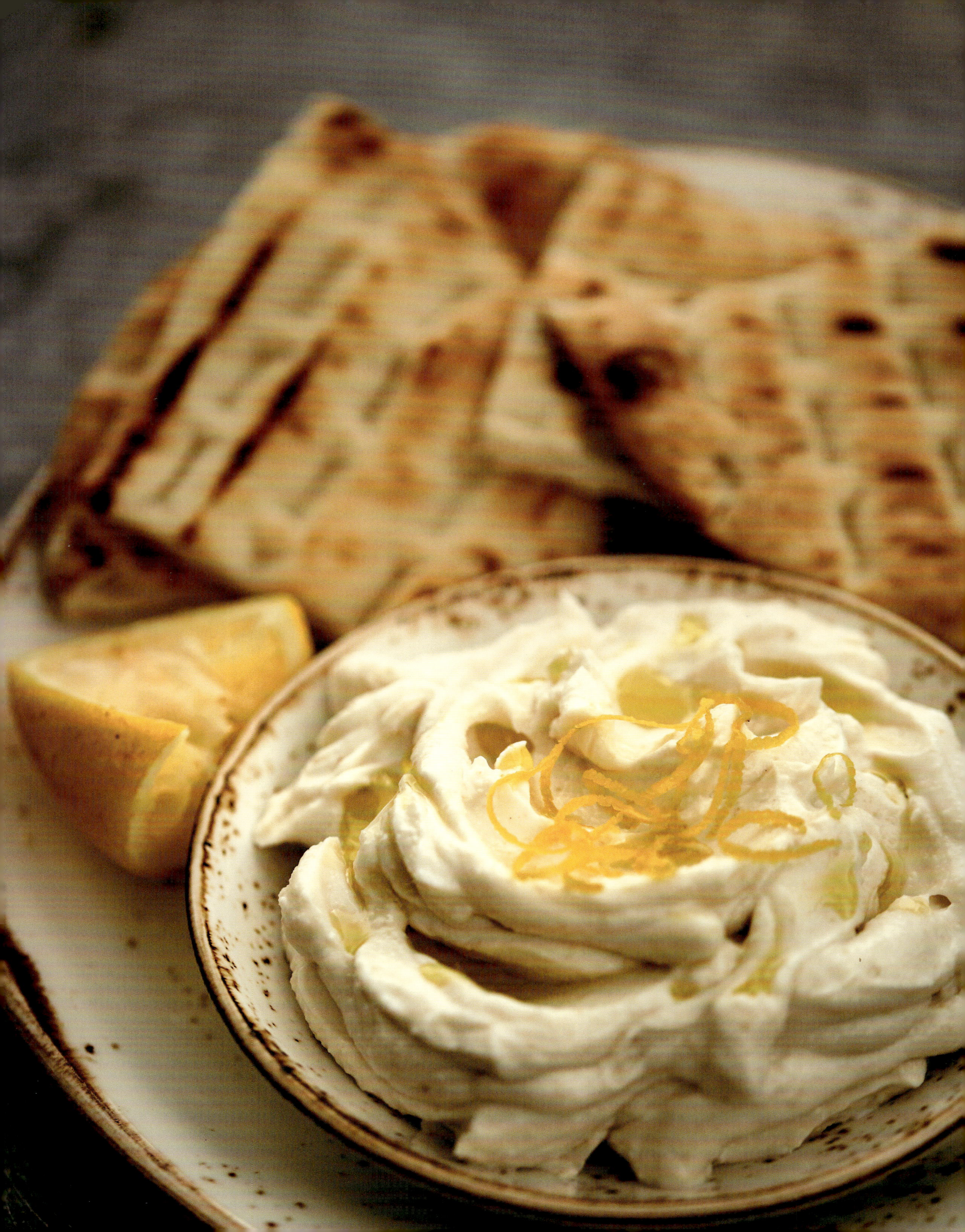

Taramas – Fish Roe Dip

serves 4

Every summer I develop the habit of eating the same dish every day. Last summer, Taramas turned out to be my unconsciously chosen daily snack. I guess this habit is the result of my favourite time of year as a child. Not summer, but Christmas! I loved opening the little doors of my advent calendar day by day and scooping out my little treat: the same piece of chocolate every day until Christmas. So, this chocolate is now Taramas, my daily treat all summer long, my advent calendar door until an undetermined Christmas Eve. It may be not the usual way but I don't allow a calendar to tell me when to have a treat, when to celebrate and what to celebrate. I don't celebrate when it is the right date, the right number on my calendar. I celebrate when the moment is right.

FOR THE TARAMAS

1	white onion, finely chopped
350ml	sunflower oil
150ml	Greek olive oil
150g	white stale bread, soaked in water
75g	taramas (fish roe)
40ml	lemon juice
1	lemon, zest
	toasted pita bread to serve

1. Put the chopped onion into a pot, add water until it is covered with 2-3 finger-widths of water and bring to the boil. Allow to simmer for 10 minutes. Reserve the onion and onion water separately.

2. Combine the sunflower and olive oil and set aside.

3. In a bowl, combine the onion, soaked bread and taramas. Sprinkle with 20 ml of the lemon juice and 100 ml of the oils. Transfer to a mixer and mix the ingredients until smooth on medium speed.

4. Little by little, keep adding the remaining oil and lemon juice. If more liquid is required, add in some of the onion water. Mix well on high speed. Sprinkle with lemon zest and serve with toasted pita bread.

Greek Fava Bean Dip

serves 4

———— ✳ ————

Fava Bean Dip was one of my first recipes accomplished in my own, private kitchen. So upon my attempt to produce a perfect Fava Bean Dip – a traditional, creamy dip, made of puréed broad beans – I welcomed a handful of friends to evaluate the result of this project. They joined obediently and gathered around the enormous kitchen table which dominates the centre of the room. The table is my own design. I wanted a multifunctional object that had to serve several purposes. I designed a table to function as a workspace, to host my friends around it, to hold their chilled glasses of wine, to lend its top for dancing and to allow people to whirl around it preparing food. Above all, it had to reside between people who share friendship and food. On that day, they shared my Fava Bean Dip. Thank heavens for that table; it has stories to tell. When I set foot in my kitchen the next morning, I smiled at seeing my table fulfilling its last purpose: holding evidence. That morning, even a whole stack of evidence – an enormous pile of dirty dishes.

FOR THE GREEK FAVA BEANS

500ml	water
200g	dried fava beans (broad beans)
1.35 l	vegetable stock
10g	unsalted butter
1	garlic clove, finely chopped
1	carrot, peeled and finely sliced
1	white onion, cut into chunks
1	pinch of sugar
	fine sea salt and freshly ground black pepper
1	sprig of rosemary
	juice of 1 lemon
5 tbsp	Greek olive oil

FOR THE GARNISH

	Greek olive oil, for frying
1	large red onion, sliced
1	pinch of fine sea salt
15g	brown sugar
45ml	balsamic vinegar
1	pinch of fresh thyme
	toasted white bread, to serve
1	handful capers, to serve

1. Start to de-colour the beans. In a medium-sized pot, bring the water to the boil. Pour the broad beans into a heat-resistant bowl. At regular intervals, pour boiling water onto the beans and stir. Let it sit for 5 minutes, then drain the beans with a slotted spoon and set aside.

2. In a large pot, bring the vegetable stock to the boil.

3. Continue with the vegetables. In a sauté pan, heat the butter over medium heat. Stir in the garlic, carrot, onion and broad beans, and season with the sugar, salt and pepper. Let the ingredients sweat for approximately 3 minutes while stirring occasionally.

4. Transfer the sautéed vegetables into the vegetable stock, season with rosemary and simmer over high heat for 40 minutes. Stir occasionally, allowing the liquid to evaporate slightly over time.

5. After 30 minutes, use tongs to remove the rosemary sprigs. Transfer the contents into a blender. Add the lemon juice and olive oil and blend the ingredients on high speed until smooth. Once the desired texture has been reached, spoon the flavourful purée onto a serving plate.

6. Meanwhile make the garnish. In a sauté pan, heat olive oil over medium heat. Toss in the red onion slices, season with one pinch of salt and cook very slowly for approximately 7 minutes until translucent.

7. When the onion slices have softened and are tinged golden, stir in the sugar and balsamic vinegar to start the caramelisation process. Cook the onion over low heat for another 7 minutes, stirring frequently, until caramelised. Immediately spoon the sticky onion slices onto the broad bean purée.

8. Lastly, sprinkle the finished dish with thyme and serve warm with toasted white bread and capers on the side.

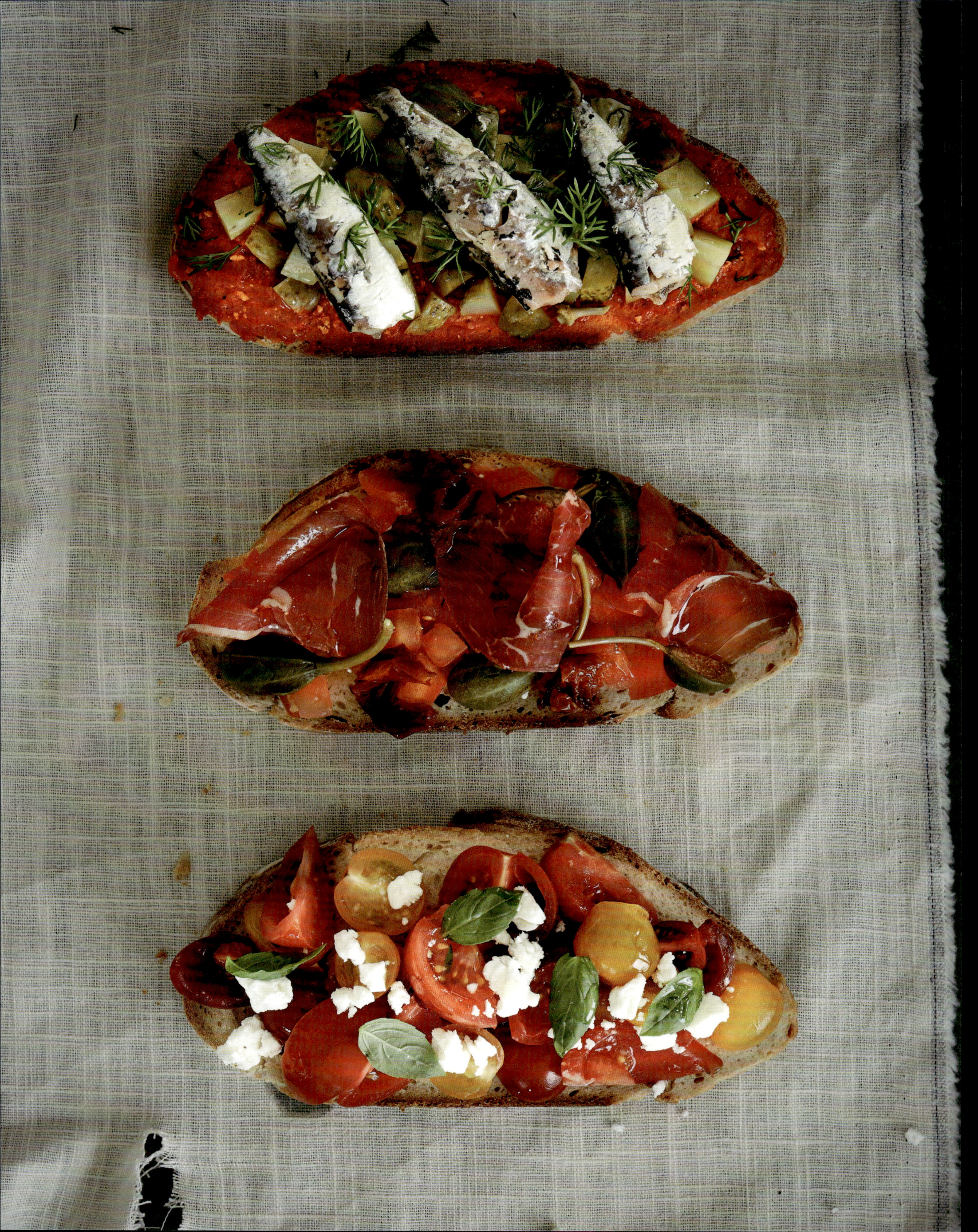

Trilogy of Cretan Dakos Toast

'Never judge a book by its cover', is an old piece of Greek wisdom. I am glad that we both agree that the cover of this book is without doubt marvellous, but truly, I am too old to be fooled by outer beauty and ignore my gut feeling when it comes to first impressions. Evoking a positive gut feeling, or ideally a full-gut feeling during the starter course is the goal, being well aware that there is no second chance for a first impression. To be on the safe side, I usually have a broad variety of first impressions ready: Trilogy of Dakos and Trilogy of Dakos for Fish Lovers. Just in accordance with another timeless piece of Greek wisdom: 'The beauty of dakos captures the eye, but their taste captures the heart.' Just in case, I packed several dakos recipes in order for you to have Plan A, B, C, D, E and F all at once, even though I keep forgetting which one is which because they are all equally tasty. But there you are, you just got six secret recipes to strike the best first, second, third, fourth, fifth and sixth impression! Thank God you proved to have good taste when shopping for cookery books …

SARDINE & RED PEPPER DAKOS

    toasted bread
    red pepper paste (see page 54)
    marinated sardines
    pickled cucumber, diced
1 sprig of fresh thyme, quartered

For the Sardine & Red Pepper Dakos

Spread the toasted bread with red pepper paste and top with marinated sardines and pickled cucumber. Lastly, sprinkle with thyme and serve.

CAPER & TOMATO DAKOS

    caper berries, halved
    sun-dried tomatoes, chopped
    tomato, diced
    louza (Greek/Myconian prosciutto)
    toasted bread
    Greek olive oil

For the Caper & Tomato Dakos

1. Combine caper berries, sun-dried tomatoes and diced tomato in a bowl and mix the ingredients by hand.

2. Place the tomato mixture onto the toasted bread and decoratively place the louza on top. Lastly, drizzle the dakos with olive oil and serve.

TOMATO & FETA DAKOS

    cherry tomatoes, halved
    fresh basil leaves
2 tsp Greek olive oil
1 pinch of fine sea salt
1 pinch of freshly ground pepper
    toasted bread
    freshly squeezed tomato juice
    feta cheese, crumbled

For the Tomato & Feta Dakos

1. Toss cherry tomatoes, basil and the olive oil in a mixing bowl. Season with salt and pepper and give the ingredients a gentle toss to mix by hand.

2. Drizzle the toasted bread with tomato juice. Carefully spoon the tomato mixture on top and, lastly, garnish with crumbled feta cheese.

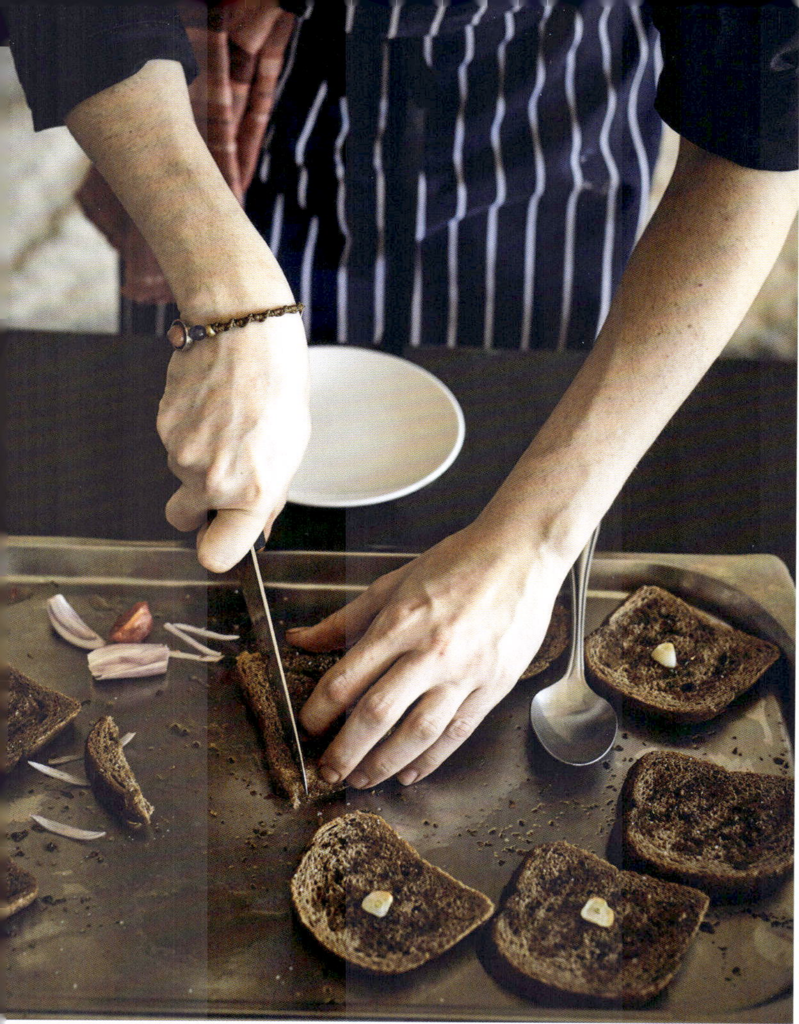
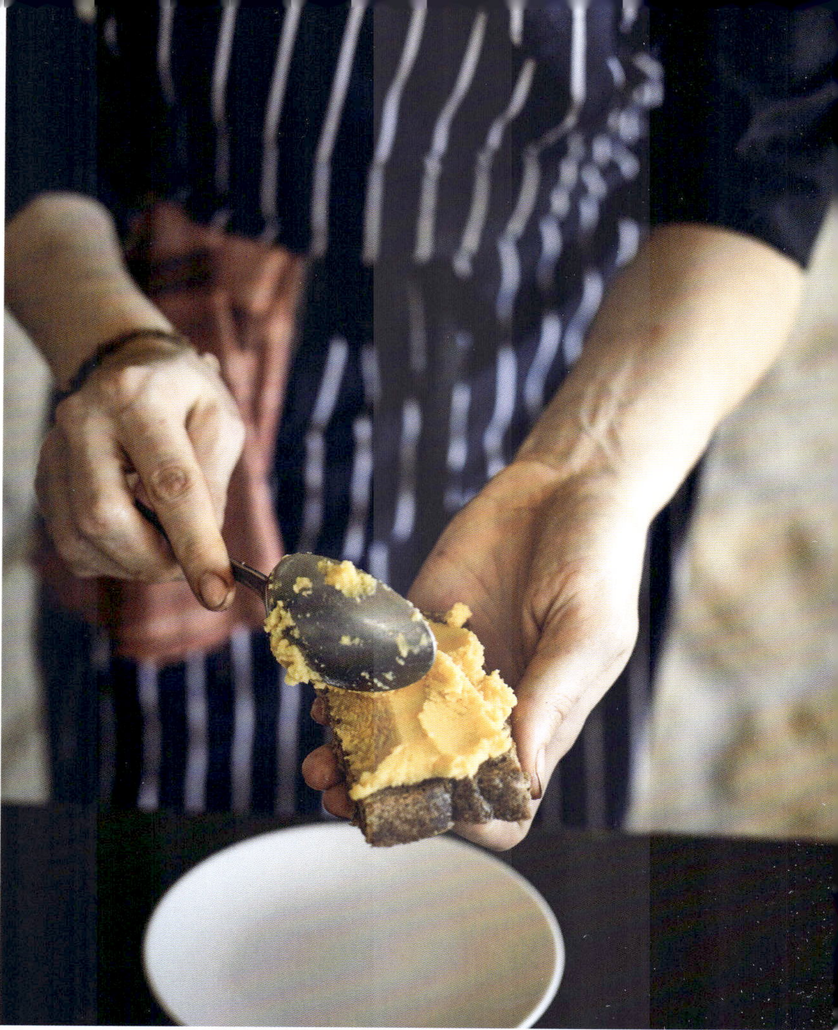
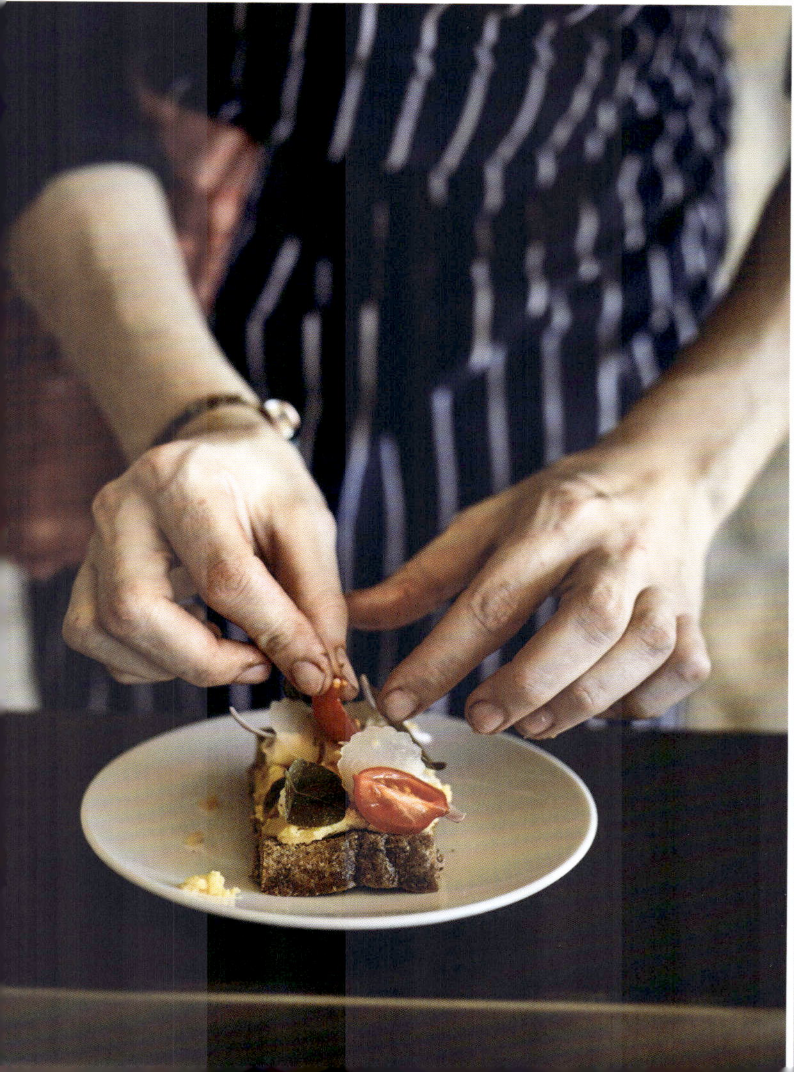
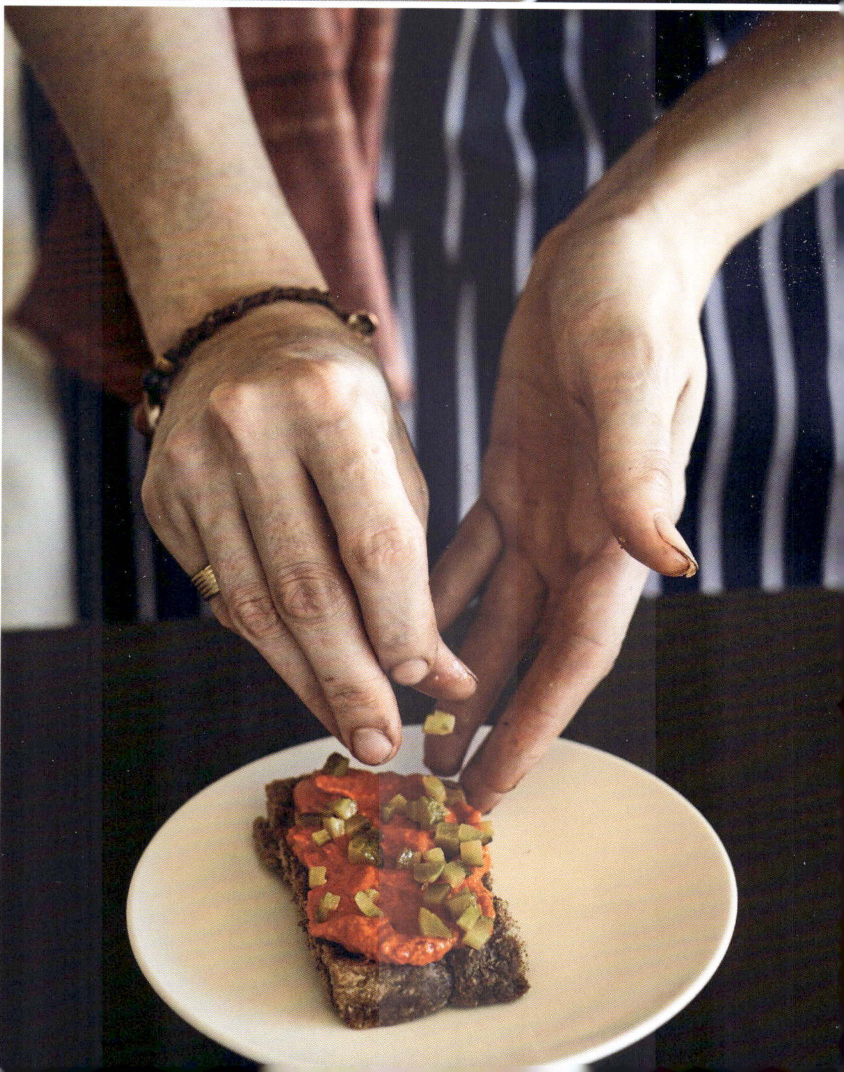

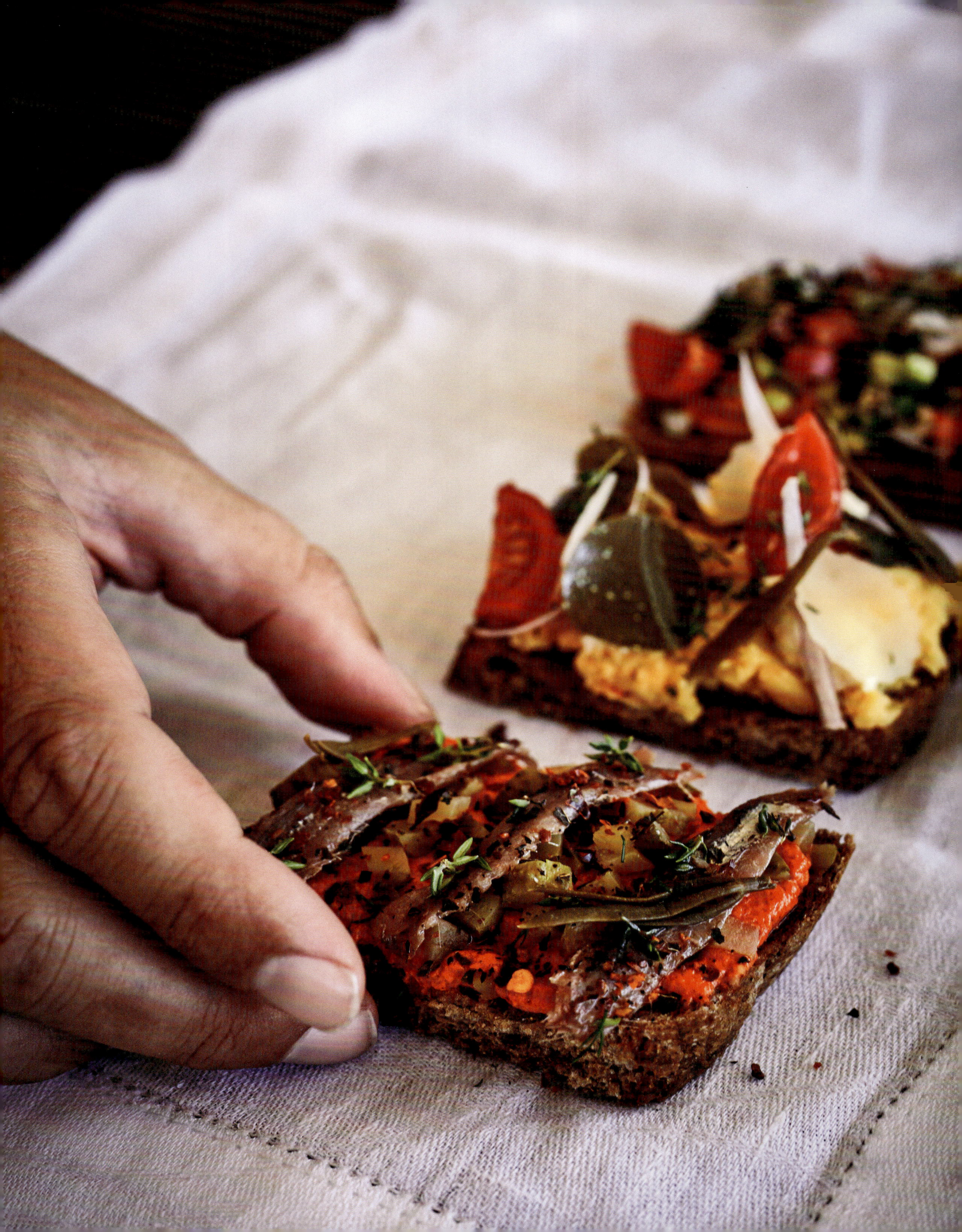

Trilogy of Cretan Dakos Toast for Fish lovers

GIANT BEAN & ANCHOVY DAKOS

1 red pepper
Greek olive oil
marinated anchovies
toasted bread
carrots, peeled and thinly sliced
cherry tomato confit
Giant Bean Dip (see page 69)
fresh basil leaves

For the Bean & Anchovy Dakos

1. First fry the red pepper in olive oil until browned. Remove the stem before finely chopping the vegetable.

2. Place marinated anchovies on the toasted bread and add carrots and the chopped pepper. Garnish with cherry tomato confit and Giant Bean Dip. Lastly, decorate the dakos with basil leaves.

FAVA BEAN & TARAMAS DAKOS

toasted bread
taramas (fish roe)
Fava Bean Dip (see page 75)
capers, chopped
black olives, pitted and sliced
pickled peppers, sliced
fresh parsley, chopped
fresh dill, chopped
Ladolemono Sauce (see page 226)

For the Fava Bean & Taramas Dakos

Garnish the toasted bread with taramas and place Fava Bean Dip, capers, olives and pickled peppers on top. Sprinkle with chopped parsley and dill and finally drizzle generously with Ladolemono Sauce.

TARAMAS & OCTOPUS DAKOS

taramas (fish roe)
marinated octopus salad
toasted bread
split peas
baby rocket leaves
Greek olive oil

For the Taramas & Octopus Dakos

Spoon a generous amount of taramas and marinated octopus salad onto the toasted bread. Add split peas and rocket leaves on top. Drizzle with olive oil and serve.

Chicken Tigania

8 pieces

Cooking can be a thrilling odyssey of navigating oneself through oceans of flavours. On his odyssey, the great Greek adventurer Odysseus had to fear Poseidon's raging waves and the Anemoi's unkind winds but, above all, he had to fear the song of the sirens. These mythological creatures had voices so beautiful, that all sailors were drawn in by the sound yet would find nothing but death when willingly navigating their ships towards the sirens' island. I am standing by the stove when I start to daydream about this ancient story: I can imagine myself standing on the deck of a creaky oak ship, gently rocked by the sea. I take a deep breath of salty air when suddenly I hear the most beautiful melody rolling towards my ship like gentle, beguiling waves and the softest tunes start to swirl within my head, flow into my heart and become the air I breathe. As I wake from my daydream I recognise, that not the song of a siren, but the aroma of my Chicken Tigania fills the air. From my pan, where the chicken glistens golden like sun rays touching the waves of the sea, comes a smell so seductive that no man could resist. With the first bite I taste the sweetness of honey blended with the spiciness of the mustard and I know that at this moment even the sirens would fall into a soulful silence.

FOR THE SAUCE

1 tsp	honey
3 tsp	Dijon mustard
	juice of 2 lemons

FOR THE CHICKEN

3	chicken thighs, filleted
	fine sea salt and freshly ground black pepper
	Greek olive oil, for frying
	sunflower oil, for frying
	unsalted butter, for frying
1	white onion, finely chopped
1	garlic clove, finely chopped
2	mushrooms, sliced
1	red pepper, finely chopped
2	sprigs of fresh thyme, leaves only
60ml	white wine
30g	unsalted butter

1. Prepare the sauce. In a small bowl mix the honey and mustard with a fork. Lastly, stir in the lemon juice and set aside.

2. Prepare the chicken by seasoning the thighs with salt and pepper before cutting them in bite-sized chunks. In a large frying pan, heat the olive and sunflower oils over a high heat and toss in the chicken. Brown on all sides until golden. Then set aside.

3. Meanwhile, heat a small pot over low heat. Reserve the cooking liquid from the frying pan by coating the bottom of the pan with water and scraping off the rendered fat. Transfer into the small pot.

4. In the same frying pan melt butter over medium-low heat. Once sizzling, stir in the chicken and fry for 1 minute on all sides. Once more, set the meat aside and reserve the cooking liquid in the small pot.

5. Continue with the vegetables by reusing the same pan and switching to high heat. In the cooking juices, sweat the onion, garlic, mushrooms and red pepper. Once cooked, add the thyme and simmer for 3 minutes before tossing in the chicken. Deglaze with the white wine and reduce to low heat. Continue to cook for another 3 minutes and, lastly, add the 30g butter. Simmer for another 2 minutes.

6. Drizzle with the rendered cooking liquid from the small pot along with the honey and mustard sauce. Give it a final, good stir and serve immediately.

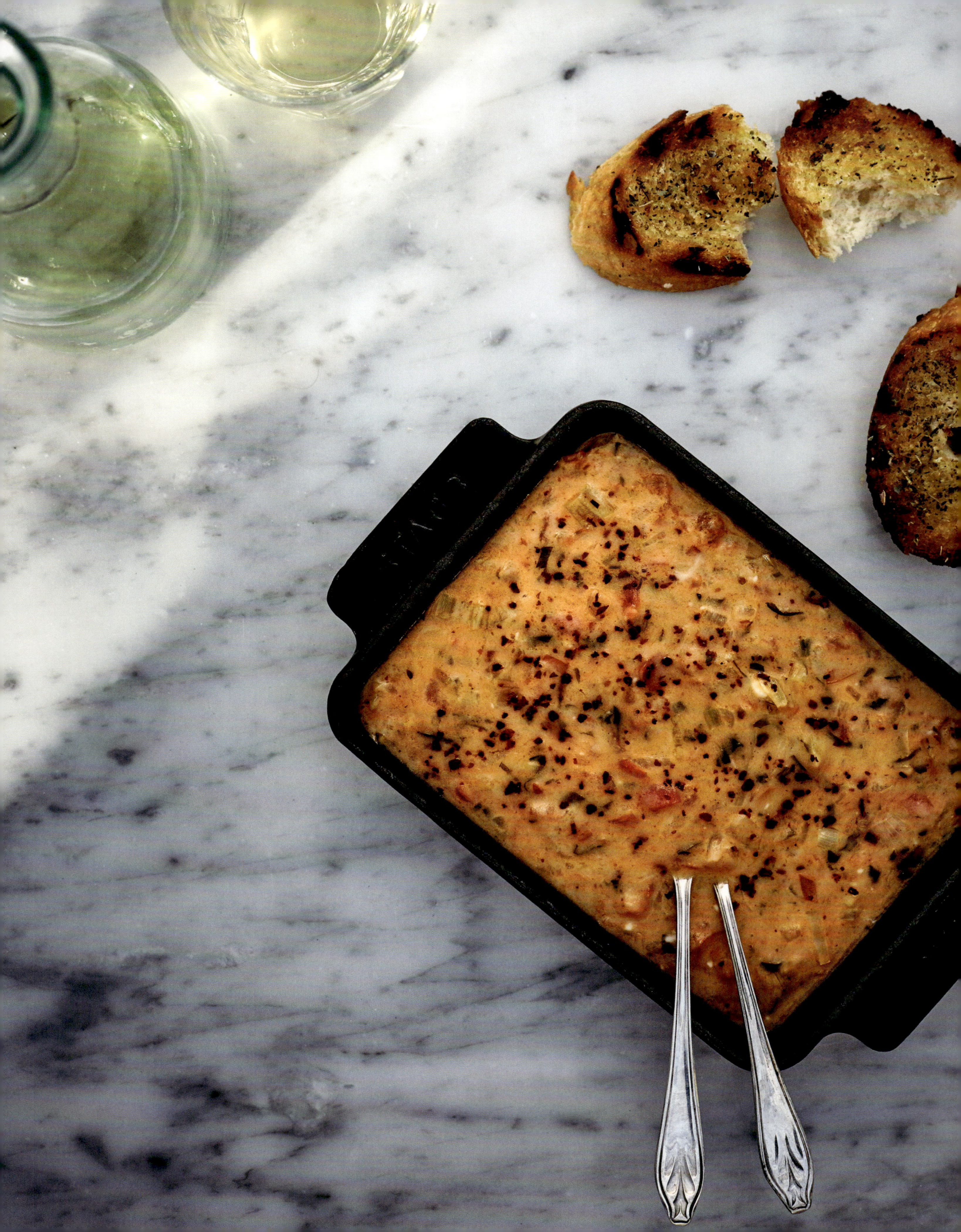

Bouyiourdi – Cheese Fondue

serves 2

FOR THE BOUYIOURDI

100g	feta cheese, crumbled
60g	Gouda cheese, grated
40g	Cheddar cheese, grated
	Greek olive oil, for frying
1	medium-sized tomato, finely chopped
1 tsp	tomato purée
1	shallot, finely chopped
1	spring onion, finely chopped
½	garlic clove, finely chopped
¼	green chilli, finely chopped
1	handful fresh parsley, finely chopped
1	pinch of chopped fresh oregano
1	pinch of dried red chilli flakes
	toasted bread, to serve

1. In a bowl, mix the crumbled feta, grated Gouda and grated Cheddar by hand.

2. In a frying pan, heat olive oil over medium heat. Sauté the tomato for 2 minutes until softening, then stir in the tomato purée. Add the shallot, spring onion, garlic and chilli, then simmer for another 2 minutes.

3. Transfer the mixed cheeses into the pan. Gradually stir the melting cheeses into the vegetables and combine with a wooden spoon until thick.

4. Lastly, stir in the parsley and season with the oregano and chilli flakes. Give it a final good stir and transfer the Bouyourdi into a small serving dish. Enjoy hot with toasted bread.

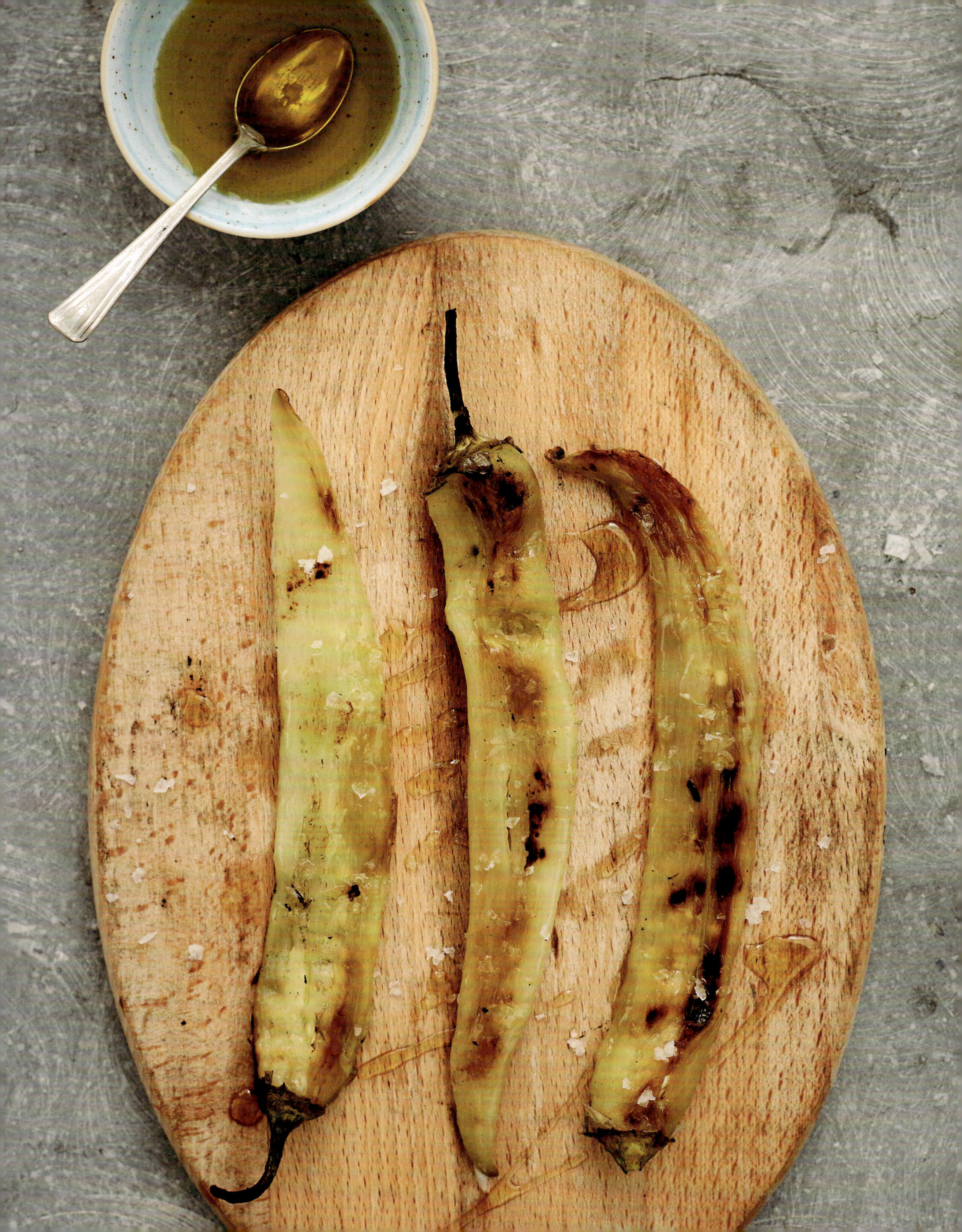

Smoky Green Peppers

serves 2

———✳———

'Those green peppers of yours are looking great', my neighbour leaned against the fence looking enviously at my garden. 'How did you get this good at gardening?' Nothing earns your watchful neighbours' attention faster than something that is none of their business. I patiently explained all I knew about growing green peppers, gave him a few of the vegetables, a smile, a brief talk about neighbourly support and a lot to wonder and talk about on his way home. My new neighbourly love is the result of a change of perspective. It started when, out of curiosity, I paid a visit to another neighbour's garden: The neighbouring peninsula of Mount Athos is a mysterious and unique place. The monk republic, a fully independent country of its own, is populated only by devoted monks. Mount Athos is known as the Garden of the Holy Mother and is also open to visitors or, in my case, open to curious neighbours. Upon my first courtesy visit I was welcomed warmly and shown around the beautiful monasteries and, of course, the fruitful grounds. 'Those green peppers of yours are looking great', I said, looking enviously at their vegetable patch. 'How did you get this good at gardening?' 'We learnt from each other', replied the monk: 'Neighbourly help basically. We look into each other's gardens to make sure we all have enough.' 'I feel mostly neighbours look into each other's gardens to make sure they have as much as the other …' 'I see. Neighbourly love is a true blessing. Sometimes all it takes is a change of perspective. Usually a perspective towards heaven.'

FOR THE GREEN PEPPERS

	Greek olive oil, for frying, plus extra for drizzling
2	spicy green peppers
1 tsp	black balsamic vinegar
1	pinch of coarse sea salt

1. In a pan, heat the olive oil over medium-high heat. Sauté the whole peppers on both sides until softened and browned. Deglaze the pan with the balsamic vinegar, cover with a lid and continue simmering for 1 minute.

2. Peel the peppers while still warm and place on a serving plate. Drizzle with olive oil and, lastly, season with a pinch of salt.

Sea Urchin Salad

serves 4

———※———

As they stick to a rock, sea urchins always remind me of shy ladies in a vintage photograph sitting lined up on the bench at a ball, waiting to be chosen. With their shiny black evening gowns, they rock from side to side with the tune of the music as if it was the rhythmic percussion of the waves. Shy ladies of an underwater nature tend to avoid having intense light on themselves. Their feelings are often as deep as the sea, and one can only discover them far beyond the shallow waters. They flee from wild open waters but choose to shelter on a solid rock where the waves brush gently over their cheeks. These shy ladies just need a safe place to hold on to, a quiet place to be by themselves.
No wonder I want to steal their hearts.

FOR THE SEA URCHIN SALAD

12	sea urchins, red or purple colouring
	sea water or salted water
2 tsp	freshly squeezed lemon juice
6 tsp	Greek olive oil

1. Use a sharp pair of kitchen scissors to cut the sea urchins into halves.

2. Rinse the interior carefully with sea water or salted water until thoroughly cleansed of sand.

3. Use a teaspoon to scoop out the sea urchin eggs and reserve them in a serving bowl.

4. Drizzle with lemon juice and olive oil and serve.

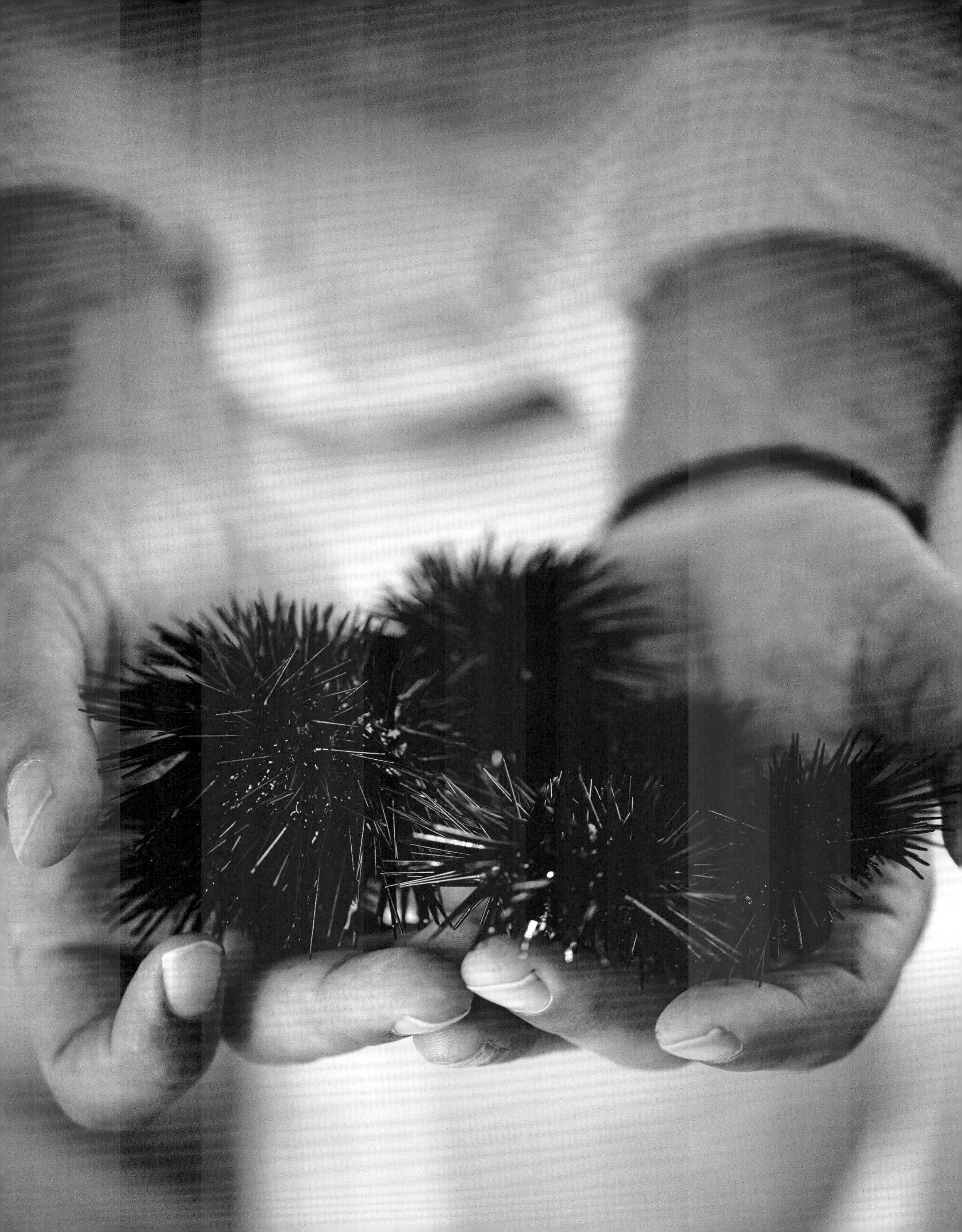

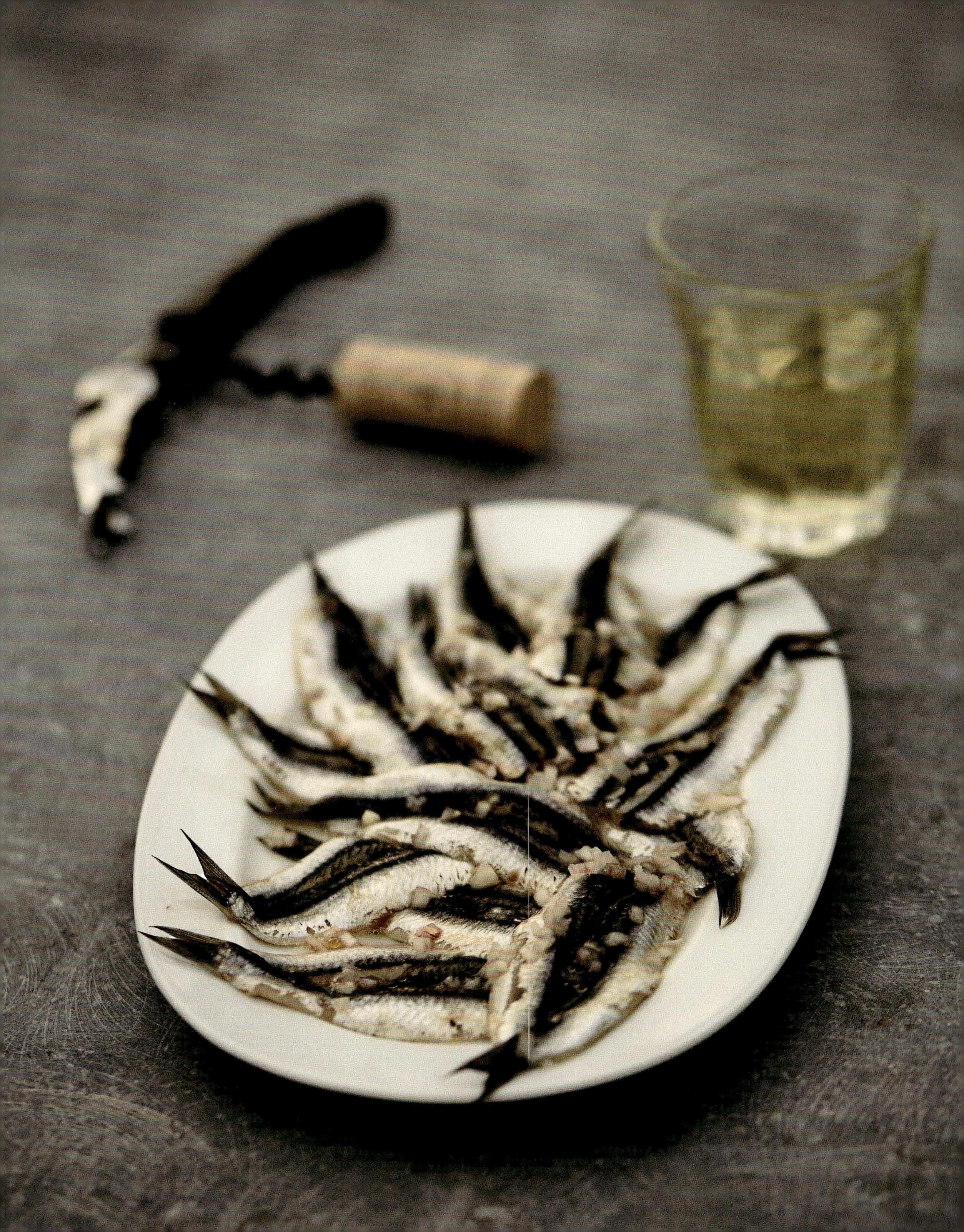

Marinated Anchovies

serves 2

I was merrily enjoying Marinated Anchovies in my favourite taverna by the harbour, until somebody gave me a more or less gentle nudge. 'Excuse me Sir, this is my table. Those are my anchovies.' Politely I apologised and threw one anchovy towards the self-proclaimed owner of my table. 'There you are. Have one.' He diplomatically accepted my offer for a start. 'Now stroke me three times', which I did two times before he kindly said, 'Thank you', by slamming his claws into my skin. One cat leads to another, some whined a few tragic meows how again lunch was served late and they had to postpone their afternoon nap because of my incompetence, others hissed spitefully that they would soon have to look for more qualified servants. I was shooed away and I meowed a heart-breaking apology while my masters licked their paws and groomed their whiskers, approving the anchovies at least. One nudged me twice on the belly and threw me one half-eaten piece of anchovy with a sweet: 'There you are. Good boy', and my services were dismissed.

FOR THE MARINATED ANCHOVIES

500g	anchovies, whole and cleaned
	white balsamic vinegar
	Greek olive oil, for frying
	sunflower oil, for frying
3	garlic cloves, sliced
2	sprigs of fresh rosemary
3	sprigs of fresh lemon thyme
1	handful fresh parsley, chopped

1. Start by preparing the cleaned anchovies. Trim the fins off all the anchovies, remove the entrails and rinse well. Remove the heads and carefully clean the fish of spine and bones.

2. In a deep bowl, marinate the fillets in the balsamic vinegar for 2 hours in a cool, dry environment. Once marinated, place on paper towels and set aside.

3. In a medium-sized pan over medium heat, heat the olive and sunflower oils. Sweat the garlic until translucent and season with rosemary and thyme. Lastly, add the parsley and the anchovies and cook until the fish are slightly browned.

Stuffed Sardines

serves 6

I know exactly what it is like to travel within a swarm of sardines, as hundreds, thousands of small, silvery darts at a time speed through the water. No space to move and no air to breathe, everybody squeezed against one another like passengers on a Thessaloniki bus ride. The swarm is usually packed with undisciplined children yelling and being loud while poking and teasing one another. If I was born a sardine, I would happily push myself into the fresh air by willingly swimming into the next fisherman's net to put an end to this journey. 'Stop pushing me.' 'I am not pushing.' 'Stuart is pushing!' 'Are we nearly there yet?' 'Stuart is pushing!' 'I need the loo …' as they rush through the water. 'Jocelyn poked my eye! Jocelyn!' 'Are we going to eat plankton again today?' 'I hate plankton!' 'Are we nearly there yet?' 'I don't want to swim anymore …' 'Jocelyn!' 'I am going to be sick …' 'Are we nearly there yet?!' That's why I eat them stuffed.

FOR THE FISH

1kg	fresh sardines, whole and boned
	Greek olive oil

FOR THE FILLING

2–3	garlic cloves, finely chopped
1	white onion, finely chopped
	Greek olive oil
	zest of 1 lemon
100g	sun-dried tomatoes
2	tomatoes, finely chopped
1	pinch of fresh lemon thyme
300ml	tomato juice
	juice of ½ lemon
	fine sea salt and black pepper
½	bunch fresh parsley, finely chopped

1. Preheat the oven to 190°C (fan).

2. Prepare the filling. In a small pot over medium heat, sweat the garlic and the onion in olive oil until translucent but not browned. Add the lemon zest and the sun-dried and fresh tomatoes. Season with a pinch of lemon thyme and stir for 2–3 minutes. Pour in the tomato and lemon juice. Reduce the heat to low and allow to simmer for approximately 15 minutes, until the ingredients have combined.

3. Season to taste with salt, pepper and more lemon juice before adding the parsley.

4. Stuff the sardines by spooning the filling into the opened fish.

5. Grease the bottom of a large cooking dish with olive oil and place the stuffed sardines inside. Drizzle with olive oil and season with salt.

6. Allow the sardines to roast in the oven for approximately 5–8 minutes and serve immediately.

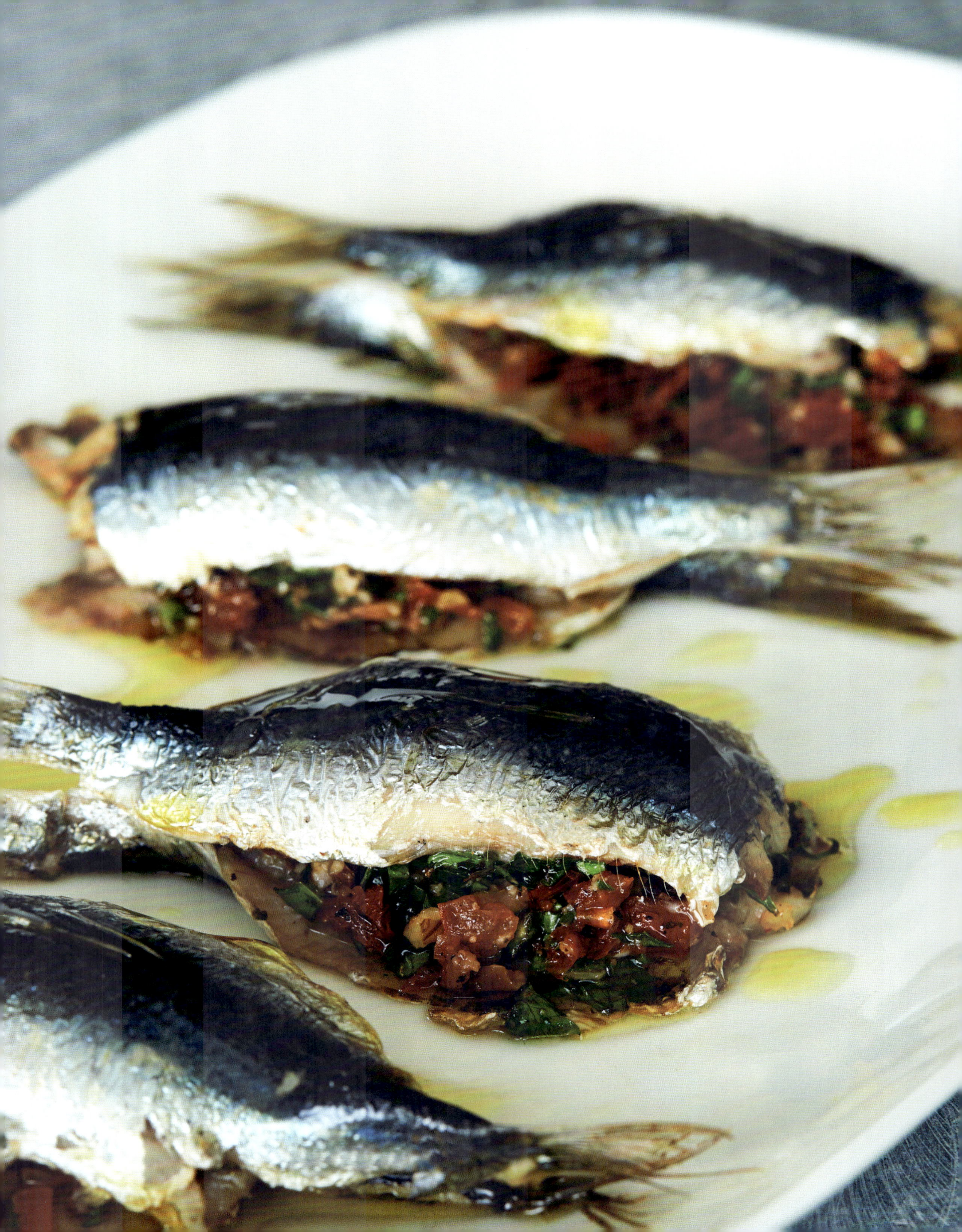

Juicy Onion Wedges with Minced Meat Filling

serves 4

———✳———

When I pull the steaming dish out of the oven, I am greeted by a lovely smell of what appears to be a tiny fleet of little ships that are rocking gently on the golden frying liquid. I can tell that my ability for proper construction of tiny model ships was not encouraged enough as a boy: my little fleet looks like they have just emerged from a raging storm. The colour of the ship's hull of white onion wedges is showing dark blister-like paint peeling off the salt-crusted wood. The top shell, like a white sail, shows severe damage as if a storm had torn them mercilessly. If a miniature crew had been on board, they would have had rain drops of the salty cooking liquid slammed into their faces as they slipped on the deck while the fanned air of the oven would mercilessly send mountains of waves. The crackling of the onion roasting, like a thunderstorm in the night, a malign laughter at their attempt to escape the ocean's hunger just when it is about to devour them at last. That is exactly the moment when I take the onions from the oven. They are too good to be shared.

FOR THE JUICY ONION WEDGES

5	white onions
	fine sea salt and freshly ground black pepper
	Greek olive oil, for frying
2	carrots, finely chopped
2–3	sprigs of fresh thyme
1	garlic clove, finely chopped
300g	minced beef
10	sprigs of fresh oregano, stripped
60ml	red wine
1	handful fresh parsley, chopped
1 tbsp	white balsamic vinegar

1. Preheat the oven to 180°C.

2. Prepare the onion shells by cutting the onions into halves to within 1 cm of the root. Boil the onions for 30 minutes. Remove them from the pot. Reserve the onion water. Separate out the onion wedges individually and reserve the centre parts on the side. Carefully remove the transparent membrane from the largest wedges. Sprinkle the wedges with salt and set aside.

3. Finely chop the reserved onion centres. Reserve approximately 1½ handfuls of chopped onion.

4. You will need two sauté pans. In one sauté pan heat olive oil over medium heat, fry the chopped onion, carrots, thyme and garlic. Meanwhile in the second sauté pan, fry the minced meat in olive oil over high heat. Brown the meat until well-cooked for about 5 minutes, and break it up with a wooden spoon. Season with the leaves of 6 sprigs of oregano and fry it for about 2 minutes while constantly stirring, then deglaze the pan with red wine. Season to taste with salt and pepper.

5. After approximately 2 minutes, add the contents of the first pan to the meat. Let the ingredients combine for 6–10 minutes before stirring in the chopped parsley and remove from the heat. If necessary, season to taste again with salt and pepper as well as the leaves from 2 more oregano sprigs. Mix in the balsamic vinegar

6. Now spoon the mince into the onion wedges. Gently squeeze the edges with your fingertips to close the opening. Place them into a cooking dish and pour the reserved onion water into the dish until it comes 1 finger width above of the onions and sprinkle with the remaining oregano.

7. Bake for 30 minutes, or until lightly browned.

Mussel Pilaf

serves 2

FOR THE MUSSEL PILAF

	Greek olive oil
1	garlic clove, finely chopped
1	white onion, finely chopped
1	red pepper, finely chopped
1	green pepper, finely chopped
3	spring onions, finely chopped
50ml	dry white wine
	zest and juice of 2 lemons
300g	basmati rice
800ml	vegetable stock, warm
300g	fresh mussels, cleaned
200g	shelled mussels
½	bunch fresh dill, finely chopped
	fine sea salt and freshly ground black pepper

1. In a large pan, heat olive oil over medium heat. Toss in the garlic, onion, red and green peppers and spring onions and sauté until translucent. Deglaze with the white wine and season with the lemon zest. Simmer until the wine has evaporated.

2. Now stir in the rice and pour in the warm vegetable stock, then let the pilaf cook for 18–20 minutes.

3. Add in the whole and the shelled mussels and give it a good stir. Allow the ingredients to combine for another 3 minutes, until the mussels slowly open.

4. Lastly, sprinkle with dill and drizzle in the lemon juice. Season to taste with salt and pepper, add another 1–2 tbsp of olive oil and give the pilaf a final stir.

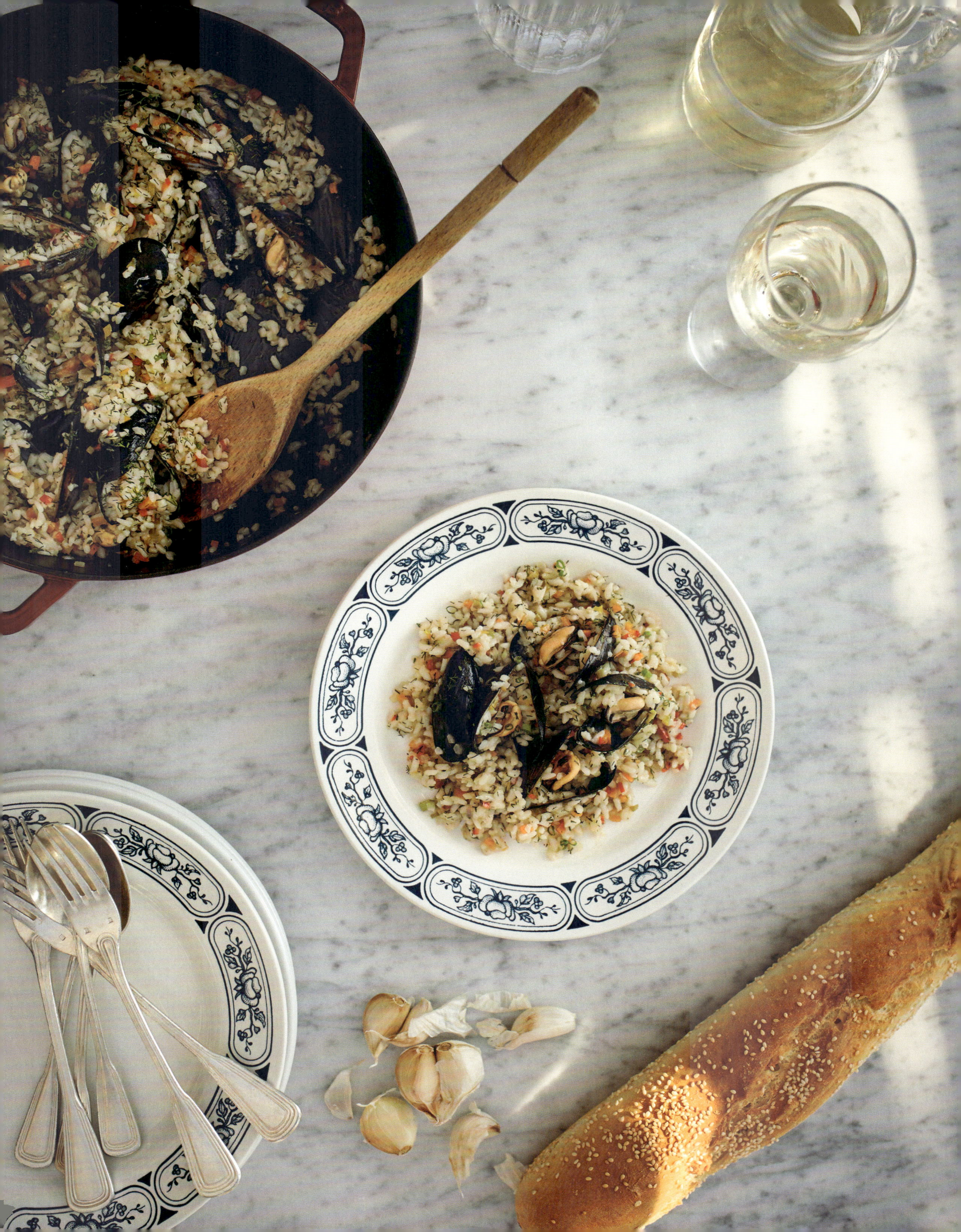

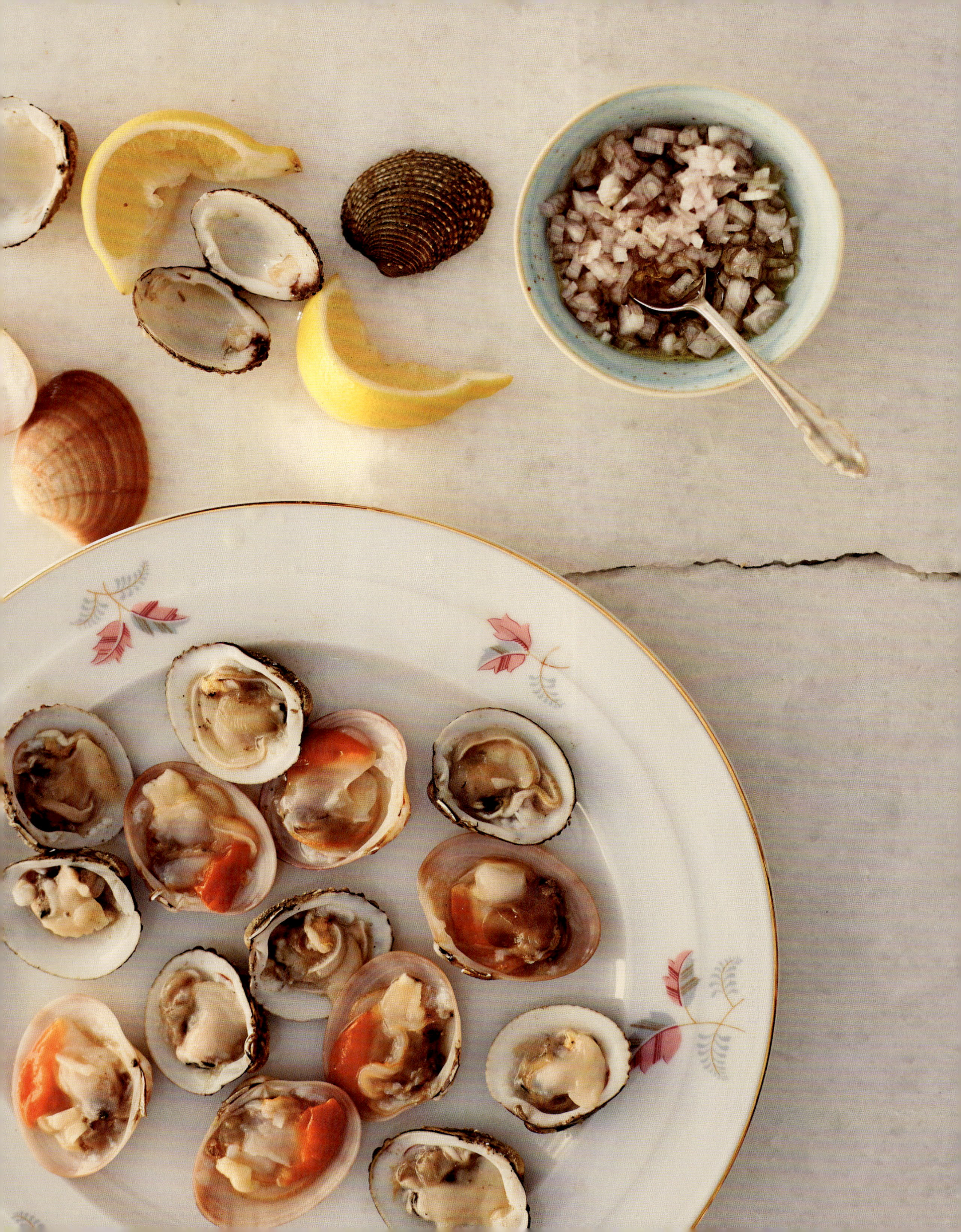

Dressing for Clams

Mother's Hands

———✻———

Each threat, each fear, the ocean's spite
Your strength, a shell, as hard, as tight
A shield, eternal, solid, steel,
Against the ocean's tides of teal

I never learnt of fear, of threat,
I never knew of dark, of dread
I the mussel, you the shell
and all you let me see,
Was humble beauty all around,
A world of yours for me.

A thousand colours' shimmer bright,
A sheltered bed to spend the night,
A mussel on cold ocean's sands,
A life, a son, a mother's hands.

———✻———

FOR THE DRESSING

3	shallots, finely chopped
½	cucumber, peeled and finely chopped
½	tomato, skin only
1 tbsp	fresh chives, chopped
½	chilli, finely chopped
	zest of 1 lemon
100 ml	white wine vinegar
2 tbsp	Greek olive oil

In a small bowl, combine the shallots, cucumber, tomato skin and chives. Now add the chilli, lemon zest and vinegar and stir the ingredients thoroughly. Lastly, add the olive oil and spoon onto the clams just before eating.

OLIVE OIL

In Greece we refer to olive oil as liquid gold. It is packed with nutrients that are beneficial to health and has several other functions in cosmetics and medicine. In Greece, we have the highest consumption of olive oil worldwide and I, too, use it in the broad majority of my recipes. When I drive my car through the streets of Sithonia, I pass by row after row of neatly lined-up olive trees on both sides of the road. When you push your trolley through the supermarket, you pass by shelf after shelf of neatly lined-up bottles of olive oil on both sides of the aisle. As fast as I drive past the trees outside my window, you should walk past those bottles. They most likely do not contain liquid gold, health benefits or drops of a Mediterranean lifestyle. They most likely contain cheaper oil, colourants and merely drops of olive oil. The business around liquid gold has turned many big farmers into large producers, and many small farmers into even smaller farmers. Luckily, when I purchase olive oil, I can visit one of these even smaller farmers, a neighbouring producer just a short drive away. And on my return trip, I usually have some glass bottles clinking in the boot of the car. Those are the bottles that contain liquid gold, the natural health benefits and 1 litre of a Mediterranean lifestyle with a hint of spice. The viscous gold and green oil burns a little going down, but does not leave an oily residue in your mouth. The farmer whose blackened hands may burn a little from hand-picking the olives ripened under the sun is a genuine producer. Genuine Producers feel sun and rain on their skins outside in a field, wear muddy boots and have that sparkle in their eyes. Perhaps customers are getting rare, but they keep fighting for what makes them happy. And that is even rarer. As rare as original Greek olive oil.

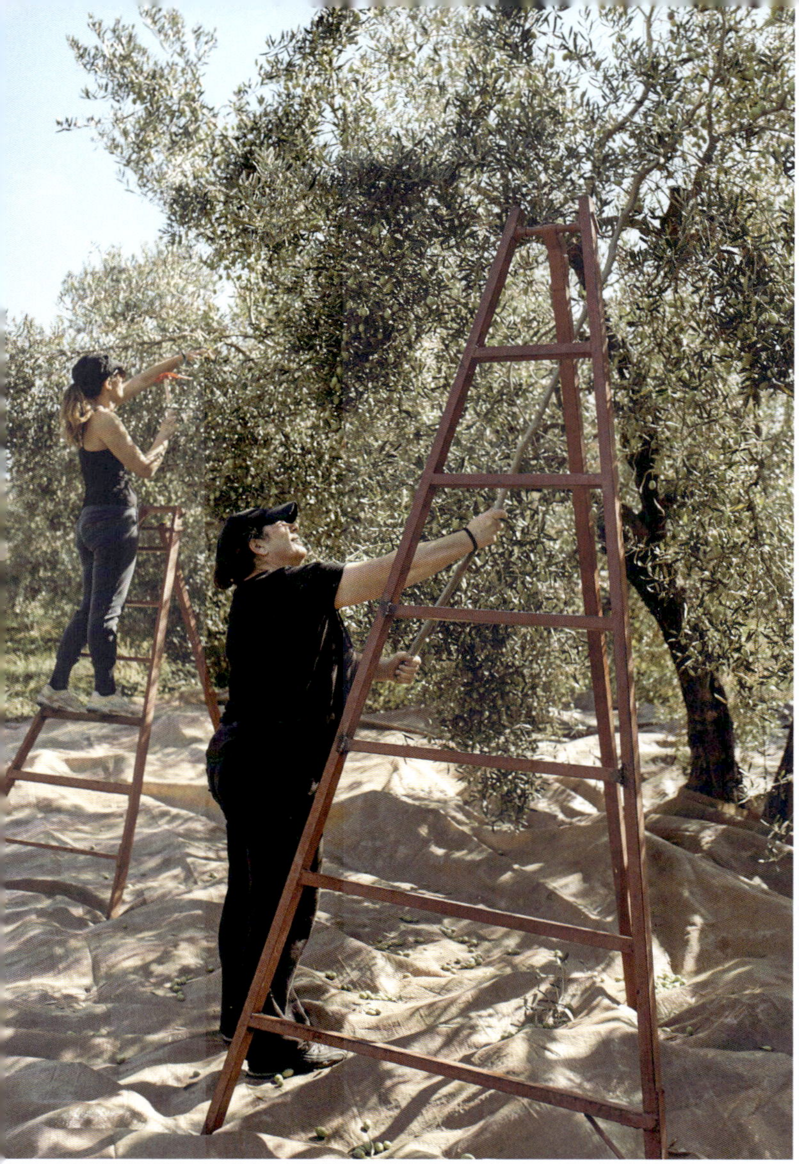
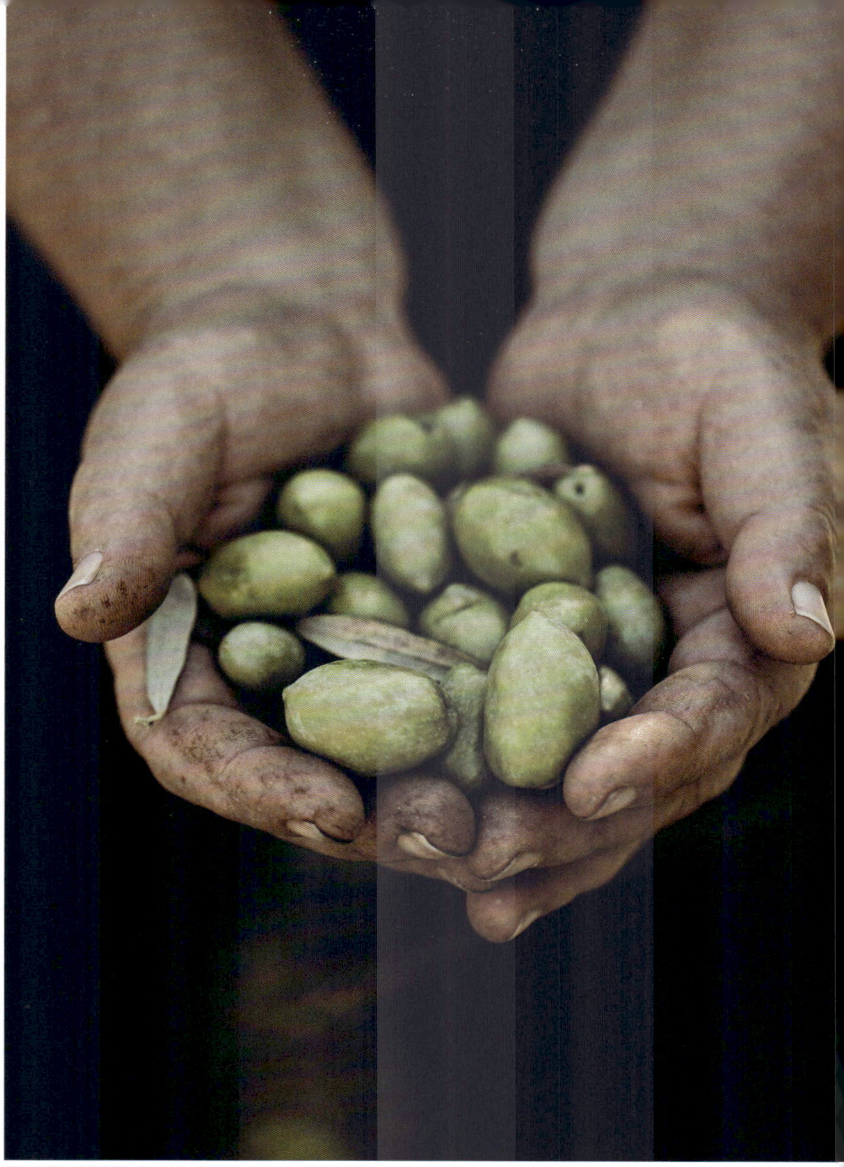
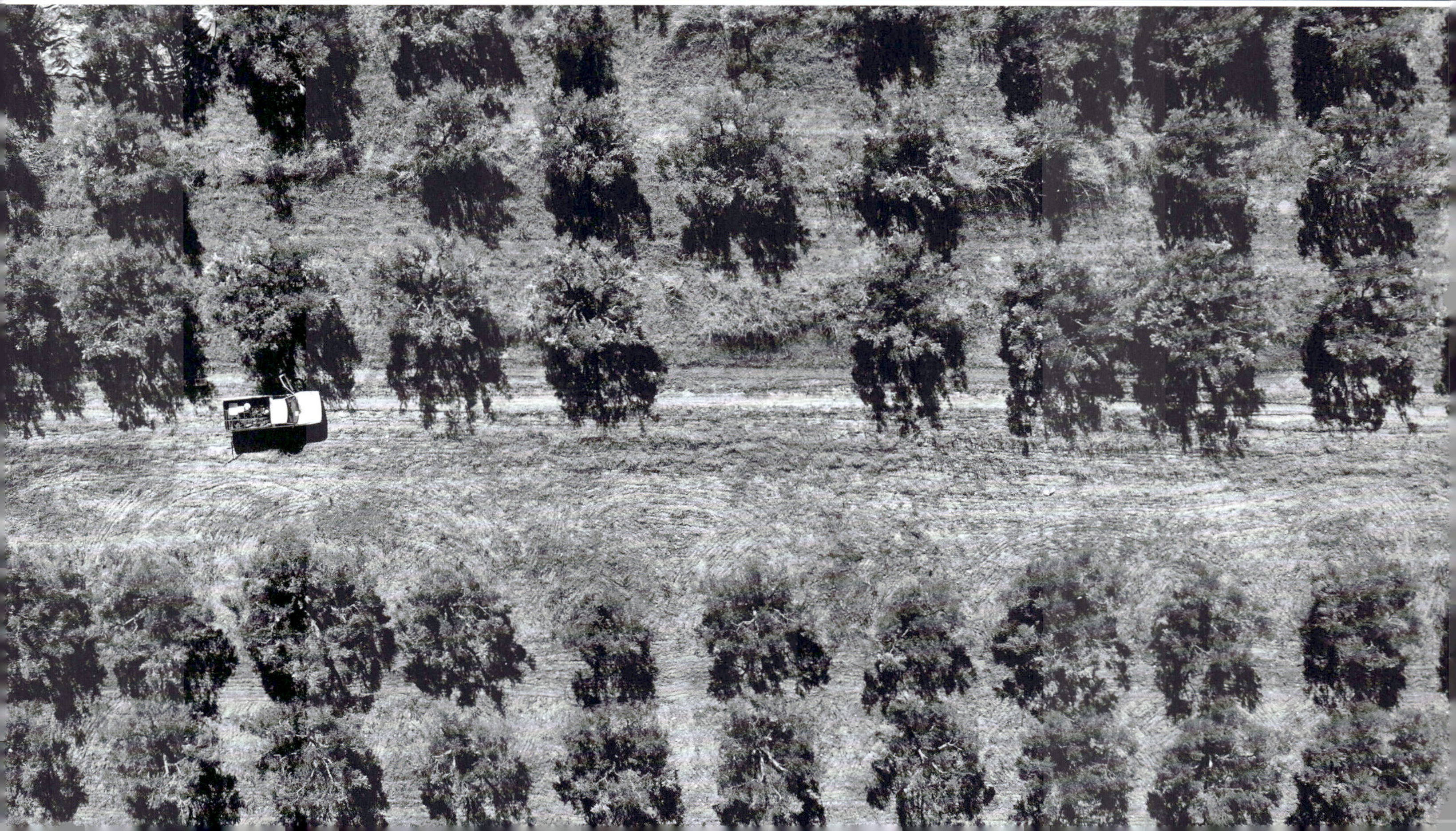

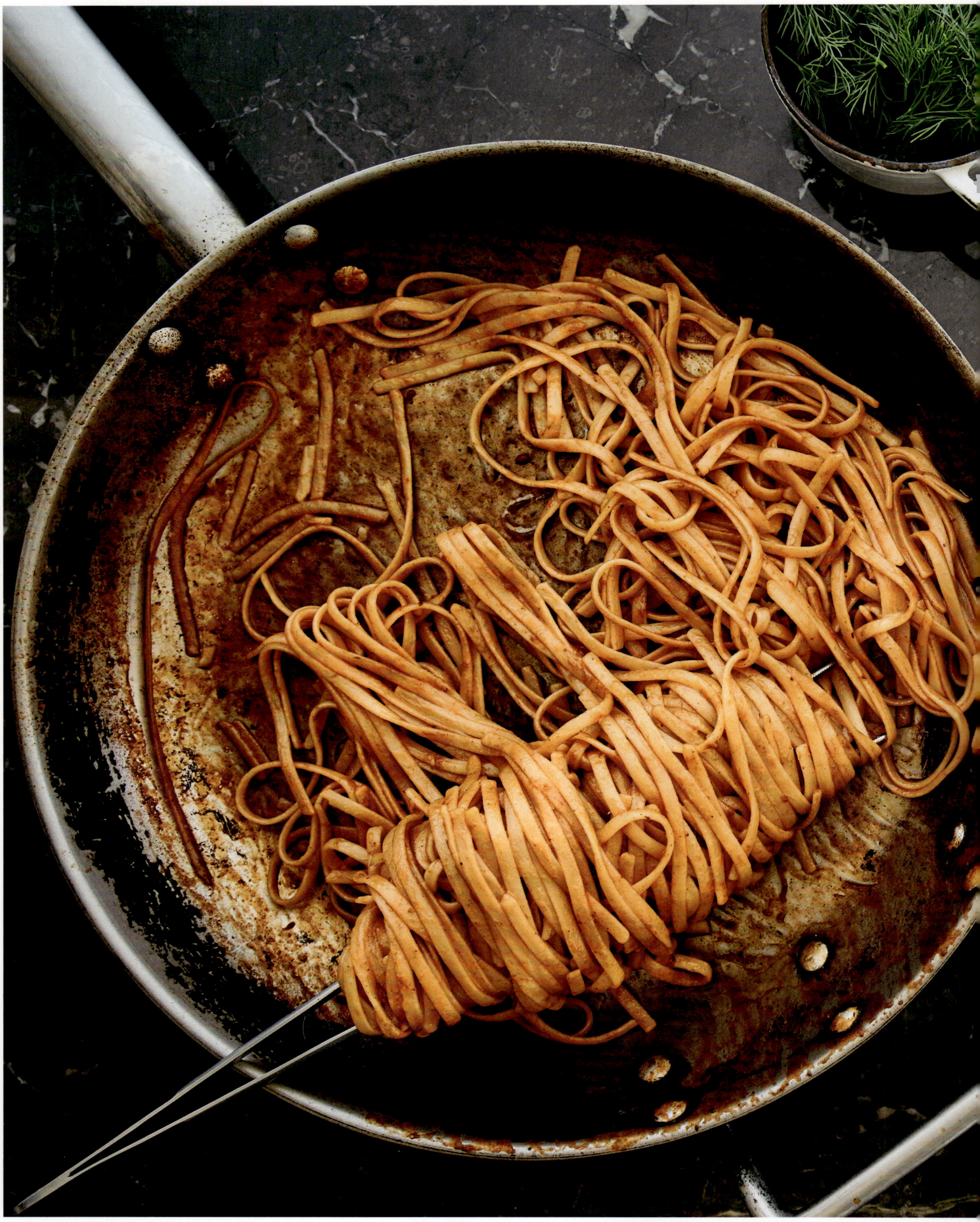

Ζυμαρικά

PASTA & RICE

The Cockerel Recipe

serves 4

―◆―

'All right, let me read it out to you once again, I thought I was quite clear! Firstly, preheat the oven. Season with salt, pepper and olive oil. Brown for 4 minutes until golden then set aside. Prepare the vegetables, you know, until a nice aroma fills the air, then deglaze with a generous amount of port – a fine port I admit … However, then roast for 30 minutes in the nice warm oven – so far so good.' 'Well …' 'No, please hear me out! After that, I demanded clearly … read for yourself …', he pointed feverishly at the piece of paper he was holding up. The clerk started hopping uncomfortably from foot to foot. 'I apologise, sir. Our mistake. You asked for another 10 minutes before …' 'Exactly! Another 10 minutes!' His face turned even redder with rage: 'I understand you are a clerk and clearly you don't know wake-up procedures as well as I do, after all I was a specialist all my life, but I assumed you could at least read instructions!' 'I … I am very sorry, I am not a chef. I understand as a cockerel you do value precise timekeeping. Please accept my apologies.' The clerk lowered his voice. 'We don't usually do this, but how about we forget that any of this ever happened? I will just expect you back here in 10 minutes?' The angry guest nodded. 'You can keep this. For next time.' He threw his testament at the clerk and stomped away from the gates of heaven. The next moment the cockerel found himself back in the warm oven. 'Heavenly', he sighed and happily snuggled into his pasta.

FOR THE COCKEREL

1	cockerel, whole
	fine sea salt and freshly ground black pepper
	Greek olive oil
	sunflower oil, for frying
2	white onions, finely chopped
1	garlic clove, finely chopped
8	sprigs of fresh thyme
1	leek, white part only, finely chopped
2	sticks celery, roughly chopped
3	carrots, peeled and finely chopped
30g	unsalted butter
2	bay leaves
1 tbsp	tomato purée
½ tsp	ground coriander seeds
350ml	port
350g	passata
1.2l	chicken stock
½ tsp	ground cinnamon
200g	xilopites or pappardelle pasta

1. Preheat the oven to 180°C. Gut the cockerel, cut into portions and season all over with salt and pepper and sprinkle with olive oil.

2. In a large sauté pan, brown the cockerel. Heat the sunflower oil over medium heat, stir in all parts of the cockerel and cook for about 4 minutes, until golden. Transfer the meat to a deep pan and set aside.

3. Discard the sunflower oil from the used pan, reduce temperature to a low heat. Heat olive oil and sweat the onions and garlic. Add the thyme and stir occasionally to combine the ingredients until the onions are translucent, for approximately 3 minutes. Stir in the leek and celery. Combine the ingredients with a wooden spoon before adding the carrots and continue to stir for another 2 minutes. Now add the butter, bay leaves and tomato purée. Let the ingredients simmer for approximately 3 minutes before seasoning with the coriander and pepper. Lastly, deglaze the pan with the port. Season to taste with salt and pepper and simmer for approximately 4 minutes. Now stir in the passata.

4. Spread the vegetables around the cockerel in the pan. Pour over the chicken stock and transfer the dish to the oven for 30 minutes. Remove from the oven, turn the meat in the sauce and sprinkle with the cinnamon. Roast for another 10 minutes.

5. Take the dish out of the oven and remove the inedible parts of the cockerel. Add the uncooked pasta next to the meat. With a fork, gently press it into the sauce. Cover the pan with a lid and return to the oven for another 10 minutes. Serve hot.

Spicy Mediterranean Linguini

serves 2

This dish is clearly no Greek classic. Yet, filling my book I chose to pick this as a recipe which is worth being included. Occasionally, you might arrive home exhausted from work on a weeknight and the idea to cook up a fussy meal just seems too much of an effort? My advice is this quick but glorious meal from my repertoire! Why bother? Because cooking is immensely pleasurable, plus you acquire a valuable life skill for yourself. Ease of approach and a vibrant blend of tasty ingredients, spicy chilli flakes, simmered in olive oil are the keys to this pasta recipe. Pour two glasses of wine and enjoy.

FOR THE PASTA

	salted water or chicken stock for cooking
300g	dried linguini

FOR THE SAUCE

	Greek olive oil, for frying
3	garlic cloves, finely chopped
3	medium shallots, finely chopped
2	spring onions, thinly sliced
⅓	green chilli, thinly sliced
14	cherry tomatoes, halved
	fine sea salt and freshly ground black pepper
2	sprigs of fresh thyme
60ml	dry white wine
½	handful fresh parsley, chopped
110ml	chicken stock
40g	unsalted butter
	zest of ½ lime
1 tsp	dried red chilli flakes, plus more to serve

1. In a medium pan, bring salted water or chicken stock to a boil and stir in the linguini. Cook until al dente.

2. Meanwhile, prepare the sauce. In a medium sauté pan, heat olive oil over medium heat. Sweat the garlic and shallots, stirring constantly, for about 1 minute, until slightly golden.

3. Stir in the spring onions, chilli and cherry tomatoes. Simmer the ingredients until translucent before seasoning to taste with salt and pepper. Keep adding olive oil if required. Lastly, toss in the thyme.

4. Allow the ingredients to combine, before deglazing the pan with the white wine. Stir in the parsley, then pour over the chicken stock. Add the butter and let it dissolve, then season with the lime zest.

5. Drain the linguini in a pasta sieve once they are al dente, then set aside.

6. When the sauce begins to simmer, transfer the linguini to the pan and season with the chilli flakes. Give it a final good stir and serve hot with more chilli flakes on the side.

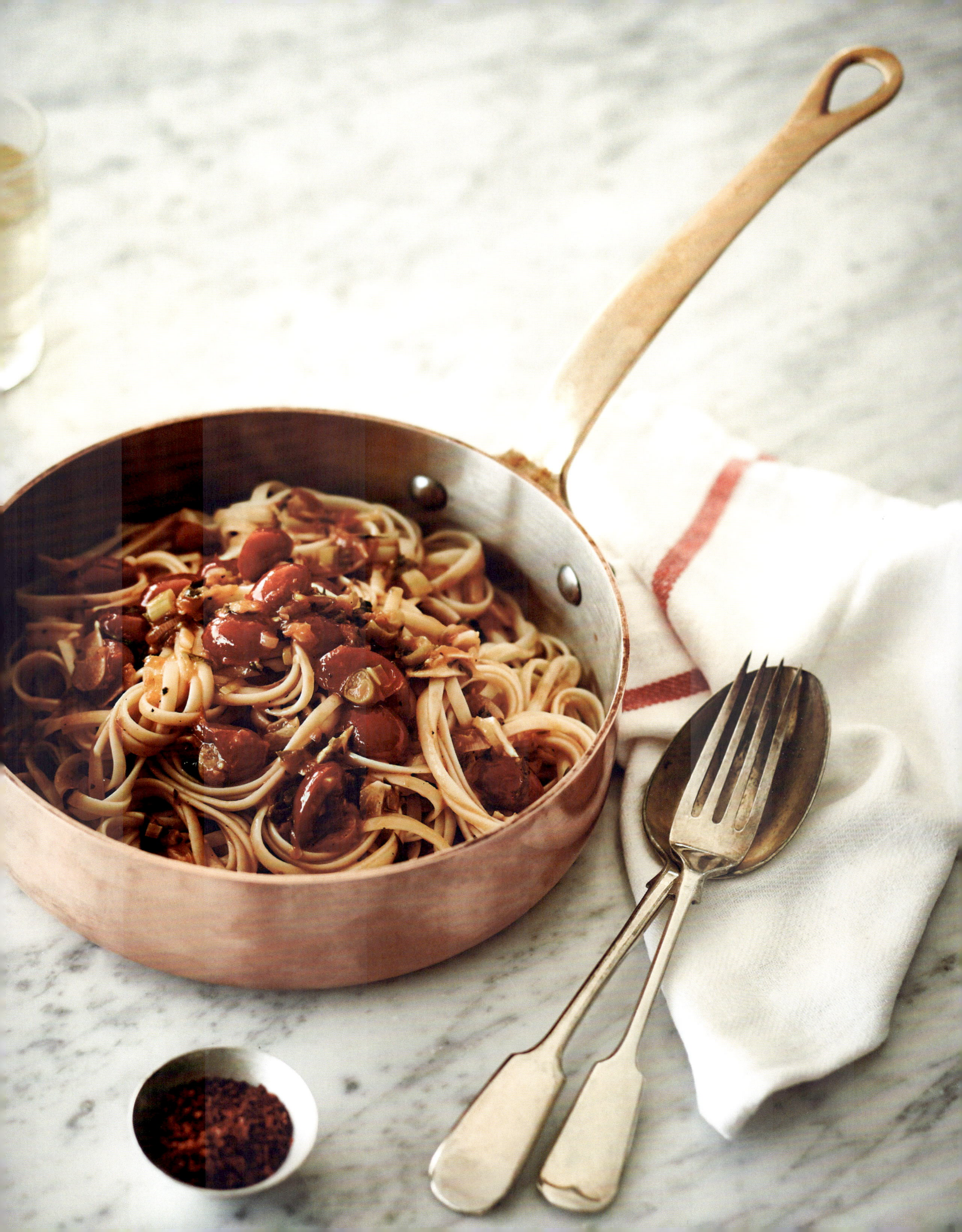

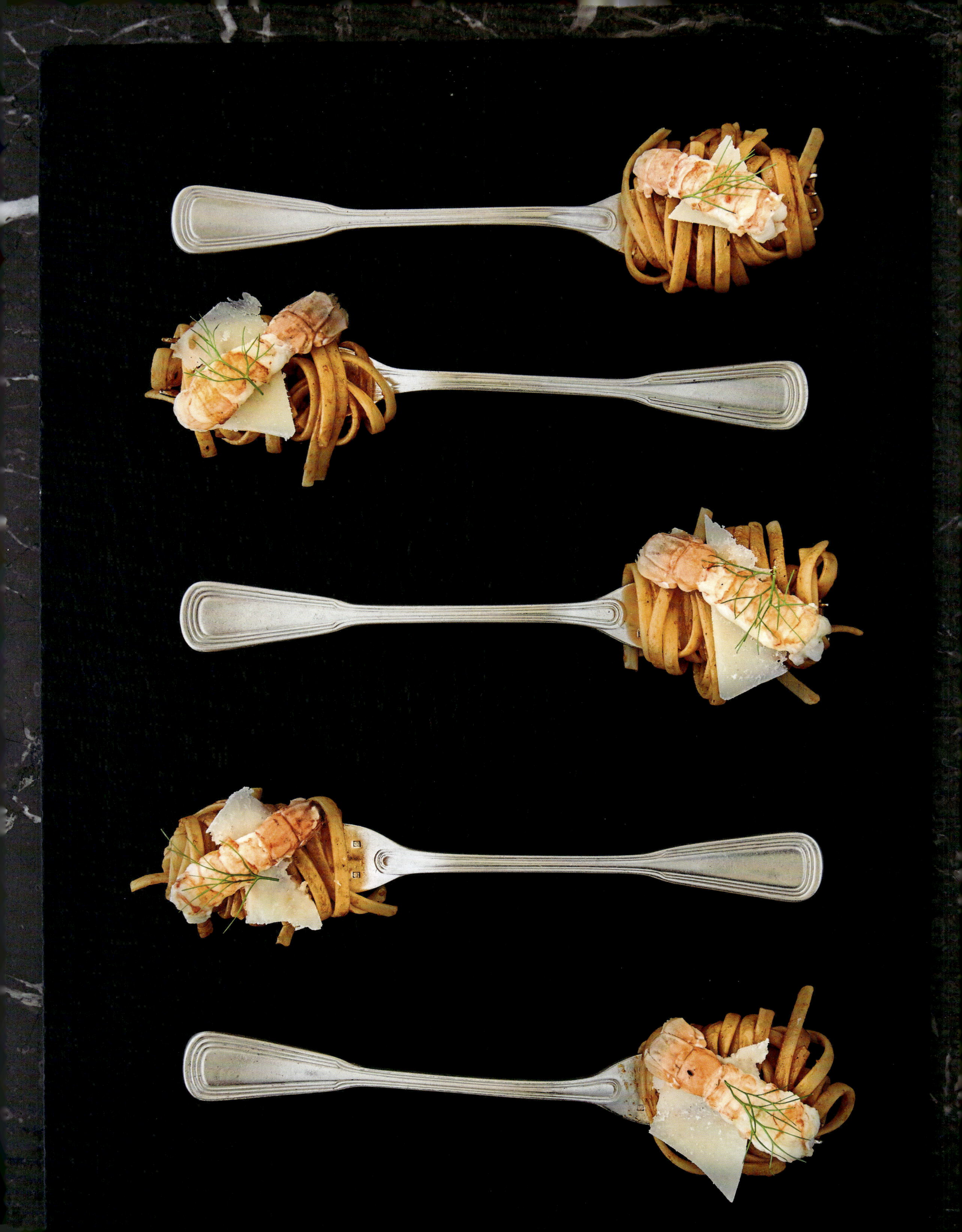

The Langoustine Linguini

serves 2

I wanted to taste it. I ate it all.

FOR THE LANGOUSTINE BISQUE

8	fresh langoustines
	Greek olive oil, for frying
1 tsp	unsalted butter
1	carrot, peeled and sliced
½	leek, chopped
1	stick celery, chopped
½	white onion, chopped
1	garlic clove, crushed
	leaves from 2 sprigs of fresh thyme
1 tbsp	tomato purée
1 tbsp	plain flour
	brandy, for deglazing
60ml	dry white wine
1.8l	chicken stock
	lemon juice
	Parmesan cheese, grated

FOR THE LINGUINI

200g	linguini
	butter, for frying

1. Start with the preparation of the bisque. Strip the heads, shells and tails from the langoustines. Set the meat aside.

2. In a casserole dish, heat olive oil over high heat and stir in the langoustine heads, shells and tails. Fry until browned. Use a potato masher to crush the ingredients, then reduce the heat to medium-low.

3. Add the butter, carrot, leek, celery, onion and garlic. Season with the thyme leaves and stir for 3–4 minutes to combine ingredients. When the vegetables are beginning to soften, stir in the tomato purée and add the flour. Deglaze the pan with brandy and shortly after with the white wine.

4. Pour in enough of the chicken stock to cover all of the ingredients. Simmer for 30 minutes, then strain the bisque through a sieve and set aside.

5. Heat a deep pan over medium heat. Add the linguini and pour in equal amounts of bisque and chicken stock until the pasta is covered. When the liquid starts to evaporate continue to add bisque and chicken stock to ensure the linguini remain covered and cook until al dente. Meanwhile, in a separate pan, brown the langoustine meat in butter over medium heat.

6. Season the linguini with a few drops of lemon juice and whisk in the Parmesan cheese as per personal preference. Give the pasta a final good stir and serve the linguini along with an extra spoonful of sauce from the pan. Once the langoustine meat is nicely browned, place it on top of the pasta and serve hot with Parmesan cheese on the side.

Stuffed Tomatoes & Peppers

serves 6

I enjoy the peppers and tomatoes from my own harvest. My small vegetable garden flourishes with green and red once the vegetables' time has come and before I process them into Stuffed Tomatoes & Peppers. If I could, I would love to use only the produce from my own garden. But, unfortunately, like all good things in life, the ripening requires time. So gardening taught me the virtue of being patient. It taught me that there is a time to plant and a time to harvest. A time for the tomatoes to be green and sour, and a time for the tomatoes to be juicy and red. A time for green leaves in spring and a time for red ones in autumn. A time to pick fruits and a time to pick weeds. A time for sun and a time for rain. A time for loss and a time for triumph. A time to nurture your garden and a time for your garden to nurture you. We always ask when the time of harvest will be. From all the things I have learnt from gardening, do you trust me if the answer is to wait?

FOR THE VEGETABLES

6	tomatoes
6	green peppers
	fine sea salt and freshly ground black pepper
	Greek olive oil

FOR THE FILLING

	Greek olive oil, for frying
500g	minced beef
2	white onions, finely chopped
2	garlic cloves, finely chopped
2	carrots, finely chopped
2 tbsp	tomato purée
350g	glazed rice
1 tbsp	granulated sugar
600ml	vegetable stock
	fine sea salt and freshly ground black pepper
1	bunch fresh parsley, finely chopped
1	bunch fresh mint, finely chopped
½	bunch fresh dill, finely chopped
2	potatoes, peeled and cut into wedges

1. Preheat the oven to 170°C.

2. First, remove the tops of the tomatoes and peppers. Keep them aside, they will later be used as lids. Core and hollow out the tomatoes and peppers carefully. Reserve the tomato flesh in a small bowl and set the hollow vegetables aside in an oven dish. Sprinkle the hollow tomatoes and peppers with salt and pepper and drizzle with olive oil.

3. Make the filling. In a medium-sized pan, heat the olive oil over high heat. Sauté the minced beef until brown, breaking it up with a wooden spoon. Reduce the heat to medium and stir in the onions, garlic and carrots. Sauté until softened. Add the tomato purée and allow ingredients to combine for 2–3 minutes.

4. Reduce the heat to low and add the rice and the reserved tomato flesh, season with the sugar and pour over 400ml of the vegetable stock. Sprinkle with salt and pepper and simmer for 5–6 minutes.

5. Remove the pan from heat and stir in the parsley, mint and dill. Now spoon the filling into the hollow vegetables so that they are up to three-quarters full, then place them back in the oven dish. Cover the tomatoes and peppers with their tops.

6. Arrange the potato wedges around the stuffed vegetables and pour the remaining 200ml of vegetable stock over the potatoes. Cover the oven dish tightly with kitchen foil and transfer it to the oven for 60 minutes.

7. Remove the foil and allow the vegetables to roast for another 10–15 minutes, until nicely browned. Enjoy hot with the golden potato wedges on the side.

Greek Orzo with Seafood

serves 2

'But grandma, orzo is the new rice!' I was only a little boy, excitedly hopping up and down with my new discovery between my little hands. '"Orzo", where does that word even come from?', my grandma's brow furrowed. 'It is a pasta. It is tiny pasta, look!' I waved the packet of orzo. 'Looks like rice to me', my grandma replied sceptically. 'That's because it is rice-shaped. Just the colour is a little different.' I continued to hold out the packet. She sighed and grabbed the plastic bag from my little hands. 'So,' she cleared her throat: 'Boil in water …' She read through the instructions. 'You cook it exactly like rice.' 'Yes, and it tastes similar!' She shook her head disapprovingly. 'Oh, my boy, your generation and your revolutionary spirit. Always wanting to replace the good old things.' I became impatient: 'But it's different! Can't you see? You just have to be open-minded, grandma! Please try it!' She looked at me unconvinced. 'The same but different.' She shook her head and mumbled under her breath: 'Makes no sense to me …' I remained quiet while I watched her boil the orzo. I was a little boy and could barely look over the counter. Eventually we sat down at the table, my grandma eyed her spoon, then took a bite: 'Looks similar. Tastes … the same. I like it. However, this is the exact same thing to me.' I chewed my orzo happily and finally broke the silence: 'It's just like people.' 'What?' she stared at me perplexed. 'The same but different.'

FOR THE ORZO

	Greek olive oil, for frying
2	garlic cloves, finely chopped
½	white onion, finely chopped
1	spring onion, finely chopped
8	prawns, heads, shells and tails removed and seasoned with salt
20	cherry tomatoes, quartered or halved
12	clams, cleaned
300g	Greek orzo
60ml	dry white wine
1l	chicken stock, warm
2	pinches of fine sea salt
	freshly ground black pepper
1	small handful fresh parsley, finely chopped
50g	unsalted butter
	zest and juice of ½ lemon

optional:

| 20g | Greek Kefalotiri or Parmesan cheese, grated |

1. In a large pan, heat olive oil over medium heat. Toss in the garlic, onion and spring onion and sauté until translucent. Add the prawns and brown them on both sides for about 45 seconds each. Remove them and set aside.

2. Stir in the cherry tomatoes. Add the clams and leave to simmer until the clams start to open slightly. Remove them as well and set aside.

3. Now add in the orzo and combine the ingredients by giving them a good stir. Shortly after, deglaze the pan with the white wine.

4. Little by little, pour the warm chicken stock into the pot, stirring constantly. During this process, season with the salt and pepper. Continue to gradually add chicken stock until you have about 100 ml left. Test the orzo for doneness.

5. Return the prawns and clams to the pan. Finally, pour in the last 100 ml of chicken stock and combine the ingredients. Stir in the parsley and butter, season with lemon zest and lemon juice and simmer for another 1–2 minutes.

6. Optionally add cheese for a thicker consistency if desired, then serve hot.

THE GOD OF WINE

Everything I know about wine, I learnt from Apostolos, the sommelier. Except for drinking it, that I figured out myself without any help from anyone.

Apostolos is a truly accomplished mastermind of wines. I am of the Orthodox faith, but if somebody told me that Apostolos was the human incarnation of the ancient Greek god Dionysus, the god of wine, I would not doubt it for a second. Especially after the first bottle. The creature Dionysus was a mischief-maker. With his charm he would seduce people to drink wine to excess, lift their moods into an ecstatic state and turn cultivated dinners into rousing orgies in the blink of an eye. In Apostolos I have recognised those exact competencies (except for arranging orgies perhaps) paired with an abundance of expert knowledge.

Wine production in Greece dates back to the Neolithic age, and developed from the 11th and 13th centuries before Christ. Even though little information is obtainable from this early period, it is said that even breakfast included a decent cup: *akratos oenos* – dipping bread into undiluted wine. Starting in the early morning, the consumption of pure or diluted wine did not cease throughout the day and played a part at all social occasions, from weddings to funerals. What a time to be alive! But don't worry, even these days us Greeks have plenty to offer.

The Grapes

AGIORGITIKO, Peloponnese: aromatic, fine and rich red grape, resulting in charming and soft red wines with a basic aromatic palate of cherries and cinnamon

LIMNIO, island of Lemnos, Halkidiki: red grape with rich, aromatic intensity, opulent taste

LIATIKO, island of Crete: among the oldest grape families in Greece, dominant and sometimes ageworthy red wines

MALAGOUZIA, mainland Greece: fine, aromatic white grape family with floral identities of jasmine and tea leaves

MANDILARIA, island of Paros, Rhodes, Crete: rich-in-taste red grape with aromas of black and red fruits, spices and animalistic flavours

MAVRODAPHNE, Patra, island of Kefalonia: among the finest Greek grapes, very aromatic, rich, fruity and earthy aroma, it is often made into sweet red wines

MAVROTRAGANO, Santorini: once close to extinction but now restored red grape from Santorini, an area formerly celebrated for its ASSYRTIKO grapes

MONEMVASIA, island of Paros: aromatic, medium-heavy, floral red wine from Paros

MUSCAT, mainland Greece: renowned family of grapes resulting in light, aromatic, grapey and floral wines

MOSCHOFILERO, Mantinia (Peloponnese): white grape resulting in light, crispy, aromatic wines with characters of rosé and white fruits

NEGOSKA, northern Greece: ageworthy red, high in acidity with firm tannins, animalistic character and a spicy aroma

NTEBINA, northern border: a white grape mostly found in the northern parts of Greece. Over the past years especially sparkling wines produced from the Ntebina grape have gained popularity

XINOMAVRO, northern border: one of Greece's finest red varieties. High acidity and dense aromatic intensity with a strong red fruit aroma and, once aged, tomato flavour. Often compared to its sisters in Burgundy (France) and Barolo (Italy)

RODITIS, Patra, mainland Greece: the grape used to produce Greece's traditional wine 'Retsina'

ROBOLA, island of Kefalonia, central Greece: white, fine grape, light, crispy, citrus taste

ASSYRTIKO, Santorini, northern Greece: rated among the finest Greek white grapes, having earned strong admiration globally

VIDIANO, Crete: a white grape which was restored after having been almost extinct. It has a pleasant peach and apricot flavour. French Viognier wines are comparable in taste

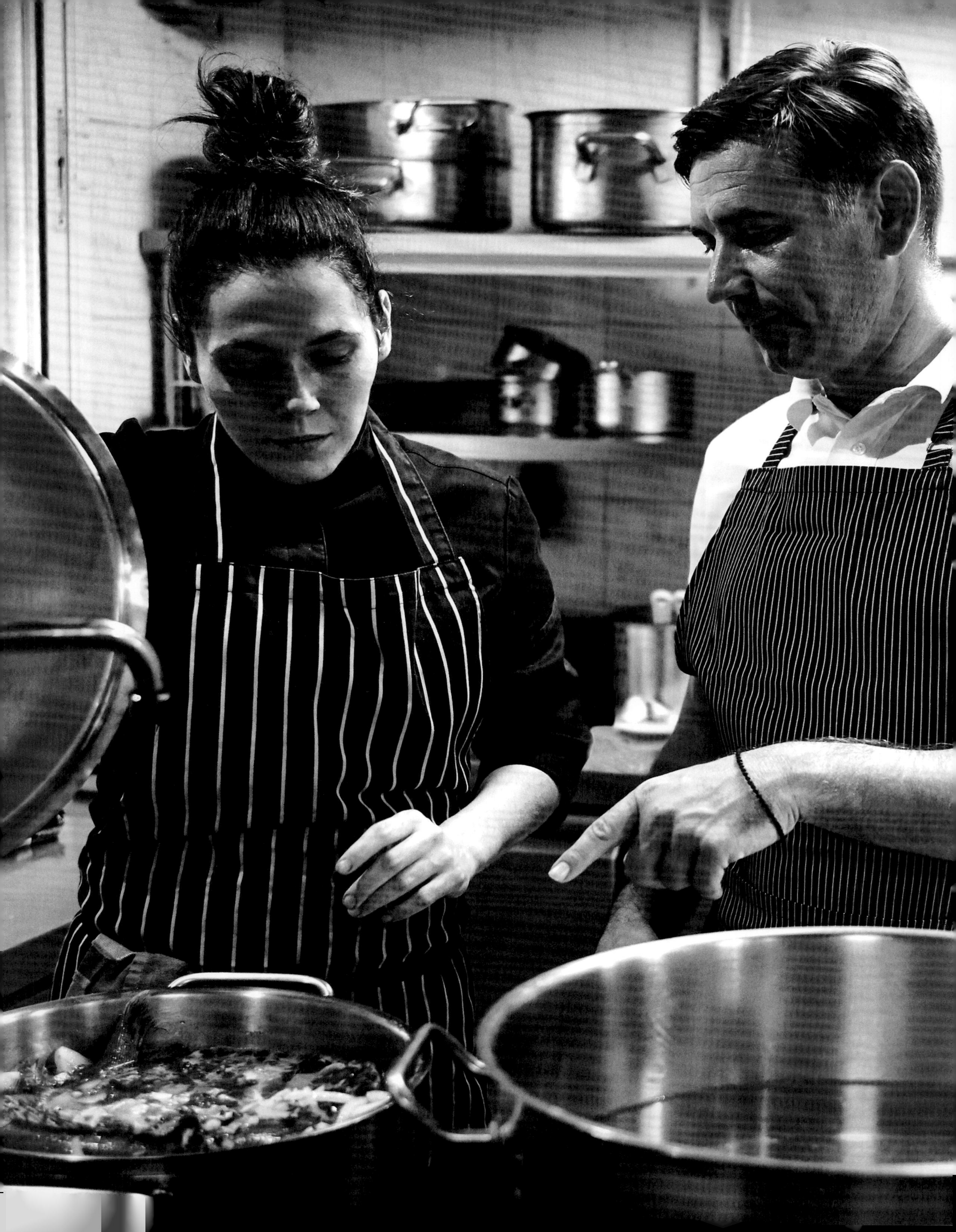

Κυρίως

MAIN COURSES

— ✤ —

MAIN COURSES

At the beginning of each of my stories, I tie on my apron, place the ingredients on my desk and start to chop them. I fire up the stove, heat a pan, uncork my thoughts and pour the oil. I take a sip from my morning coffee and the onions start to sauté: the scent of wonderful words fills my head and my kitchen. I continue mixing flavours, combining ingredients, combining sentences and I pick out the seasonings from my shelf as I pick out pieces of my life from my memory and blend them in with the rest. Over the sizzling of the oil and the crackling of the browning meat I hear unspoken words and whispers of unwritten lines from my pen. At the table, a white, cold, empty porcelain plate awaits me like a blank sheet of paper demanding to be filled with a story. In the end I wash my hands and the water runs over my fingers washing away some traces of food, invisible ink and the memory of how I did it. I never thought cooking was much different from writing. To me cooking is, in fact, exactly like writing. It is the passion of filling a blank page with a story: a steaming, emotional, tasty and deliciously unique story of my own, written in my thoughts and told in my own words through my hands …

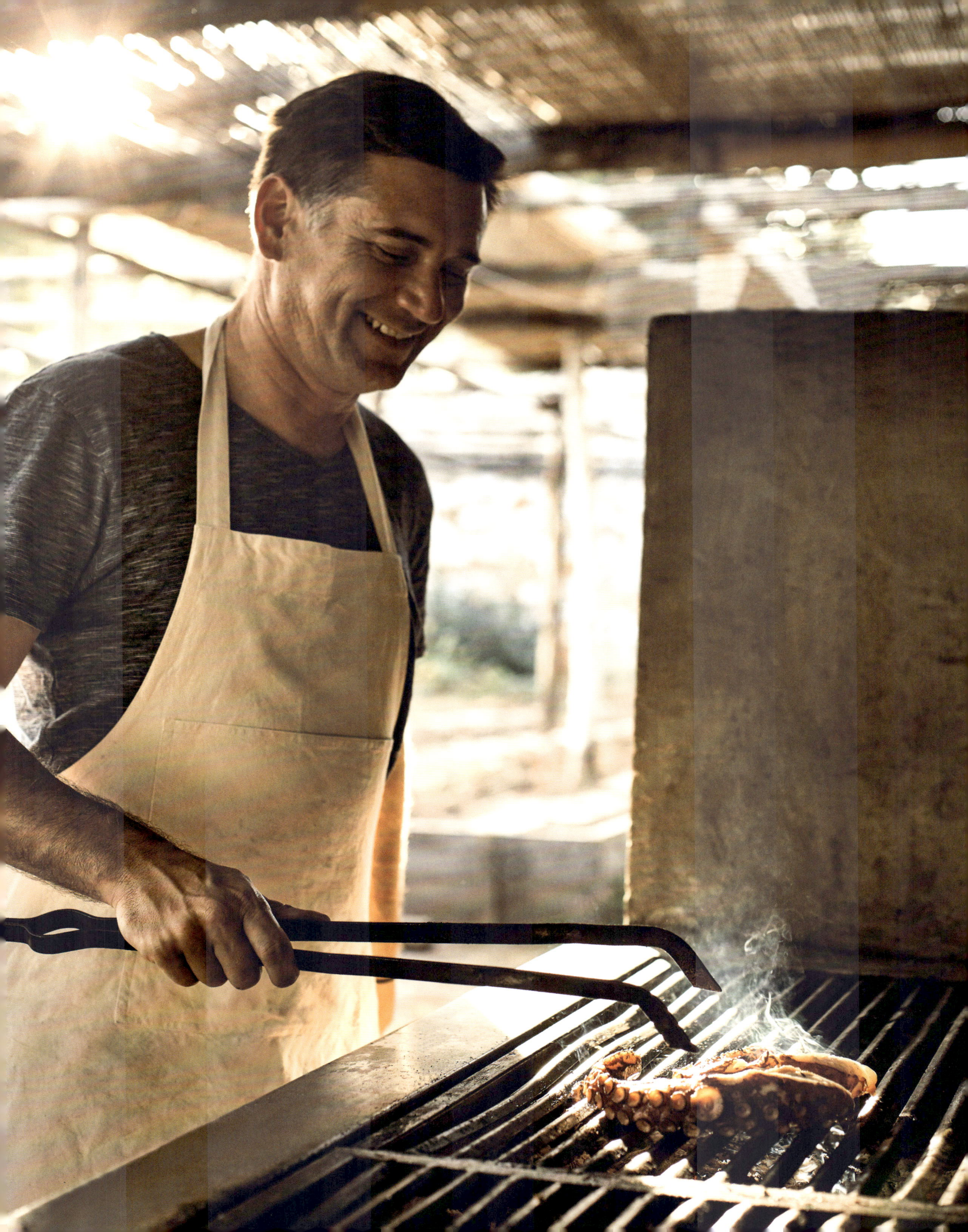

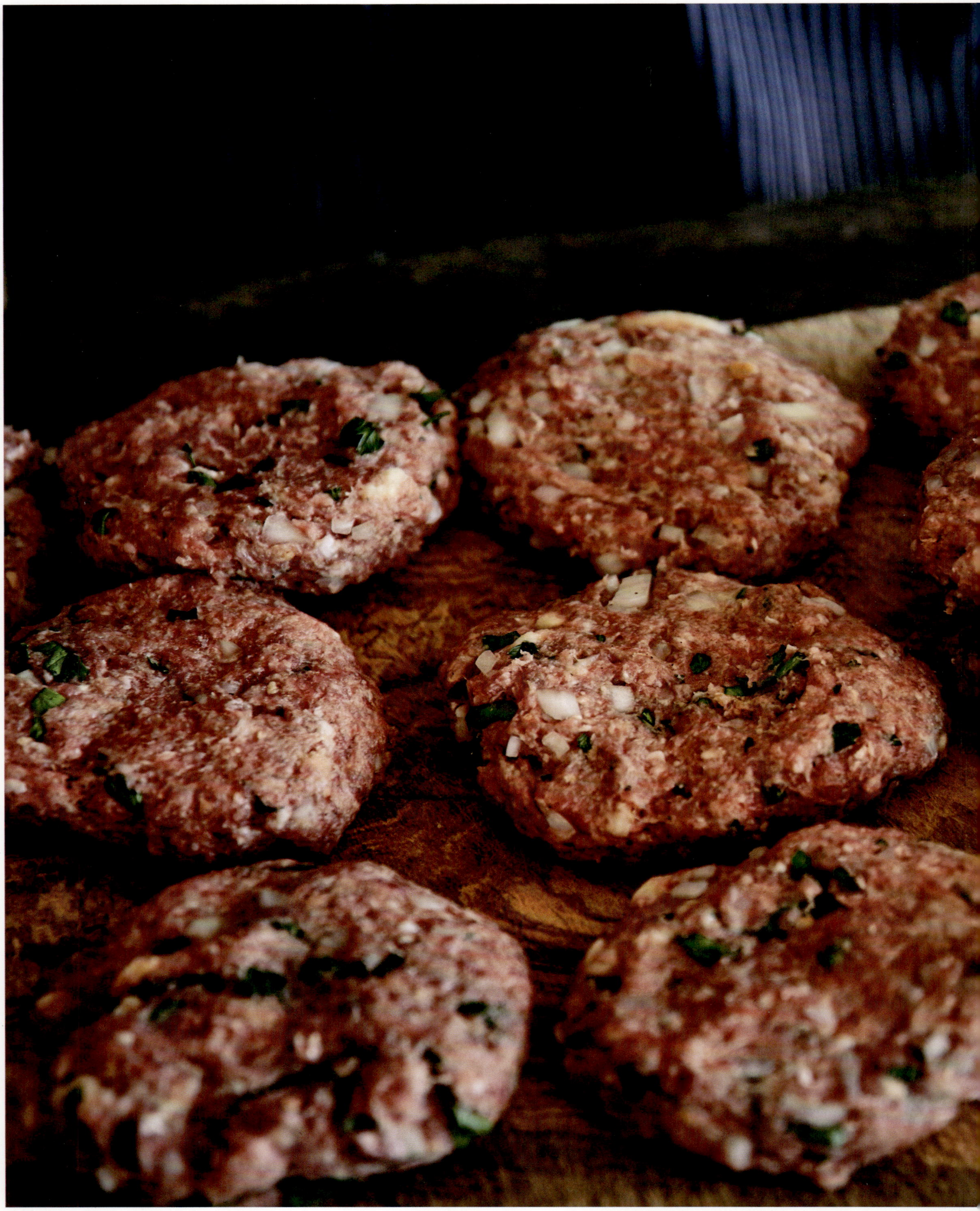

Κρεατικά

MEAT

Traditional Moussaka

serves 6

—✻—

Sitting in the airport hall, my suitcase in one hand, my saxophone case in the other, and in my pocket a ticket home. When going home I travel to more than a house. With home I associate the warmth of a fireplace in the living room, but even more the warmth of the people inside. With home I associate food. A traditional, hearty Moussaka is a classic dish in Greek households like our own. Because a Moussaka contains more than a recipe can reveal. The bottom layer consists of minced meat simmered with garlic and onion, a first familiar smell that will greet me at the door and lead my way over the creaking floorboards to the kitchen. The minced meat is topped by vegetable layers harvested from our own garden, which I can admire through the open windows. All topped by a final layer of white béchamel sauce, as thick in consistency as our walls are against any storm that may come. Lastly, it is sprinkled with cheese and baked until golden, for the times I spend at home are golden days indeed.

FOR THE FILLING

	Greek olive oil, for frying
3	aubergines, sliced
3	medium-sized potatoes, peeled and sliced into finger-width pieces
	fine sea salt and freshly ground black pepper
1	white onion, finely chopped
3	garlic cloves, finely chopped
2	pinches of granulated sugar
1	pinch of grated nutmeg
1	sprig of fresh thyme
1	sprig of fresh rosemary
1	pinch of ground cinnamon
600g	minced beef
3 tbsp	passata
1 tsp	tomato purée
½	bunch fresh parsley, finely chopped
4	leaves fresh basil, finely chopped

1. Preheat the oven to 180°C. Sprinkle two baking trays with olive oil. On one of the trays place the aubergine slices and cook them in the oven for 35 minutes. On the second, place the potato slices. Season generously with salt on both sides and cook in the oven for 30 minutes.

2. To prepare the rest of the filling, in a large sauté pan heat olive oil over medium heat. Sauté the finely chopped onion and garlic until translucent. Season with the sugar, nutmeg, thyme, rosemary and cinnamon. Stir in the meat and allow to brown, breaking it up with a wooden spoon. Once the meat is browned, stir in the passata and tomato purée. Season to taste with salt and pepper and allow the ingredients to combine before adding in the parsley and basil.

3. Switch off the heat. Remove the rosemary sprigs using tongs and discard them. Set aside the sauté pan.

4. In a clean pan, fry the sliced onion along with the cherry tomatoes in olive oil until the onions are translucent. Keep this pan aside, too.

1	white onion, sliced
6	cherry tomatoes, quartered
50g	Parmesan cheese, grated

FOR THE BÉCHAMEL SAUCE

110g	unsalted butter
120g	plain flour
600ml	milk
50g	Parmesan cheese, grated
1	pinch of nutmeg
1	medium egg
1	sprig of fresh thyme, stripped

5. To make the béchamel sauce, heat the butter on high heat in a pan. Once melted, whisk in the flour and stir until thick. Now pour in 600ml of the milk and stir briskly. Lastly, add the cheese and season with the nutmeg. Continue to stir the ingredients for approximately 3 minutes, then remove from the heat and immediately stir in the egg. Set the béchamel sauce aside.

6. Meanwhile, the potato and the aubergine slices will have softened. Remove from the oven and increase the heat to 200°C.

7. Begin to layer the moussaka. Brush the base of a large baking dish with a generous amount of olive oil. Begin layering the slices of potatoes, then continue with a layer of aubergine. Spread a thin layer of minced meat on top, then proceed with the tomato and onion slices. Sprinkle with salt, pepper and thyme. Spread with the remaining minced meat. Finally, cover with béchamel sauce and, lastly, one layer of Parmesan cheese. Place the moussaka in the oven and bake for 45 minutes, until the cheese is golden brown.

Kleftiko – Savoury Parcels of Lamb & Vegetables

serves 4

—✻—

Kleftiko is a mixture of vegetables and tender meat, wrapped tightly inside a paper parcel and firmly tied up with string, then cooked slowly. The highlight of the preparation process is when you open the little parcel when the dish is ready and you get to see the final result. I generally like to compare food with aspects of life and the characteristics of people, since it is all somehow connected. Humans can relate to Kleftiko. Generally, everyone enjoys opening objects, like presents. At the same time, we fear opening up our emotions and feelings and thoughts. All of us hold these concealed inside like Kleftiko, wrapped tightly and tied firmly, slowly simmering until we are ready to open the knot and release the heat. So all – emotions, feelings, thoughts and Kleftiko – need to be opened when ready. The key ingredient is time and patience. But be careful not to allow the parcel to overheat. Then you will just burn your fingers.

FOR THE KLEFTIKO

3	garlic cloves, crushed
	juice and zest of 1 lemon
100g	unsalted butter
	leaves from 3 sprigs of fresh oregano
	leaves from 1 sprig of fresh rosemary
1½kg	leg of lamb
	fine sea salt and freshly ground black pepper
1kg	potatoes, cut into bite-sized pieces
1	red pepper, sliced
1	leek, chopped
250g	Graviera Kritis or Gruyère cheese, diced

The previous day

1. Combine the garlic, lemon zest and 50g of the butter in a blender. Season with the oregano and rosemary. Blend on high speed into a thick paste.

2. Prepare with the meat. Remove all visible fat from the leg of lamb and put it into a roasting pan. Season with salt and pepper and rub the meat with the butter mixture until it is completely covered.

3. Cover or seal the roasting pan tightly with a lid or kitchen foil and refrigerate, ideally overnight or for at least 3–4 hours.

The following day

4. Preheat the oven to 150°C.

5. Remove the lamb from the refrigerator and keep at room temperature for one hour.

6. In a pan, combine the potatoes, the red pepper, leek and cheese. Season with salt and pepper. Place the lamb onto the potatoes and spread the remaining spiced butter all over the ingredients.

7. Cut four pieces of baking parchment each large enough to hold one-quarter of the ingredients. With a soup ladle, spoon a portion of the ingredients onto each one. Form them into parcels and seal with a length of kitchen string. Wrap each one in kitchen foil before placing them on a baking tray and transferring them to the oven.

8. Allow the Kleftiko parcels to roast for 3 hours, until well cooked.

9. Once the suggested cooking time has passed, increase the temperature to 200°C and allow the Kleftiko to cook another 30 minutes until tender. Carefully cut the string and undo the parcels. Enjoy!

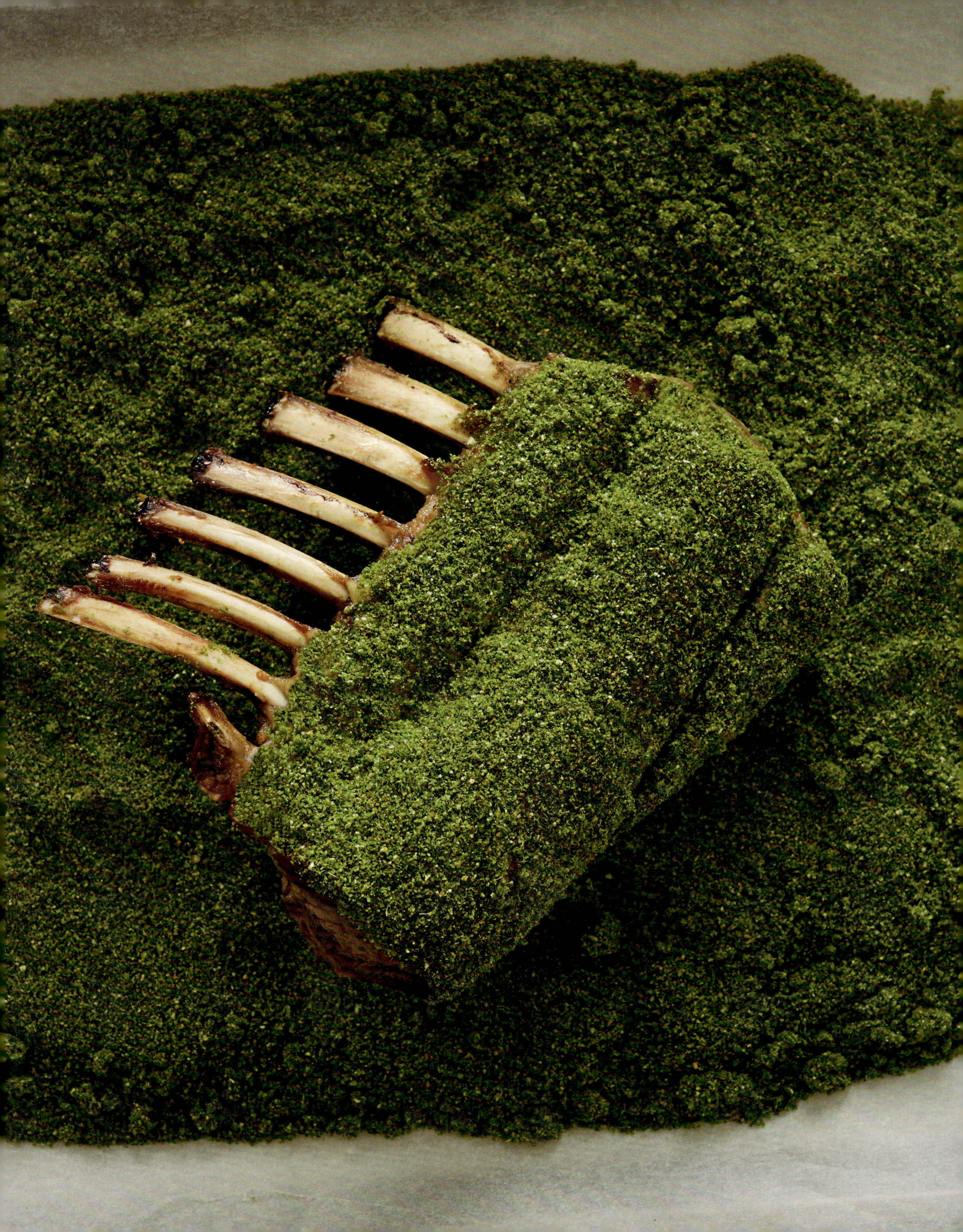

Rack of Lamb

6 pieces

—✤—

A tender rack of lamb is what we traditionally eat at the Greek Orthodox Easter, the holiest period in our faith. In Orthodox families, these days are commonly filled with traditions, but the most important one is the Resurrection of Christ, which is celebrated in a nearby monastery shortly before midnight. The inside of the colourful Orthodox church is usually packed with people, all holding long candles in one hand. The visitors listen to the tranquilising melody of the Byzantine songs sung by the priests while praying, until suddenly all the lights are extinguished. We stand still in the darkness.

After a few long moments, in the distance, somewhere at the front of the church, a single flame appears. A priest has lit a single candle and slowly the flame is passed from one to another, each lighting their own. Outside, the visitors gather, exclaiming a joyful 'Christos anesti' – Christ has risen – and exchange kisses. It is truly an experience, I must say. But it is an even more remarkable experience to actually be a believer. To reach a point in your life when you stand in the darkness, trusting that a light will appear, and the amazement when it always does.

FOR THE COATING

160g	breadcrumbs
1½	bunches fresh parsley, chopped
20g	fresh mint

FOR THE LAMB

1	rack of lamb
	fine sea salt and freshly ground black pepper
	sunflower oil
	Dijon mustard

1. Preheat the oven to 180°C. Start with the coating. Combine the breadcrumbs, parsley and mint in a blender and blend on high speed until powdery. Transfer to a bowl and set aside in a cool, dry place for 30 minutes.

2. Meanwhile, continue with the lamb. Season with salt and pepper before sprinkling with sunflower oil. In a hot pan, fry for approximately 1 minute on each side until fully browned.

3. Transfer the lamb to the oven and roast for 10–14 minutes, until the centre reaches a temperature of 55°C when measured with a meat thermometer.

4. Remove the lamb from the oven and use a pastry brush to dab it all over with Dijon mustard.

5. Lastly, coat the lamb on all sides with the herbal breadcrumbs. Wrap the meat in aluminium foil and allow to rest for approximately 5 minutes, then serve.

Keftedes – Meatballs

serves 6

All my childhood memories of my father standing at the stove, cooking, are of him making Keftedes. Standing by his side I enjoyed watching him produce meatballs, using the same recipe always. Back then his hands were bigger than mine, and only he could reach the top shelf of the kitchen cabinet. The recipe has not changed over the years, neither has anything else. His large hands have always had this gentleness, when forming meatballs, when holding my own hands leading me to places, or when rested on my shoulder, guiding me through life. Growing taller over the years, I could easily reach the top shelf myself, but I never stopped looking up to him no matter how tall I grew. And he is standing where he has always been standing, right by my side. And yes, I did not always follow your advice. Even today, I don't always follow your advice. But I follow your example. Always.

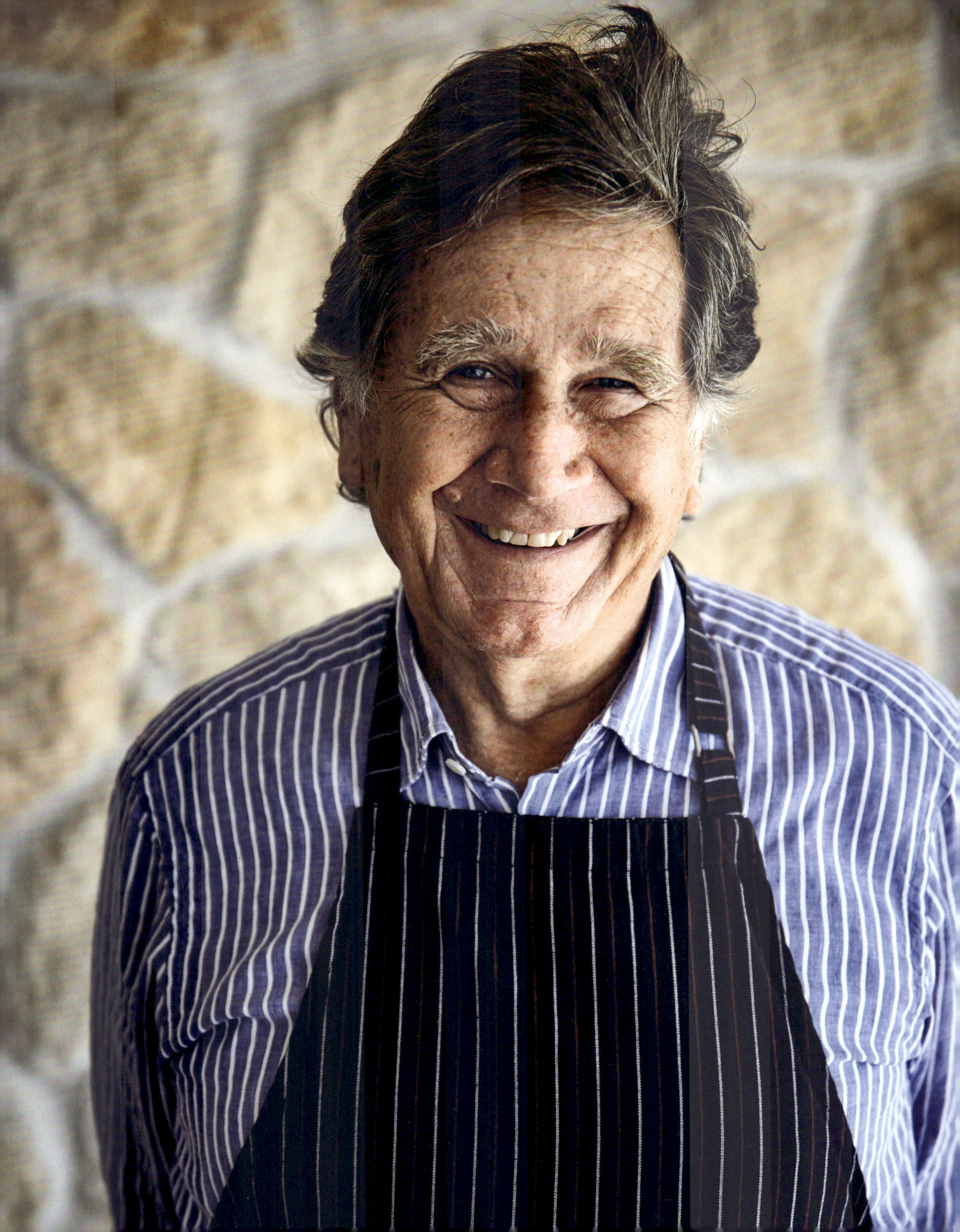

FOR THE KEFTEDES

380g	loaf white bread
700ml	water
1kg	minced beef
500g	minced pork
2	medium onions, finely chopped
1	handful fresh parsley, roughly chopped
1 tbsp	Greek olive oil, plus extra for frying
4 tsp	fine sea salt
4 tsp	freshly ground black pepper

1. Crumble the white bread roughly into a large plastic bowl. Add the water and knead by hand until the bread has swelled. Squeeze the bread to remove any excess water.

2. Add the minced beef and pork, onions, parsley, 1 tbsp olive oil, salt and pepper to the bowl and mix with your hands until you have a uniform mixture. By hand, form into oval patties, each weighing about 150g.

3. In a pan, heat a generous amount of olive oil over medium heat. Place the meat patties inside and cover the pan with a lid. After approximately 4 minutes, when the meat has taken a crispy, golden brown crust, flip over to the other side, replace the lid and fry for another 4 minutes. Fry on each side for 1 minute more before removing them from the pan.

MAIN ~ Meat { 131 }

Tender Lamb with Lemon Potatoes

serves 8

In Greek, *filoxenia* is the term for a strong sense of hospitality. We never refuse guests at the door who happen to be in the area, instead we welcome them and feed them well. We cherish having visitors but, every other Sunday, I enjoy having a Sunday meal at our home within the idyllic setting of a moment of family bonding with my parents and sisters. Like every other Sunday, the aroma of the crispy lamb and potatoes streams through the open windows and my sisters tie on their aprons when the phone rings. 'Kimon, are you having lamb today? I am just asking because in – darling, how much longer do you need? Ah, in about 30 minutes we just happen to be in the area. We'll just say hello …' 'I will keep two portions aside', I reply when my sister rushes past me with several emptied plates. 'Another table of five, distant friends who happened to be in the area.' I squeeze through the queue of waiting neighbours and more distant friends who happened to be in the area and open the door to the postman delivering on a Sunday, as usual. 'Today I'll have an extra helping of potatoes!' He passes me the mail of the week. 'Oh, and three portions to take away, the neighbours asked for delivery because they won't make it to happen to be in the area today …'

FOR THE POTATOES

3kg	potatoes, peeled and cut in wedges
2 tbsp	Dijon mustard
	juice and zest of 2 lemons
200ml	Greek olive oil
240ml	water
4	sprigs of fresh thyme
2tbsp	fine sea salt
2	pinches of freshly ground black pepper

FOR THE LAMB

2.5kg	lamb shoulder
	fine sea salt and freshly ground black pepper

1. Preheat the oven to 180°C. Start with the potatoes. Place the potato wedges in a large dish and set aside. In a small bowl thoroughly combine the mustard, lemon juice and zest, olive oil, water, thyme, salt and pepper. Pour the mixture over the potato wedges and leave to marinate for 30 minutes.

2. Meanwhile prepare the lamb. Pat the meat dry, then rub in a generous amount of salt and pepper.

3. Transfer the marinated potato wedges to a large roasting pan and place the lamb on top. Pour the marinade over the top. Cover the dish with a sheet of baking parchment and then a sheet of kitchen foil.

4. Roast in the oven for 2¼ hours. Check at least twice, adding more water if necessary.

5. Lastly, remove the baking parchment and foil and roast for another 10–15 minutes, until the potatoes and lamb are tender and golden.

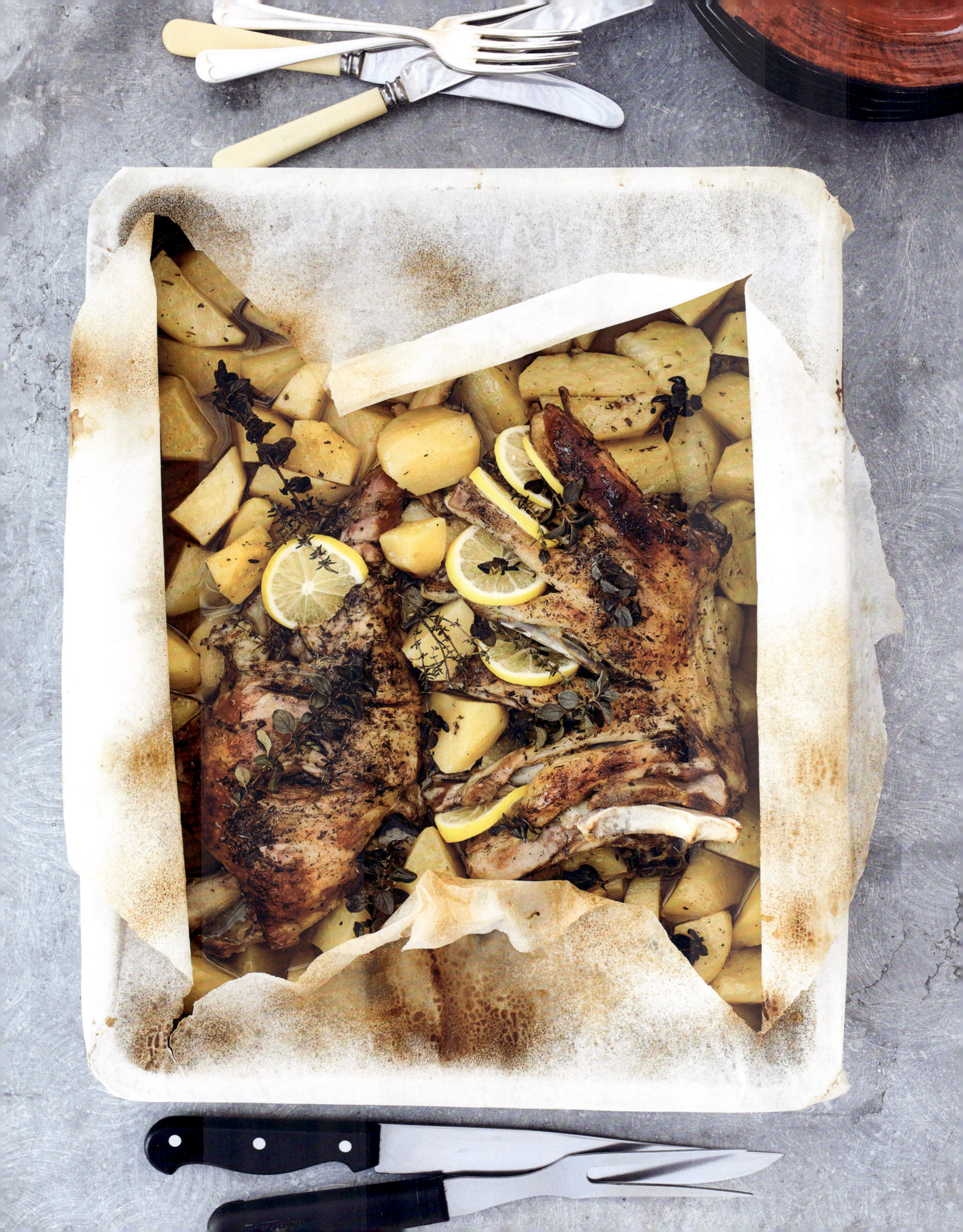

Pork Neck with Vegetables & Rice

serves 4

FOR THE RICE

500g	white basmati rice
	salted water
	Greek olive oil, for frying
80g	pine nuts
4	mushrooms, finely chopped
80g	raisins
½	bunch fresh dill, chopped
20g	unsalted butter
	fresh oregano
	fine sea salt and freshly ground black pepper
½	bunch fresh parsley, finely chopped

1. Preheat the oven to 180°C.

2. Prepare the pork. Remove all visible fat from the meat and put it into a large roasting pan. Rub all over with the olive oil and mustard and generously season with salt and pepper, oregano and smoked paprika seasoning.

3. Place the onion, garlic, apple, tomatoes, celery, green pepper, lemon, carrots, thyme, rosemary and 20g of the butter in the roasting pan, spreading them evenly around the meat. Sprinkle the parsley over all the ingredients.

FOR THE PORK

1.6 kg	pork neck
100 ml	Greek olive oil
1 tbsp	Dijon mustard
	fine sea salt and freshly ground black pepper
1	pinch of fresh oregano
2 tbsp	smoked paprika seasoning
1	white onion, roughly chopped
6	garlic cloves, halved
1	green apple, roughly chopped
3	tomatoes, roughly chopped
2	sticks celery, roughly chopped
1	green pepper, roughly chopped
1	lemon, peeled and halved
2	carrots, peeled and roughly chopped
2	sprigs of fresh thyme
2	sprigs of fresh rosemary
40 g	unsalted butter, roughly chopped
10	sprigs of fresh parsley, roughly chopped
1 l	chicken stock

4. Pour enough chicken stock over the vegetables to cover them. Season again with a pinch of salt and pepper.

5. Cover the pan with one sheet of baking parchment and one sheet of kitchen foil. Transfer to the oven and bake for about 2½ hours. Check for tenderness after 2 hours.

6. Once the meat is ready cooked, place the pork neck on a serving plate.

7. To make the sauce, spoon the vegetables and cooking liquid from the pan into a blender. Blend until smooth. Place a sieve over a pan and strain the blended mixture through it. Discard the vegetables in the sieve and add 20 g of butter to the sauce in the pan. Bring the sauce to a simmer.

8. Meanwhile, prepare the rice. Boil the rice for 9 minutes in salted water. Drain and cool in cold water.

9. In a frying pan, heat olive oil over high heat and fry the pine nuts until browned. Add the mushrooms and raisins and sauté for 3–4 minutes.

10. Remove from the heat and add the dill without stirring. Whisk in the remaining 20 g of butter and allow it to almost completely melt.

11. Combine the nuts with the rice and season to taste with the oregano, salt and pepper. Lastly, sprinkle with parsley before serving.

12. Carve the pork into slices and arrange on the plate. Pour the sauce over the pork slices and serve immediately with the rice.

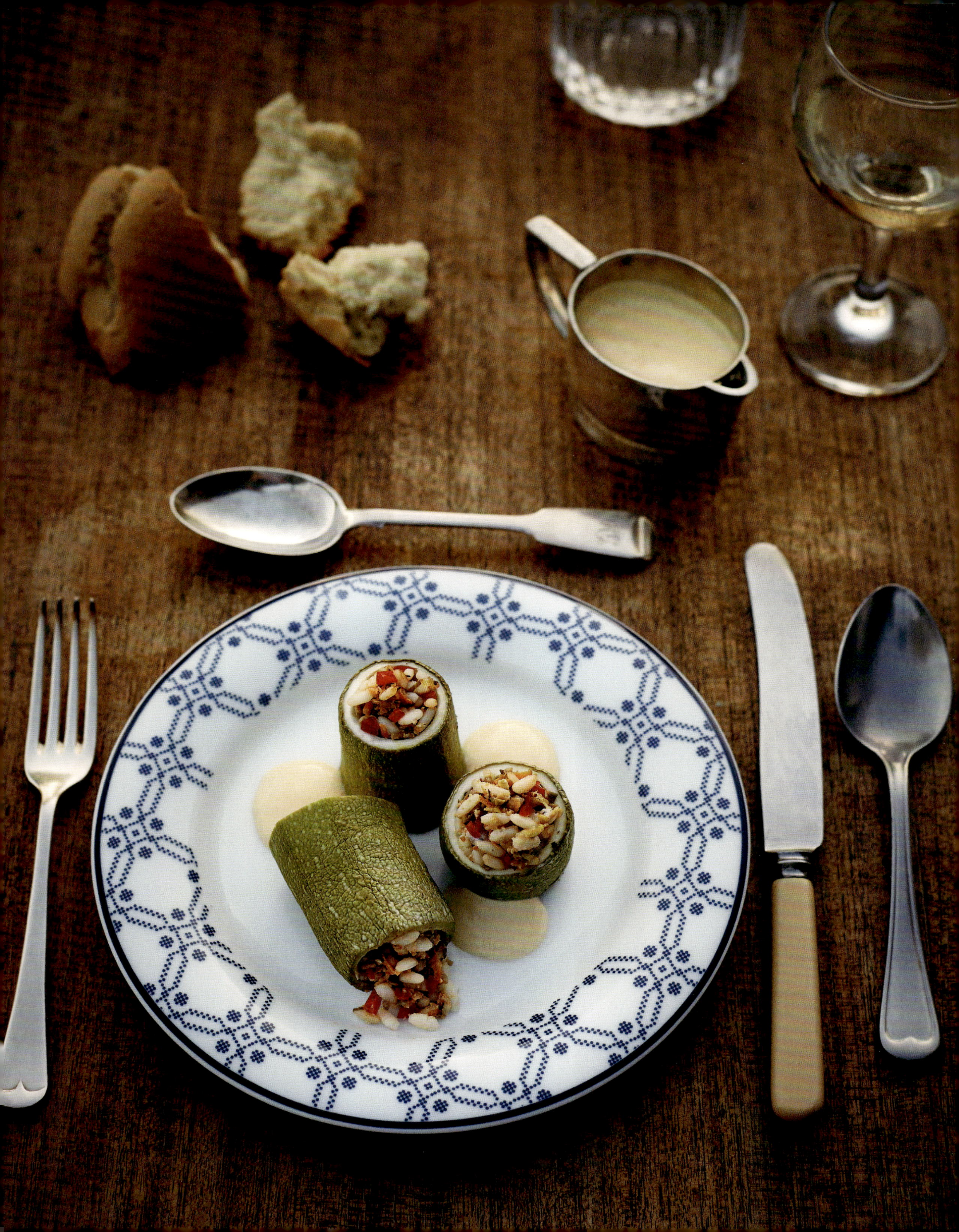

Stuffed Courgettes with Avgolemono Sauce

serves 4

FOR THE STUFFED COURGETTES

8	courgettes
400g	minced beef
150g	long-grain white rice
1	white onion, chopped
1	garlic clove, sliced
1	carrot, peeled and finely chopped
1	red pepper, finely chopped
1	bunch fresh parsley, chopped
1	bunch fresh dill, chopped
2	pinches of saffron
6 tbsp	Greek olive oil
	chicken stock
	fine sea salt and freshly ground pepper
	juice of ½ lemon
	Avgolemono Sauce (see page 227)

1. Start with the preparation of the courgettes. Cut off the ends and use a vegetable corer to remove the interior. Set the hollow courgette tubes aside.

2. Make the stuffing. Combine the minced beef, rice, onion, garlic, carrot, red pepper, parsley, dill, 1 pinch of saffron and 3 tbsp of the olive oil in a bowl. Mix the ingredients thoroughly by hand. Spoon the stuffing into the courgette tubes and place the stuffed vegetables into a large pan.

3. Gradually pour chicken stock into the pan until the stuffed courgettes are just covered. Season with salt, pepper, 1 pinch of saffron and drizzle with the lemon juice. Lastly, cover the pan with a lid or plate and cook over low heat for 1¼ hours.

4. Once the stuffed courgettes are cooked, remove the pan from heat and reserve the cooking liquid in a separate bowl for the Avgolemono Sauce.

5. Prepare the Avgolemono Sauce.

6. Serve the stuffed courgettes surrounded by the sauce.

Pork Shoulder with Leek & Celery

serves 4

FOR THE PORK SHOULDER

	water
	Greek olive oil, for frying
2kg	pork shoulder, cut into chunks
1	white onion, chopped
	freshly ground pepper
1	celery, chopped
1½kg	leeks, chopped
1	bunch fresh dill, finely chopped
	Avgolemono Sauce (see page 227)

1. Bring a medium-sized pan of water to a boil while preparing the meat.

2. Heat olive oil in a large pan over medium heat. Toss in the pork and sauté until nicely browned on all sides. Stir in the onion and sweat for 3 minutes.

3. Pour enough boiling water into the pan to cover the pork and onion. Season with a pinch of pepper, then simmer for 30 minutes. From time to time use a small soup ladle to remove any foam that rises to the top of the pan.

4. Once the meat is tender, place a layer of celery on top of the pork, followed by a layer of leeks and, lastly, another layer of celery. Cover with a lid and simmer for another 30–40 minutes.

5. Meanwhile, prepare the Avgolemono Sauce.

6. Remove the pan from the heat. Sprinkle with the dill, then use a wooden spoon to stir the Avgolemono Sauce into the pan until fully combined with the broth. Serve immediately.

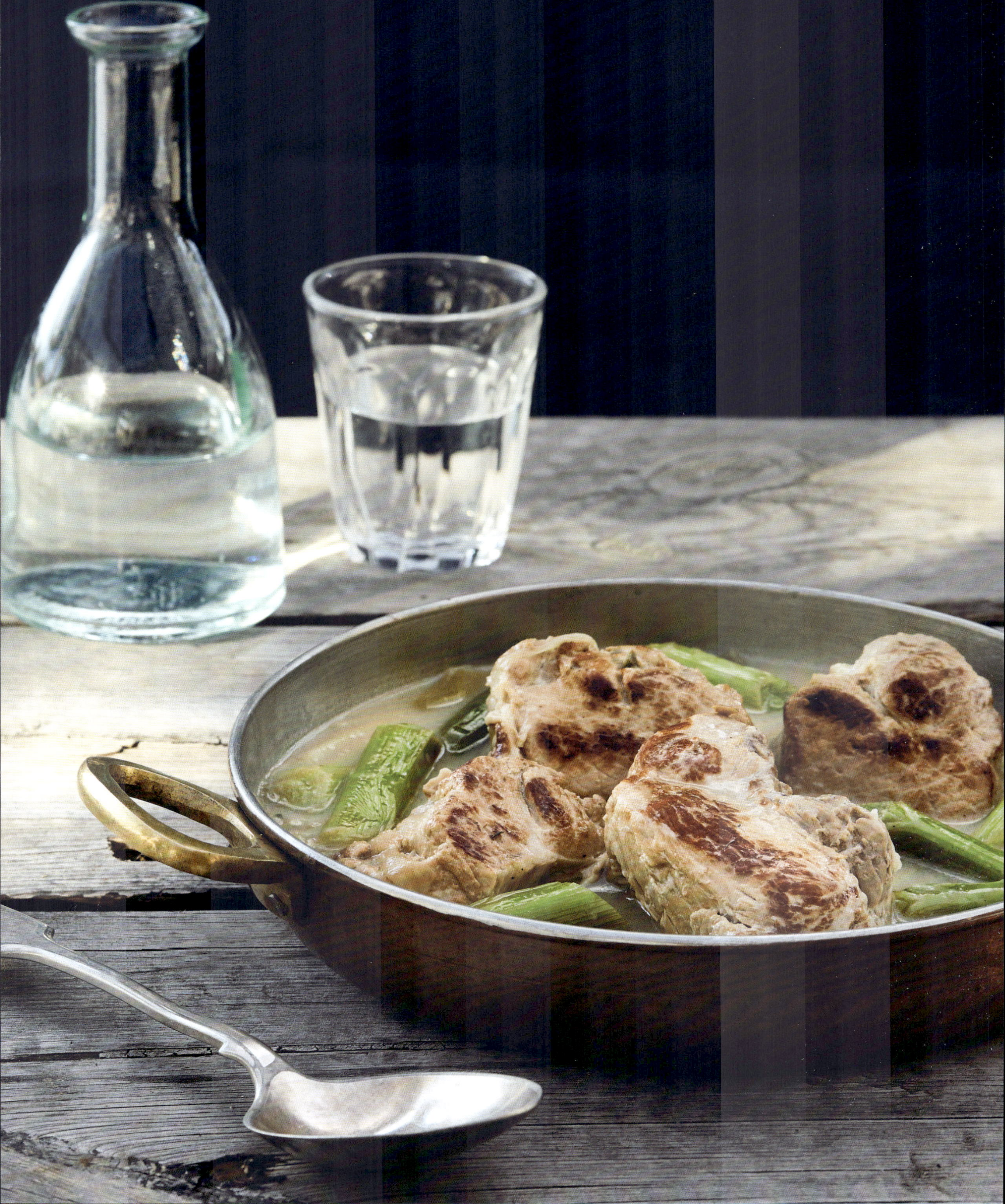

Rib Eye Steak with Marinated Cherry Tomatoes

serves 4

———— ❈ ————

'Kimon', she stared at me with sad eyes: 'Please, just look at me! Let's talk about this.' I felt guilty but continued eating my steak with a fiery red face, ignoring her pleas. She sobbed: 'I thought you loved me. At least you said so. Many times. Was that even true?' The scenario was heartbreaking, but I decided to remain firm this time: 'Stop. Just sit down, please. We will talk about it at home.' 'After all these years I don't even deserve an answer? Have you forgotten our cosy evenings cuddling up on the sofa? Our holidays? Our walks in the park?' Her voice broke and she started crying. 'Spitha, be quiet. We are in the middle of a restaurant! People are staring already …' 'That's all I am for you? An embarrassment? Just look at me. Look me in the eyes and tell me that you really don't love me anymore.' She started howling. 'For god's sake.' I dropped another piece of rib eye which she devoured instantly. 'This was the last time I ever took you to a restaurant. Now, you've just had another piece, don't give me that look, no! Spitha, behave! Sit!' She sat down obediently. I continued eating my steak. 'Kimon …' I ignored her but my Jack Russell pressed one of her soft paws against my shin: '… Please, just look at me!'

FOR THE MARINATED CHERRY TOMATOES

24	cherry tomatoes on the vine
2	garlic cloves, sliced
1½ tbsp	Greek olive oil, for frying
1 tbsp	black balsamic vinegar
1 tsp	fine sea salt
1 tsp	freshly ground black pepper
1 tsp	granulated sugar
3	basil leaves, whole

FOR THE STEAKS

	Greek olive oil
1	garlic clove, crushed
1	sprig of fresh rosemary
4	rib eye steaks

1. Start with the cherry tomatoes. Combine the cherry tomatoes and garlic in a bowl, sprinkle with the olive oil and season with black balsamic vinegar, salt, pepper, sugar and basil. Gently mix the ingredients by hand.

2. Allow the vegetables to marinate for 30 minutes before transferring them to an ovenproof dish.

3. Preheat the oven to 180°C.

4. Roast the tomatoes in the oven for 7–8 minutes.

5. Meanwhile, proceed with the steaks. In a grill pan, heat olive oil over medium heat. Add the garlic, rosemary and steaks. Brown the meat for approximately 1–1½ minutes on each side.

6. Transfer the steaks to a baking dish and roast in the oven alongside the cherry tomatoes for 4 minutes.

7. Allow the steaks to rest for 4 minutes before placing them on a serving plate with the cherry tomatoes.

Chicken in Yoghurt Marinade

serves 4

———✳———

'I said I wasn't ready yet!' 'Then why did you keep saying 5 more minutes?' 'Because you kept asking every 10 minutes!' The clerk still held open the door: 'Madam, would you please come inside.' With a dramatic gesture she held out a piece of paper. The clerk skimmed through the instructions. 'Whisk yoghurt in a kitchen bowl … Mix ingredients … add olive oil …' 'For my complexion. It works miracles for my skin …' 'I don't mean to argue with you, madam, but …' The chicken stopped him, holding up a wing. 'I am not arguing! I am simply explaining why I am correct! It would be easier if you agreed with me. Give me the 6 more minutes I asked for!' '6? I thought you said …' 'Then you should have listened better!' She tapped her feet impatiently. The clerk replied: 'Madam, I cannot send you back. I just had a cockerel a while back who …' 'Aha! So a cockerel is granted more time, but not a chicken? Young man, let me tell you about women's rights, the necessity for the social, economic and political equality of the sexes! Women's rights at heaven's gate should be equal to those of men and I will not …' With a little 'pop' sound the chicken disappeared, only one feather was left, floating towards the ground. 'Outrageous! Cutting me off in mid-sentence', the chicken repositioned herself for 6 more minutes of relaxation in the oven. Meanwhile, at the gates of heaven, the clerk was making a call: 'Is this Mr Kimon Riefenstahl? Yes? Call from heaven: I just had your Chicken in Yoghurt Marinade here. I think it needs more than 6 minutes. We should double, even triple that. Make it 18! Great. Thank you.' The clerk ended the call. 'Heavenly!' he sighed.

FOR THE POTATOES

1.5kg	baby potatoes, halved
3	garlic cloves, crushed
	juice of 1½ lemons
7	sprigs of fresh thyme
3	sprigs of fresh rosemary
100ml	Greek olive oil
1 tbsp	fine sea salt
	freshly ground black pepper
1 tbsp	wholegrain Dijon mustard
1 tbsp	Dijon mustard
	dried oregano
1l	chicken stock, warm, plus extra if required
100g	unsalted butter, roughly chopped

FOR THE CHICKEN

300g	plain Greek yoghurt
2	garlic cloves, grated
	juice and zest of ½ lime
	juice of ½ lemon
1 tbsp	dill, finely chopped
1 tsp	ground coriander seeds
1 tsp	ground cumin
1 tsp	red chilli powder
1 tsp	fine sea salt
1 tsp	freshly ground black pepper
6 tbsp	Greek olive oil
4	250g chicken breast fillets
	sprigs of fresh rosemary, to garnish

1. Preheat the oven to 180°C.

2. Put the potatoes into a roasting pan. Stir the garlic, lemon juice, thyme, rosemary, olive oil, salt, pepper, mustards and oregano into the warm chicken stock. Lastly, add the butter.

3. Pour the chicken stock over the potatoes. Set aside to marinate for 30 minutes.

4. Cover the roasting pan with kitchen foil, then transfer to the oven and roast for 45 minutes. Remove the foil and, if required, add more chicken stock.

5. Meanwhile, prepare the marinade for the chicken. Place the yoghurt in a bowl with the garlic, lime juice and zest, lemon juice and dill. Season with the coriander, cumin, chilli, salt and pepper. Mix the ingredients with a spoon.

6. Lastly, add the olive oil, a tablespoon at a time and stirring between each spoonful.

7. Coat the chicken breasts thoroughly with the marinade. Cover them with cling film and marinate in the fridge for 35 minutes.

8. Meanwhile return the potatoes to the oven for another 45 minutes, until they are golden.

9. Remove the cling film and transfer the chicken breasts to the oven. Allow them to cook for about 20 minutes until tender. Serve garnished with sprigs of rosemary.

THE JOURNEY FROM BOAT TO PLATE

I grew up listening to the tales of the fishermen of the Aegean waters. My grandfather was a casual fisherman. Some days he left the house at 5.30 a.m. – before sunrise – and while the rest of the village and I were still sleeping, my grandfather and his crew were firing the engine and slipping into the darkness of the Aegean Sea, anxious to see another successful day's catch. On his return I would not miss out on a freshly hooked lunch nor on an exciting story of the rugged outdoorsmen testing their luck over and over again.

Occasionally I accompanied my grandfather, and even today I relish joining some of the fishermen from the village on an excursion. We go out early. The best chance to have a good catch is to shoot out the nets during the quiet of dawn. That's when the fish are making their way to the seabed in order to feed. While on board, there is barely room to think of anything else than the boat's speed, the selection of the bait and the weather conditions. Once on the water, it seems like the crew and I, even though we all have responsibilities on land, are swept off into a different world, leaving life behind at the shore; we could catch up with it later. We focus only on the present, because everything that needs our fullest attention that moment is right around us. My mind just slips occasionally to what I will do with today's catch once I am back in my kitchen.

Once the day's work is completed, I enjoy the view of the harbour coming closer. The fishermen throw all the fish guts over the side of the boat, and I see some happy seagulls darting down in order to snatch their part of the catch. Once the fish are washed and placed on layers of ice, they are sent straight to the fish markets and very small local shops, which are commonly guarded under the watchful eyes of numerous cats. Those are the places I turn to when I am not lucky enough to catch fish myself. I am glad that living on the shores of the Aegean Sea enables you to essentially select your lunch or dinner the freshest way possible, choosing from the broadest selection all spread out in front of you at the food market. Often, I smile at the amazement of tourists who loudly wonder how the fish get their fresh-from-the-sea look.

I have first-hand proof of how they get that look. Luckily, from where I live, I have an excellent view over the Aegean Sea. Every morning I spot some fishing boats in the distance, knowing well that those men have been braving the elements since before the sun rose and the sea has warmed. More than enjoying the view, I enjoy the taste. I am a purist when it comes to the freshness of any ingredient, and I am blessed to live in a part of the world where I can rely on this ideology. In fact, I witness it morning after morning with my very own eyes.

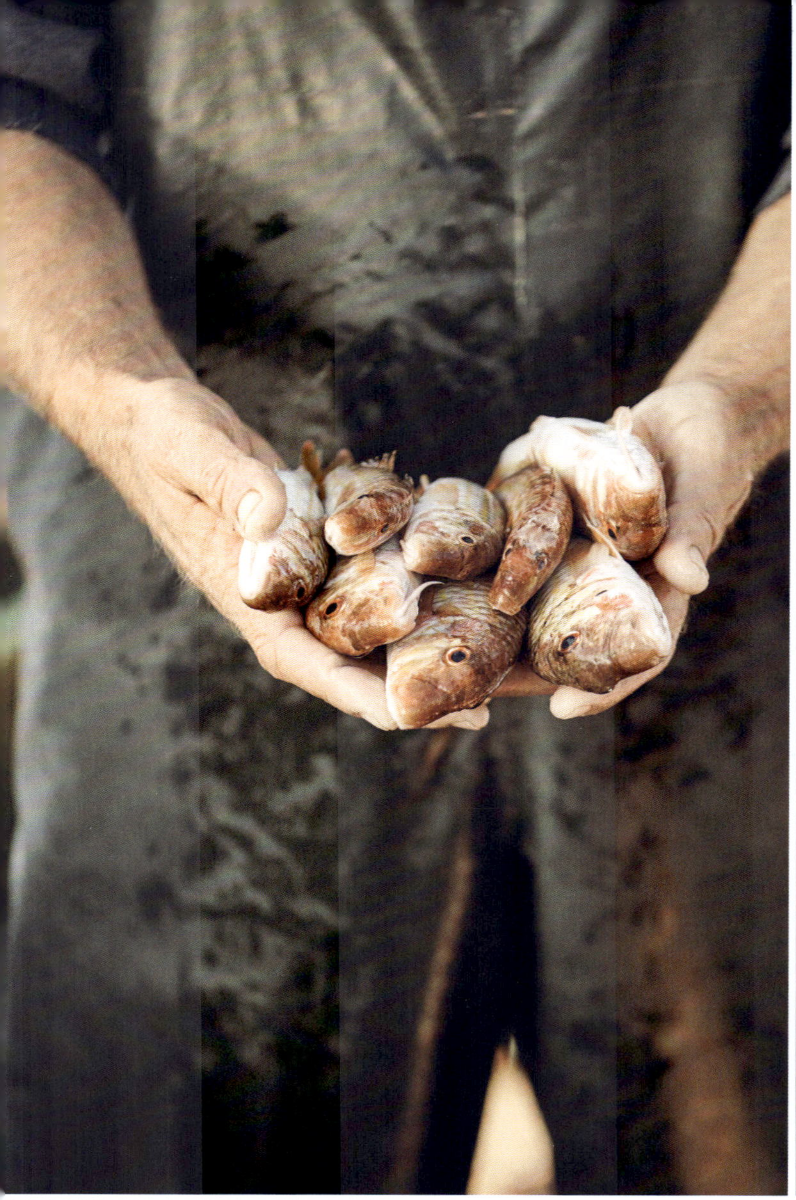
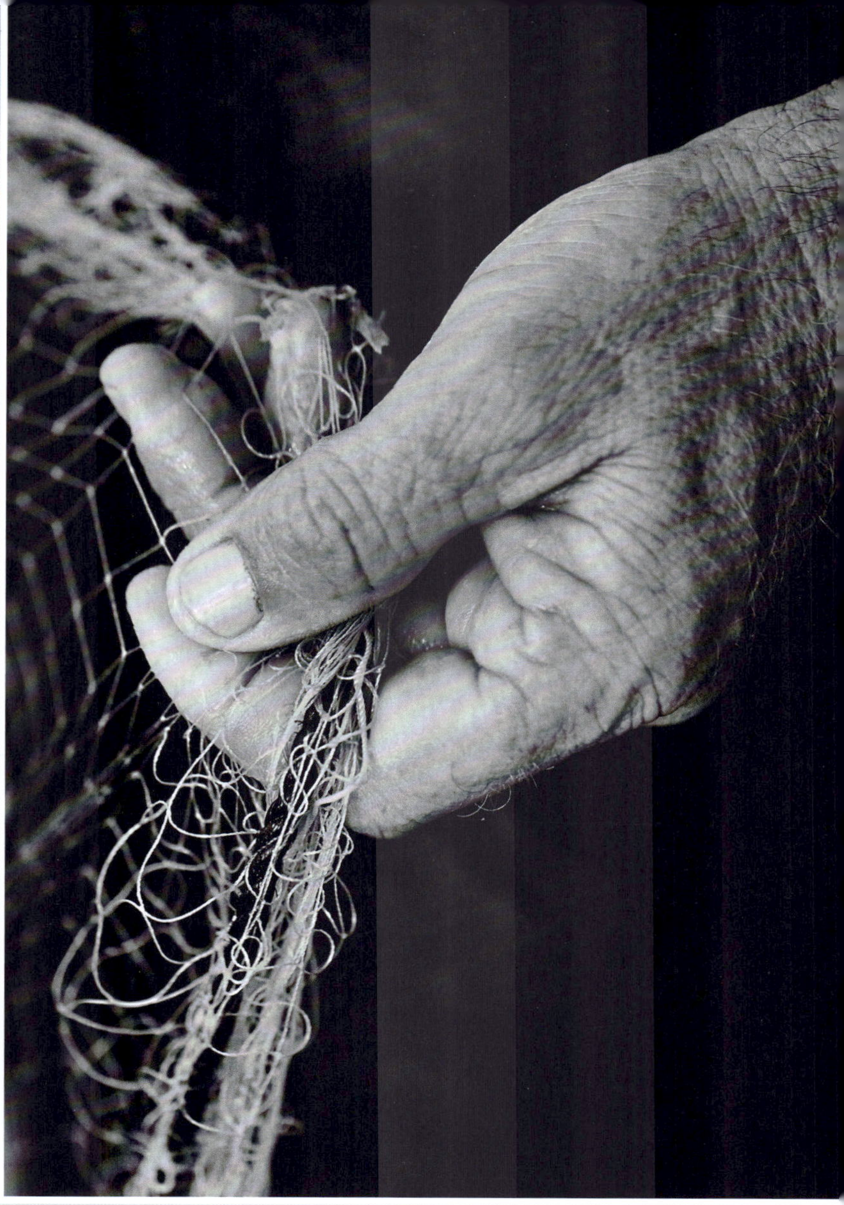
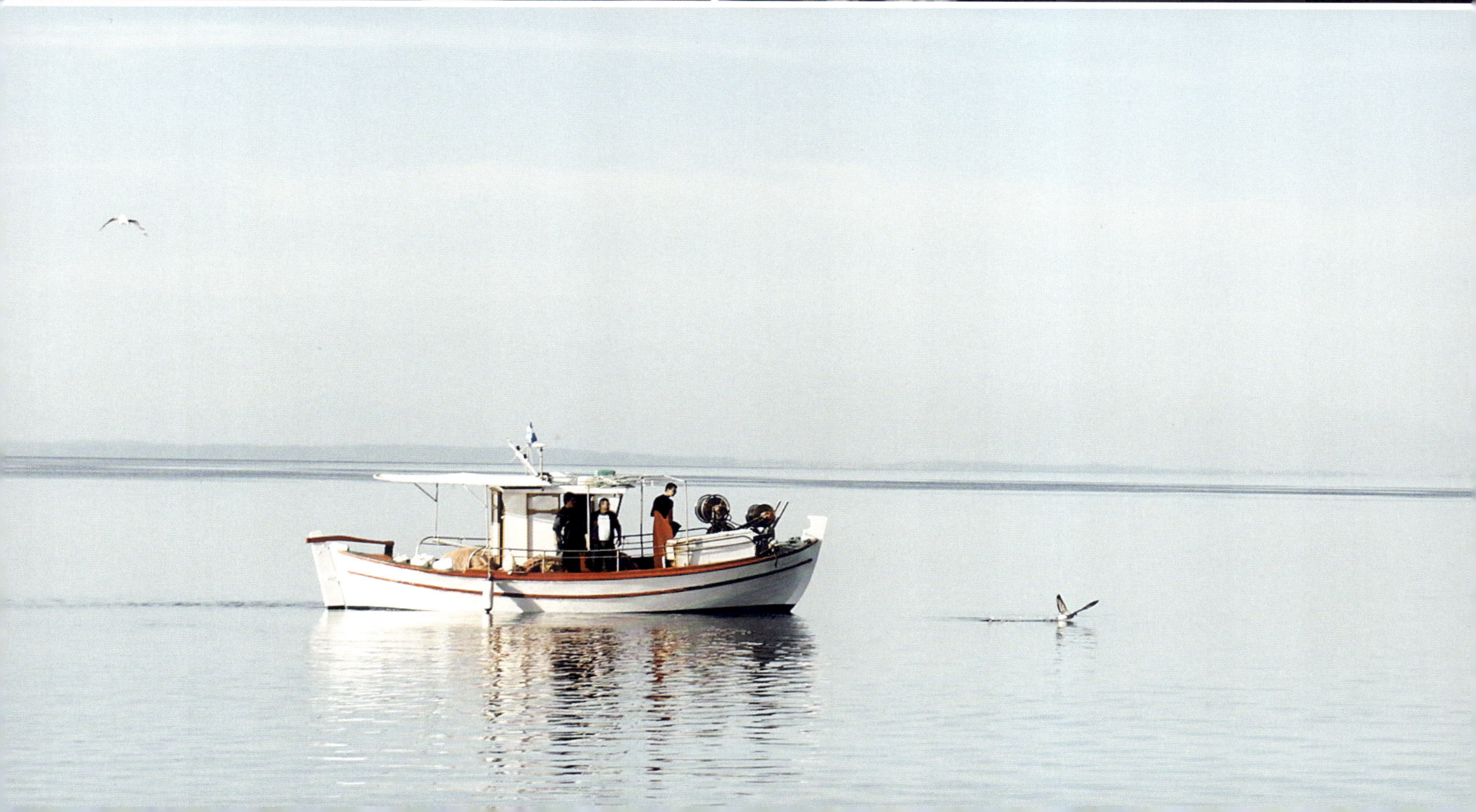

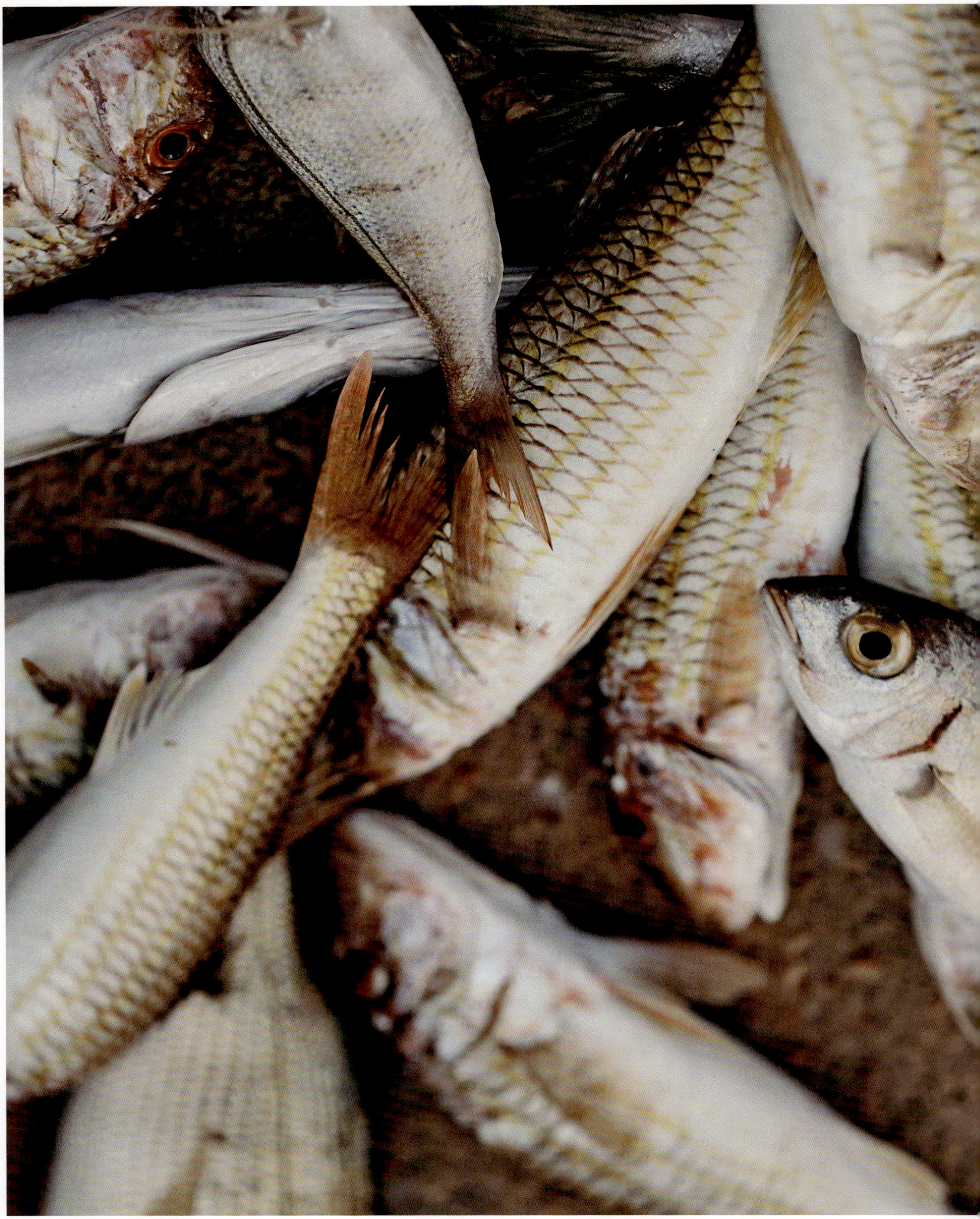

θαλασσινά

FISH & SEAFOOD

Fish in Sea Salt Crust

serves 2

———✴———

I will never forget the day I was after the big catch. Wondering what to make out of that fish, I cast my fishing line with a vigorous motion and held my rod with a confident posture. That was when I noticed the old fisherman not far from my position by the shore. A smug smile flitted across his weathered face when he asked me, 'You're after the big catch today, eh?' I nodded and he slowly laboured along through the shallow water towards me. 'You getting married, son?' I hesitated. 'Then I better tell you how to make a Fish in a Sea Salt Crust', he continued and gave me the recipe for this dish. 'I will never forget the day I myself learnt this recipe. I was a chap like you, knowing like all men that there are many fish in the sea. But I was after that one big catch. That is the moment you cross that fine line between fishing for real and standing by the shore like an idiot hoping for any fish at all to bite. It was a day like today when, finally, I got the catch of my life …' His cloudy grey eyes tiredly gazed out into the distance '… and I have been married ever since.' For a moment we remained silent. He took a deep breath of the salty air and continued: 'It was the day I realized that I myself had been the bait all along. It was me biting the hook, unaware of the consequences. It was the last day I opened my mouth, ever since I keep it shut to avoid trouble. I stand here day after day fishing and thinking of my wife's complaining before going home to my wife's complaining thinking about fishing. The only ray of light in a man's life then, son, is that Fish in a Sea Salt Crust. Its salty taste reminds me of the days, when I was still a young chap, free like a fish of the Aegean with freedom in my heart and tasting the sea salt on my lips …'

We listened to the sound of the waves coming and going as they please when I broke the silence: 'But how did you learn the recipe?' He paid me a meaningful look and said: 'That day I walked over by the shore, dreaming of the big catch and wondered what to cook with it. So I had been standing by the shore like an idiot holding my rod like I didn't have a clue about fishing. And there was that old fisherman wondering loudly whether I was after a big catch today. I nodded when he asked:

'You getting married, son?'

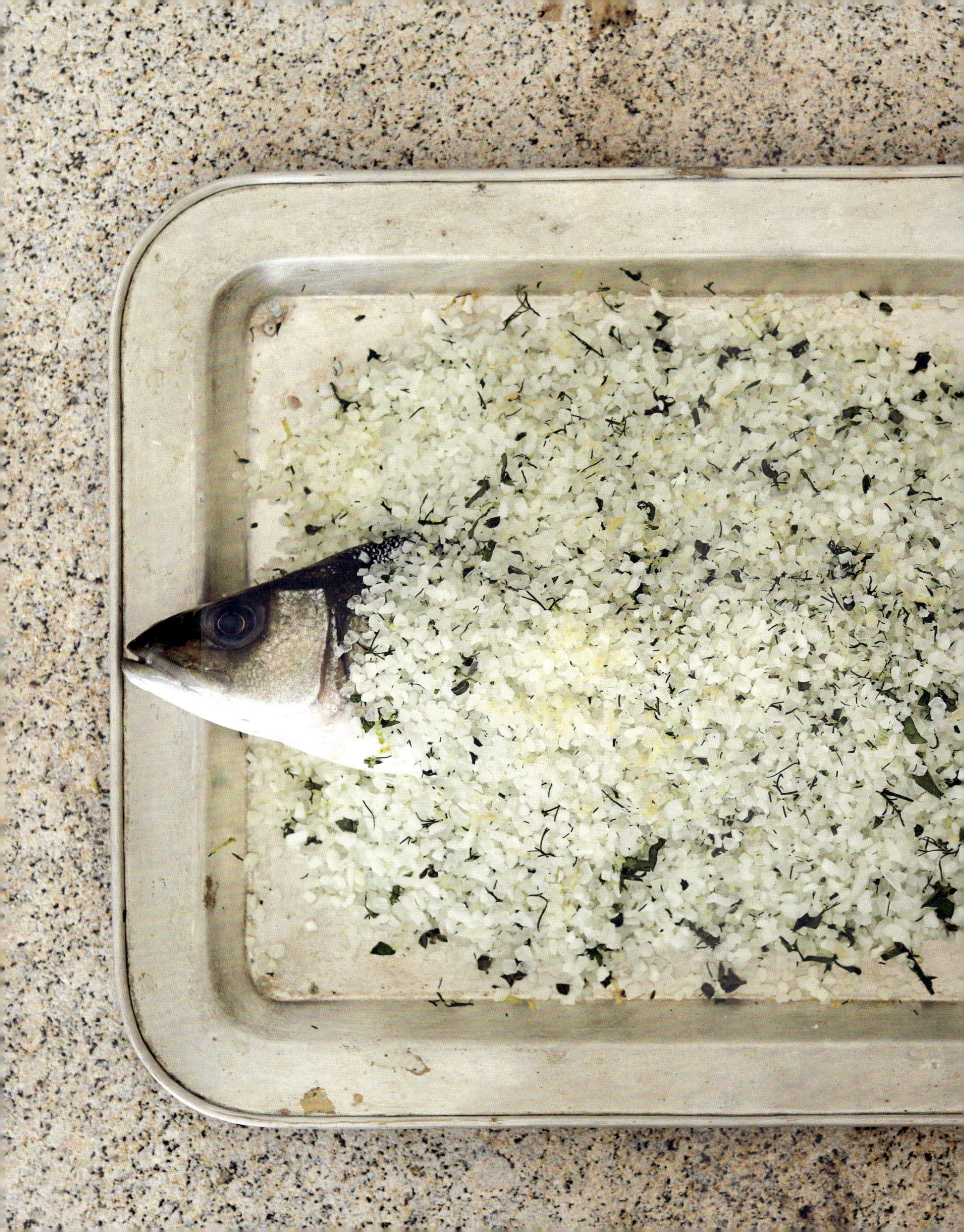

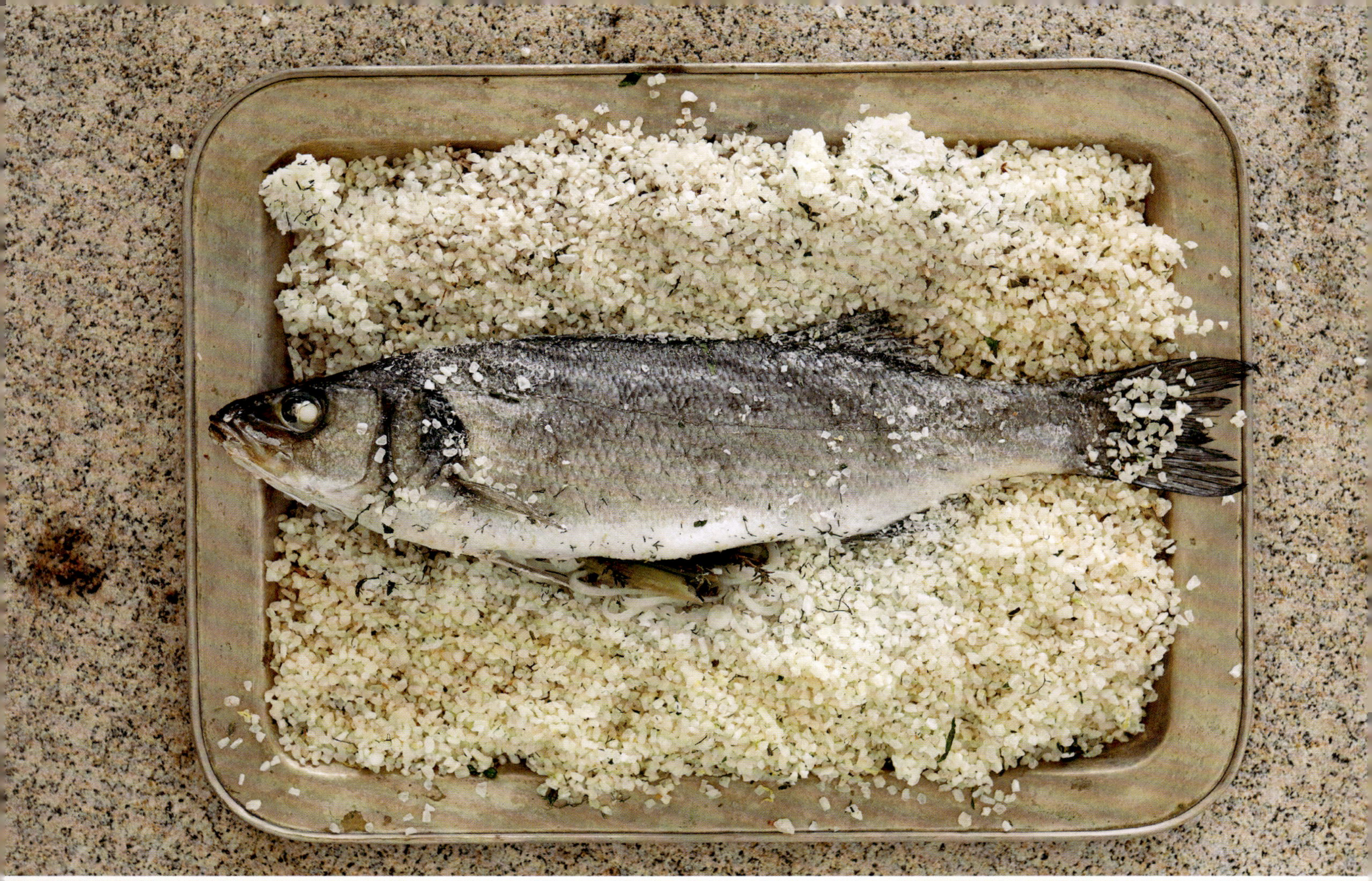
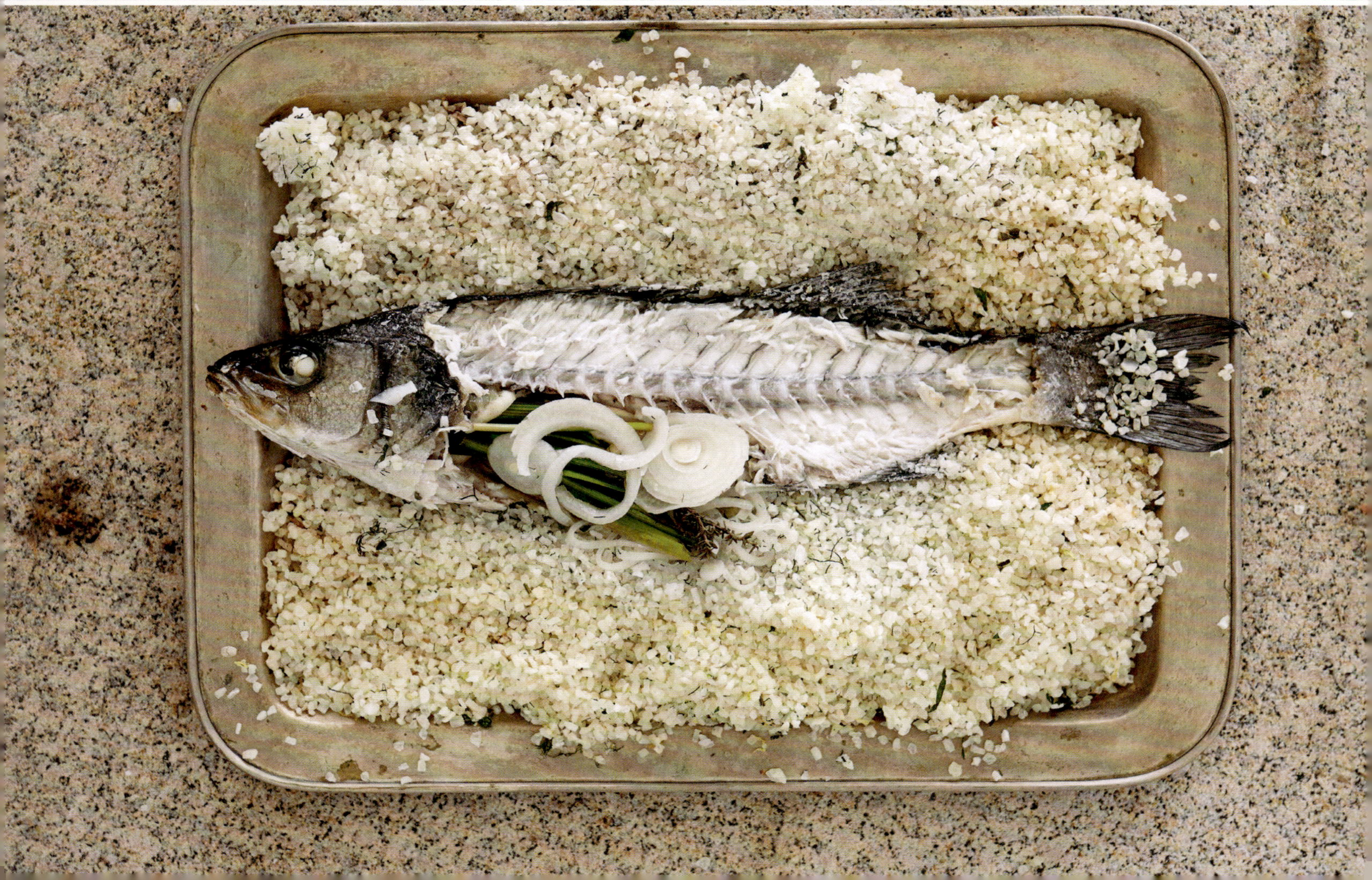

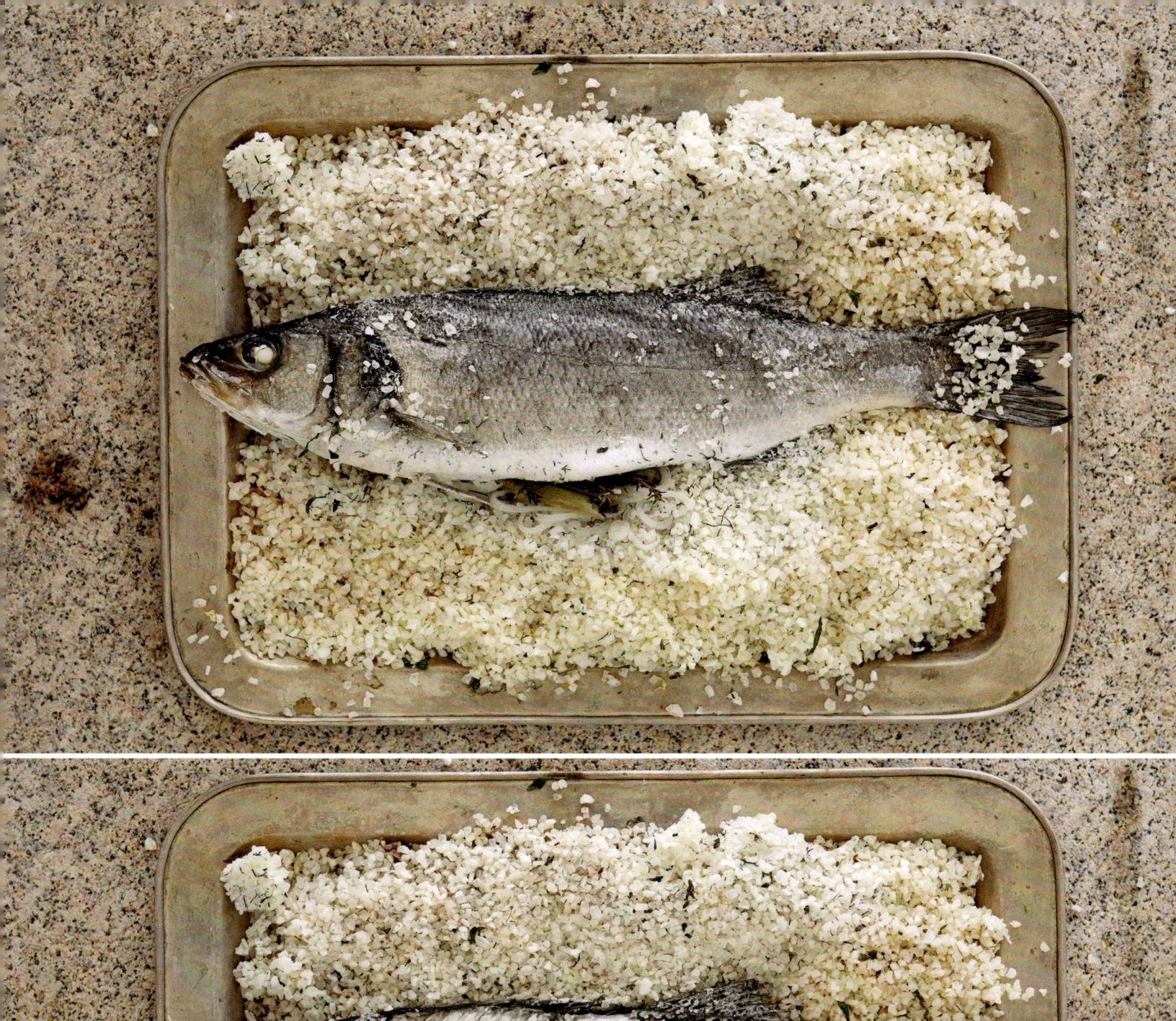

FOR THE FISH

1kg	white fish, whole
4 tbsp	Greek olive oil, plus extra for seasoning
	fine sea salt and freshly ground pepper
1	sprig of fresh rosemary, chopped
1.5kg	coarse sea salt
5	egg whites
	zest of 1 lemon
1	sprig of fresh thyme
	Ladolemono Sauce (see page 226)
½	bunch fresh parsley, finely chopped

1. Preheat the oven to 180°C.

2. Firstly, cut the fish lengthwise to clean and gut it, but do not bone them.

3. Season the flesh with 2 tbsp of the olive oil, the fine sea salt, pepper and rosemary.

4. Combine the coarse sea salt, egg whites, lemon zest, thyme, pepper and the remaining 2 tbsp of the olive oil in a bowl. Use a wooden spoon to mix the ingredients thoroughly.

5. Drizzle a baking dish with olive oil and add a thin layer of the salt mixture. Carefully place the fish onto it and spread the rest of the salt mixture on top of the fish until the body is fully covered in salt.

6. Transfer the dish to the oven and cook for 25 minutes. The roasting time may vary depending on the weight of the fish. Test whether the meat is well cooked after the suggested cooking time.

7. Remove the dish from the oven and transfer the fish to a serving plate. Generously garnish with Ladolemono Sauce and sprinkle with the parsley.

Sea Bass with a Crunchy Bread Crust, Summery Tomatoes and Courgette Purée

serves 2

Trying to describe this dish in words, I would jump to adjectives such as luscious, delicious, scrumptious, yummy, licking-your-lips-in-anticipation. But then again there is no necessity to use a fancy line, I might as well simply say: just go ahead and serve this recipe. You will find this one of the best meals that ever crossed your lips.

FOR THE COURGETTE PURÉE

- 4 large fresh basil leaves
- 2 sprigs of fresh thyme
- Greek olive oil, for frying, plus extra for seasoning
- 2 courgettes, unpeeled and grated into thin slices with a cucumber slicer
- fine sea salt and freshly ground black pepper
- 80g unsalted butter, roughly chopped
- juice of ½ lemon

FOR THE TOMATOES

- 2 large tomatoes, whole
- 4 tbsp Greek olive oil, plus more for frying
- 1 white onion, finely chopped
- 1 garlic clove, finely chopped
- fine sea salt and freshly ground black pepper
- 20g unsalted butter
- 1 pinch of fresh thyme
- 1 pinch of granulated sugar
- 3 large basil leaves, finely chopped
- 1 tsp white vinegar
- 3 drops lemon juice

FOR THE FISH FILLETS WITH A BREAD CRUST

- 1 stale baguette, placed in the freezer about 1 day before you want to prepare the meal
- 4 sea bass fillets, about 100g each
- Greek olive oil, for frying and for garnishing

1. Prepare the courgette purée. Toss the basil and thyme in a large bowl. In a roasting pan, heat olive oil and stir in the courgette slices. Season with salt and pepper and cover the pan with a lid. Cook for approximately 6 minutes, until soft, stirring frequently but keeping the pan covered in between. Check the courgettes for softness by gently squeezing the edge of one slice.

2. Transfer the contents of the pan to the bowl and combine with the thyme and basil, adding a few drops of olive oil. Cover and keep warm until shortly before serving.

3. Continue with the tomatoes. Boil water in a pan over high heat. Add the tomatoes and leave in the hot water for no more than 1 minute. Remove from the water and carefully strip off the skins, halve and remove the seeds using a knife. Chop the soft flesh into fine pieces and set aside.

4. In a roasting pan, heat olive oil and lightly sauté the onion until golden. Add the garlic, salt and pepper and stir. After 2 minutes, add 2 tbsp of the olive oil, the butter, thyme and, lastly, the tomato flesh. Season with the sugar, basil, vinegar, lemon juice and remaining 2 tbsp of olive oil and cook the mixture over medium heat for another 2 minutes. Stir and keep warm.

5. Finish the courgette purée. Place the aromatic courgettes in a blender with the butter and blend at the highest speed until smooth. Season with the salt, pepper and lemon juice and blend again to combine the flavours.

6. For the fish fillets, use a sharp kitchen knife to cut thin, full-length slices from the frozen, stale baguette. The number of slices required must equal the number of fillet pieces. Cut off the crusts to create rectangles and gently press the pieces of bread onto one side of the fillets.

7. In a roasting pan, heat olive oil. Firstly, fry the side covered with the bread crust until crispy and light brown, then flip over to the other side.

8. To serve, arrange the courgette purée in the centre of the plate and place the fish fillets on it, the bread side facing upwards. With a tablespoon, spread the tomato vegetables into a round form or simply around the fish. Lastly, sprinkle with olive oil before serving.

Tuna on a Bed of Quinoa & Lentils

serves 4

I discovered quinoa when I was searching for the perfect element to accompany tuna. My strategy was to find a not-too-complex-yet-delicious addition to the fish. Quinoa at that time was making headlines as being the 'super grain of the future', an easy-to-handle product that belongs to the group of complex carbohydrates. And oh boy, it truly is complex this carb! The first hurdle to my research was how to even spell 'kee-NO-ah'. Thanks to autocorrect, I quickly found information on how the grain of the future was controversially discovered 5,000 years ago and back then called the 'ancient grain'. Its colour is different from other grains, not uniform but red, black, beige, white ... I kept reading and understood that at least it is cooked and eaten like all grains but – oh! What's next? Quinoa is in fact not a grain at all! It is a seed. It is related to spinach. At least that makes it packed with nutrients, which is how it earned the title of 'super grain of the future'. Even though it is not a grain. And it is ancient. And for sure it's the most complex carbohydrate I know. The one thing I really understand about quinoa is that it tastes delicious with lentils and tuna.

FOR THE QUINOA

200g	black lentils
	salted water
200g	quinoa
	Greek olive oil, for frying
2	spring onions, finely chopped
10	cherry tomatoes, quartered
	zest of ½ lemon and juice of ½ lemon
1	pinch of fresh dill, finely chopped
1 tbsp	Greek olive oil
1 tsp	fine sea salt

FOR THE FISH

1kg	tuna fillet, chopped into strips the width of two fingers
	fine sea salt
	Greek olive oil, for frying, plus more to serve

1. In a large pan, bring water to a boil. Stir in the lentils and let them simmer for 15 minutes until softened.

2. Meanwhile in a second pan, bring the salted water to a boil. Add the quinoa and let it simmer for 3 minutes over high heat until crunchy.

3. Drain the lentils and quinoa. Transfer both to a bowl of cold water and set aside.

4. In a large sauté pan, heat the olive oil. Stir in the spring onions, cherry tomatoes, lemon zest, lemon juice, dill, 1 tbsp olive oil and salt. Combine for 30 seconds

5. Drain the quinoa and lentils and add to the pan. Stir thoroughly and reduce the heat to low.

6. Now continue with the fish. Season the tuna fillets by rubbing them gently with salt and then sprinkle with olive oil. In a large sauté pan, fry the tuna in olive oil. After two minutes, flip the fish and cook for another 2 minutes on the other side. Test the fillets are done by inserting a toothpick.

7. Give the quinoa and lentil mixture another good stir and serve in the centre of the plate. Once the tuna is cooked, place it on top of the bed of quinoa and lentils. Serve immediately with more olive oil on the side.

Prawn Saganaki

serves 4

FOR THE PRAWNS

8	prawns
	Greek olive oil, for frying
2	garlic cloves, finely chopped
¼	spicy green pepper, finely chopped
1	tomato, peeled and diced
2 tbsp	Napolitano sauce
1	bunch fresh parsley, chopped
60ml	dry white wine
1 tbsp	skordalia (Greek garlic paste), optional
100ml	prawn stock (see steps 2 and 3) or chicken stock
100g	feta cheese, crumbled
1 tsp	turmeric, optional
	toasted white bread, to serve

1. Prepare the prawns. Remove the heads, shells and tails. Set the flesh aside.

2. Continue with the prawn stock. In a roasting pan, heat olive oil over high heat and stir in the heads, shells and tails of the prawns and fry until browned. Use a potato masher to crush the ingredients during this process. Reduce the heat to medium-low and cover with water.

3. Simmer for 30 minutes, then strain through a sieve and set aside 100ml for the sauce.

4. In a large frying pan, heat olive oil over medium-high heat. Sweat the garlic and green pepper for about 1 minute until translucent. Stir in the tomato, Napolitano sauce and half of the parsley. Combine the ingredients with a wooden spoon before deglazing with the white wine.

5. Stir in the skordalia if using, before adding the prawn flesh. Cover the ingredients with the prawn or chicken stock and simmer for 3–4 minutes.

6. Lastly, add the feta cheese. Once the sauce is starting to thicken, stir in the remaining parsley and season with turmeric if desired. Give the Saganaki one final good stir and remove from the heat. Serve hot with toasted white bread.

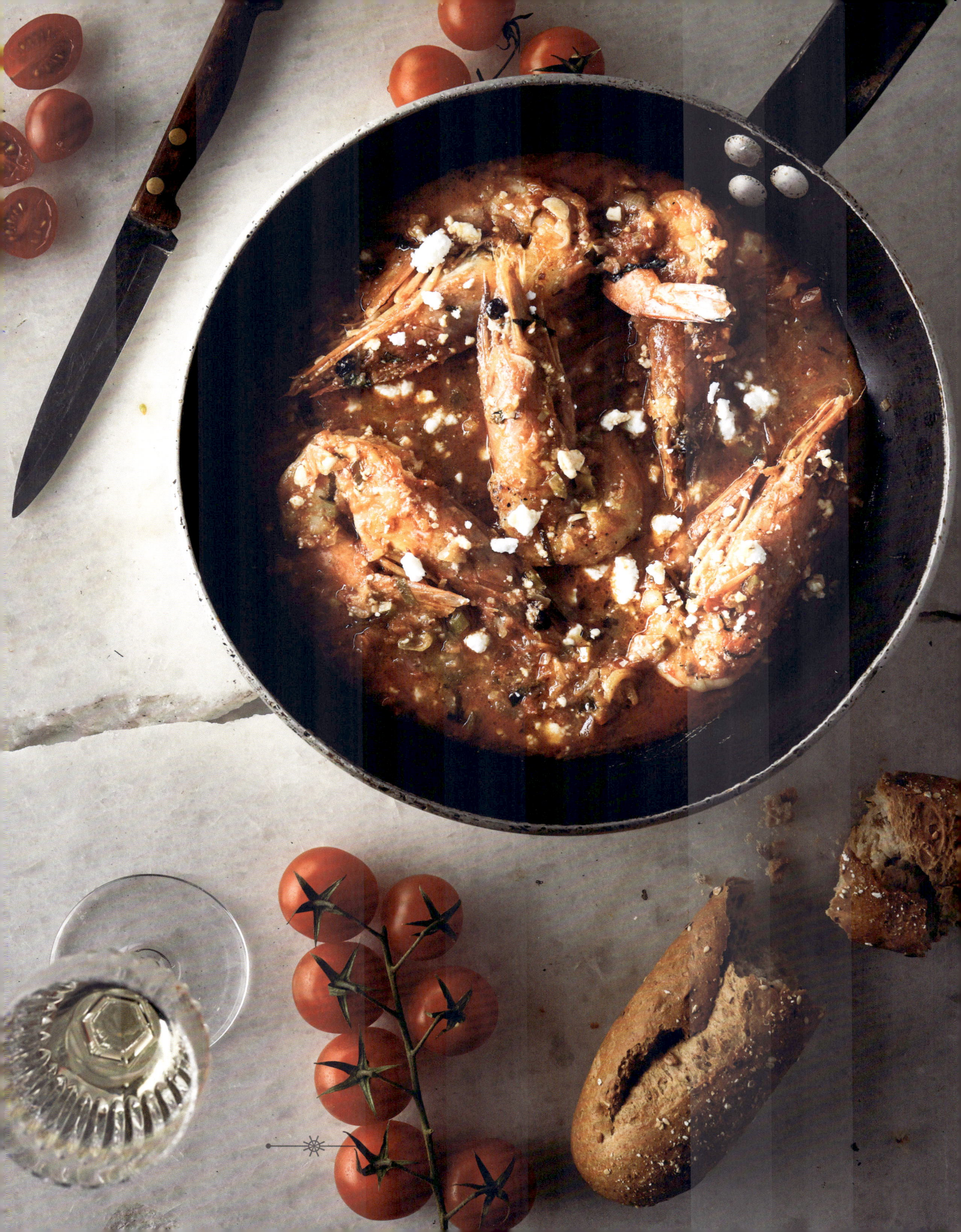

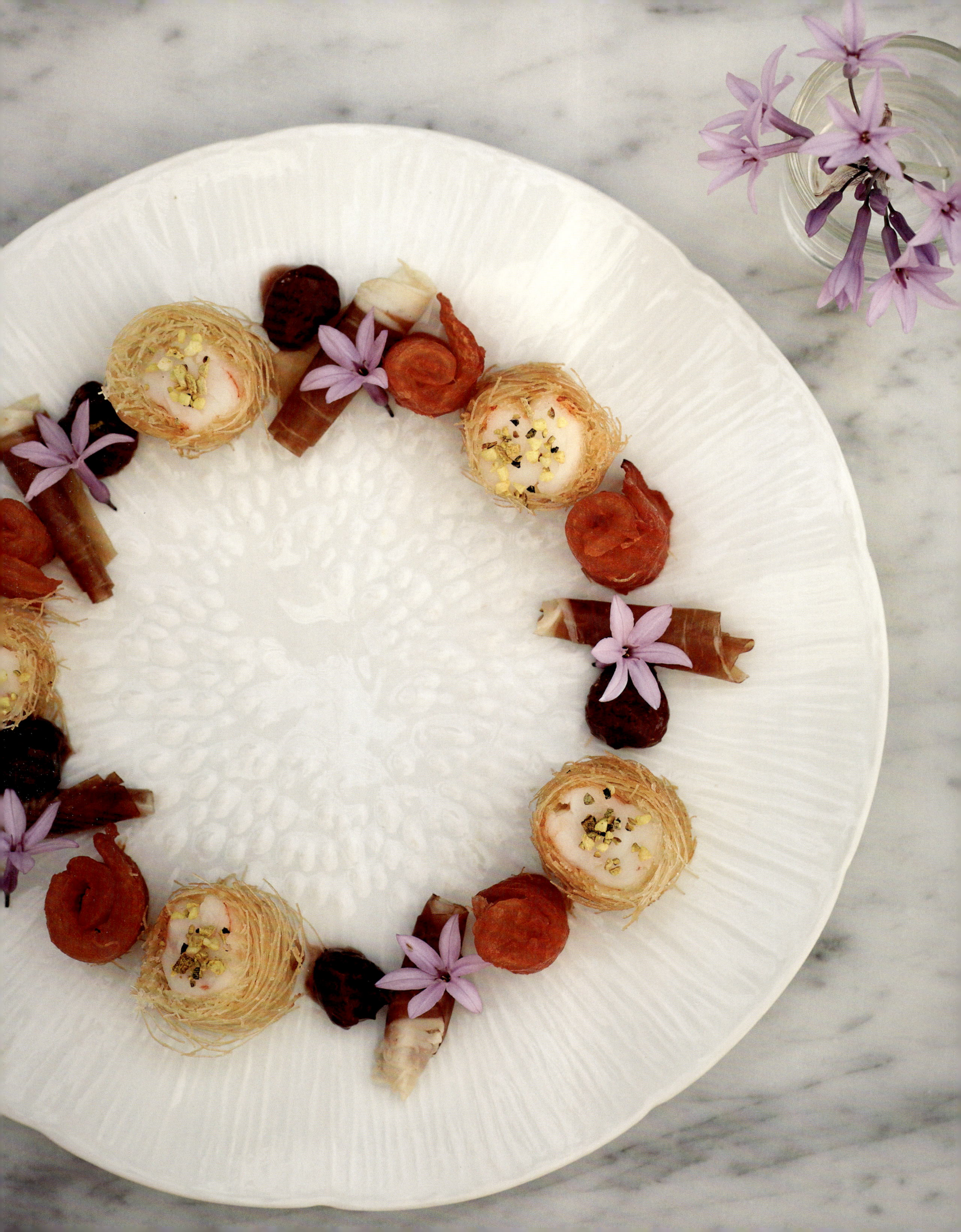

Langoustines in Angel Hair with Strawberry Gazpacho

serves 4

Beauty is in the eye of the beholder. To me this dish is undoubtedly very appealing in both its colourful optics and diversity of flavours. Fresh langoustines, wrapped in crispy angel hair, garnished with a sweet blend of juicy strawberries and honey, and artfully decorated with flowers. This dish tested my culinary abilities. But it is in exactly this challenging process of preparation that the true beauty of this dish lies. Once I travelled across Australia. I visited markets and admired the colourful pieces of local art, embraced the variety of the local cuisine and celebrated the diversity of culture in the cities and in the very heart of Australia. I admit this trip sometimes overextended my personal level of adventurousness. But the beauty of the experience was not in just travelling to a different continent, it was in this exact act of travelling beyond my personal limits, stepping outside my comfort zone. Dare to challenge your abilities and to never taste the bitterness of regret. Dare to attempt this recipe, to taste the sweetness of achievement. Oh, and even better: the sweetness of honey and strawberries.

FOR THE LANGOUSTINES

2	medium-sized tomatoes
2	pinches of fine sea salt
1	pinch of freshly ground black pepper
1	pinch of icing sugar
1 tsp	white balsamic vinegar
2 tsp	Greek olive oil
5	basil leaves
2	garlic cloves, 1 whole and 1 sliced
100g	angel hair for pastry
20	fresh langoustines, heads, shells and tails removed
	unsalted butter
	pistachio nuts, finely chopped
3	slices of Greek prosciutto, cut into strips
6	black olives, dried and thinly sliced

1. Start with the tomatoes. Place the tomatoes on a chopping board and divide them into quarters. Remove the seeds and set aside.

2. Season the tomatoes with the salt, pepper and icing sugar. Sprinkle them with the balsamic vinegar and olive oil and let them marinate with the basil leaves and 1 sliced garlic clove. After 45 minutes, preheat the oven to 130°C.

3. After approximately 1 hour of marinating, place the tomato fillets on a baking tray. Sprinkle with some of the marinade and roast for 30 minutes.

FOR THE STRAWBERRY GAZPACHO

1	slice white toast, crust removed and chopped
	Greek olive oil, for frying
	fine sea salt and freshly ground black pepper
1	red pepper, chopped
3	sprigs of fresh thyme
1	garlic clove
500g	fresh strawberries, halved
1	large gherkin pickle, finely sliced
3	leaves fresh basil
1 tbsp	icing sugar
1 tbsp	honey

FOR DECORATION

edible flowers, optional

4. Meanwhile, start the gazpacho. You will need two sauté pans. In one sauté pan and over medium heat, fry the toast from both sides in olive oil and season to taste with salt and pepper. Meanwhile in the second sauté pan, heat olive oil over medium heat and stir in the red pepper. Season with a pinch of salt, thyme and the whole garlic clove. Stir for about 3 minutes, until the pepper has softened. Now add the strawberries, pickle and basil and season with 2 pinches of salt and 2 pinches of pepper. Stir briskly and, with a wooden spoon, gently smash the strawberries. After 3–4 minutes remove the thyme, basil and garlic. Season with the icing sugar.

5. Mix the strawberry mixture and fried toast in a blender along with the honey. Blend until smooth and strain through a sieve for an even more velvety texture. Keep warm.

6. Continue with the langoustines. Spread out the angel hair and season the langoustines with salt and pepper. Place the langoustines on the angel hair and roll them into cylinders so they are entirely enveloped. Add a small piece of butter to each one and bake for 7 minutes in the oven.

7. Take out the langoustines, cut off the ends of the rolls to create perfect cylinders. Slice the cylinders and arrange them artfully in a circle on the serving plate. Sprinkle the flat top of each one with the finely chopped pistachios.

8. Roll the prosciutto strips into small tubes and place between the langoustine cylinders.

9. Place the tomato fillets in the gaps. Lastly, fill the empty spaces with black olive slices. If liked, decorate with edible flowers. Serve the plates with the strawberry gazpacho in a dish on the side and pour it in the centre of the plate once served.

MAIN ~ Fish & Seafood { 161 }

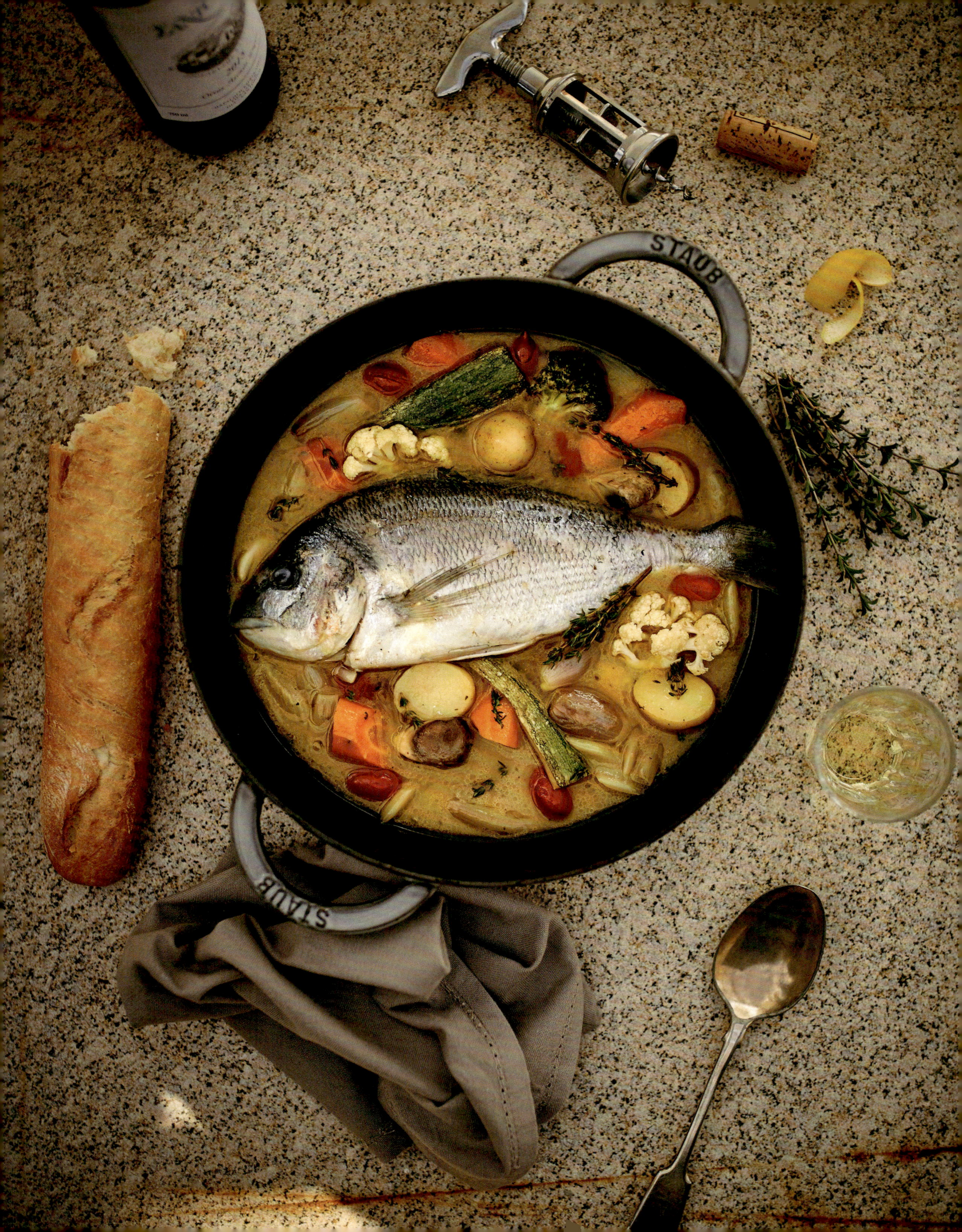
STAUB
STAUB

One-Pan Sea Bream on a Bed of Mediterranean Vegetables

serves 2

I love eating. I adore cooking. But I do not really get my kicks from washing dishes. One-pan or one-pot meals just sounded too appealing to not experiment with them. I was tempted by the ease of the procedure – putting the lid on, walking away from the stove and lingering over a glass of white wine while the magic happens on its own. After a few attempts and over a few glasses, I discovered this sea bream recipe which appeals even to the snobbiest of fish lovers, such as me. I worship fish. It is packed with vitamins and protein; it is irresistibly tasty and versatile enough to create quick and simple meals for every day of the week. For this recipe, I chose the simplest way to sit the bold flavours of sea bream on some of my favourite colourful Mediterranean vegetables!

FOR THE ONE-PAN SEA BREAM

600g	sea bream, whole and cleaned
	fine sea salt and freshly ground black pepper
40g	unsalted butter, roughly chopped
1 tbsp	Greek olive oil
1	white onion, roughly chopped
4	garlic cloves, halved
1	potato, peeled and roughly chopped
2	sticks celery, roughly chopped
10	cherry tomatoes, halved
1	mushroom, sliced
½	courgette, sliced and the seeds removed
1	carrot, peeled and sliced
1	spring onion, roughly chopped
10	cauliflower florets, roughly chopped
4	sprigs of fresh thyme
1 tbsp	Dijon mustard
60ml	dry white wine
400ml	fish stock
	juice and zest of 1 lemon
10	sprigs of fresh parsley, roughly chopped

1. Prepare the fish by seasoning it on both sides with salt. In a large sauté pan, heat 20g of the butter and the olive oil over medium heat. When the butter is sizzling, stir in the onion, garlic, potato and celery. Season with salt and pepper and simmer for 3–4 minutes.

2. Add the cherry tomatoes, mushroom, courgette, carrot, spring onion, cauliflower florets and thyme. Stir and continue to simmer for another 2 minutes.

3. Add the mustard and another 20g of the butter and combine the ingredients. Deglaze the pan with the white wine and simmer for another 3–4 minutes.

4. Gradually pour the fish stock over the ingredients until they are entirely covered. Season with the lemon juice and zest. Simmer for another 2 minutes.

5. Finally, add the sea bream. Sprinkle the parsley into the pan and cover with a lid. Simmer for 7–8 minutes, until the fish is tender. Ensure that all the ingredients are covered by liquid, adding more fish stock if required. Serve hot with the vegetables arranged around the fish and a few extra spoonfuls of sauce.

Dorado with a Duo of Colourful Beetroot Purées

serves 2

When I started painting this dish, I stood in front of a white canvas, the plate like an unwritten book. The taste of this recipe is delicious, but its colours make it art. My book was a white canvas too, before colour, shapes, space, photographs and calligraphy slowly soaked into the paper, unaware of their part in the grand design. There is green grass growing between the pages, yellow sunshine blinding the eye, there is a silver flavour of seafood, a turquoise smell of the sea and a delicious, sweet purple taste. Green and yellow are mingling friends, grey and pink chatting neighbours, orange and red lovers strolling hand in hand, and black and white are shaking hands.

FOR THE BEETROOT PURÉES

	Greek olive oil
	fine sea salt and freshly ground black pepper
500g	each red and yellow beetroot, leaves removed
40g	unsalted butter, roughly chopped
200ml	chicken stock
	juice of ½ lemon

FOR THE FISH

2	dorado fillets
	fine sea salt
	Greek olive oil, for frying

1. Preheat the oven to 180°C.

2. To make the Red and Yellow Beetroot Purée, cut pieces of kitchen foil approximately 40 x 20 cm for each beetroot. Sprinkle the foil generously with olive oil and salt. Now place them in the centre of each one and wrap into small parcels. Ensure that the end is closed tightly but allow space for air to circulate around the beetroot. Bake for 90 minutes. Towards the end of the cooking time, check softness by inserting a toothpick.

3. Once the beetroot are cooked, carefully undo the parcels. Peel the vegetables while still warm. Separate the red from the yellow ones, then chop the peeled beetroot roughly and combine the red beetroot in a blender with half the butter and stock. Blend on high speed until smooth. Season with salt, pepper and half the lemon juice and blend again to combine the flavors.

4. Repeat with the yellow beetroots to make the Yellow Beetroot Purée.

5. Season the dorado fillets with salt. Heat olive oil over medium heat. Fry the dorado fillets on both sides until crisp. Serve hot and garnished with the Red and Yellow Beetroot Purées for a colourful meal.

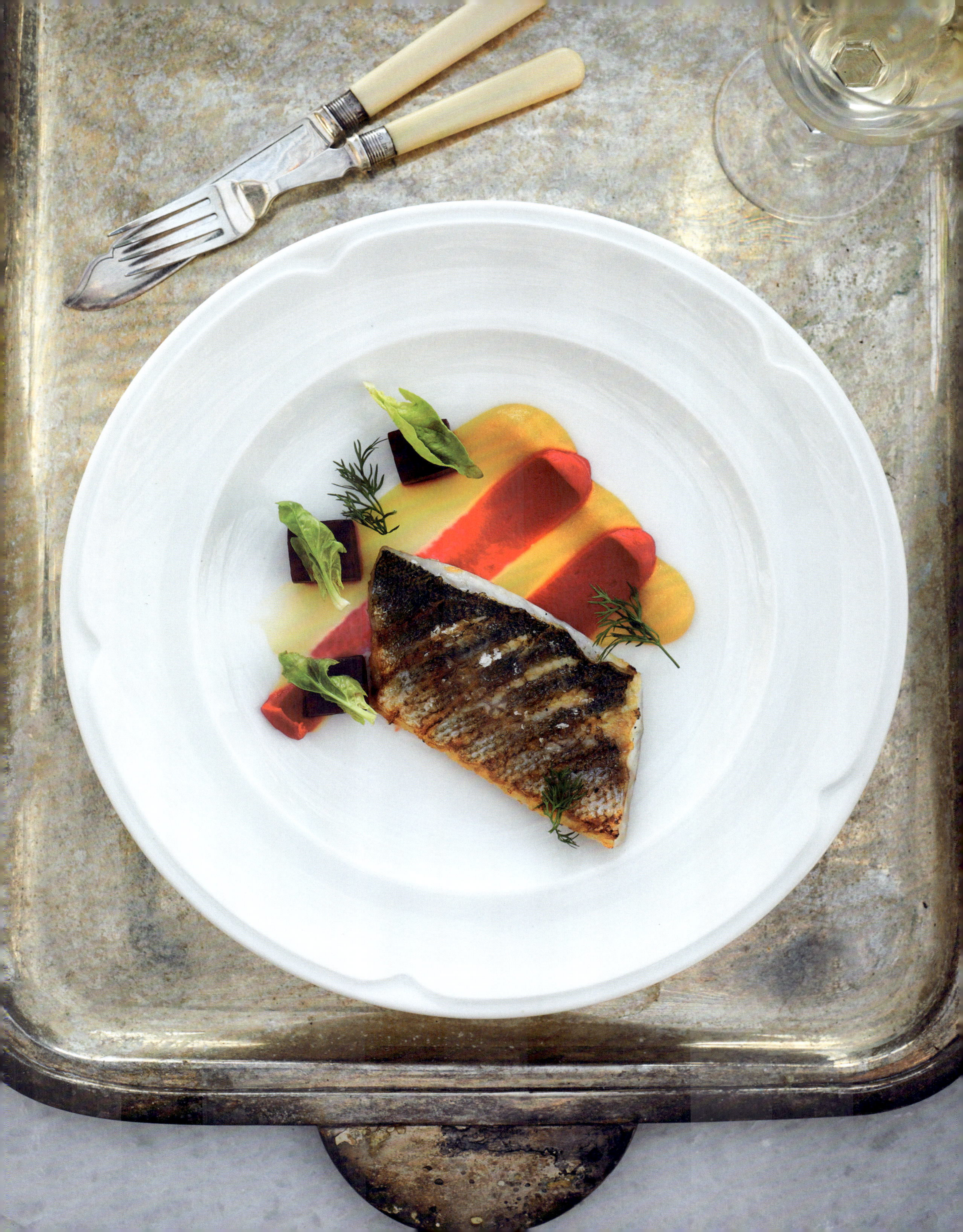

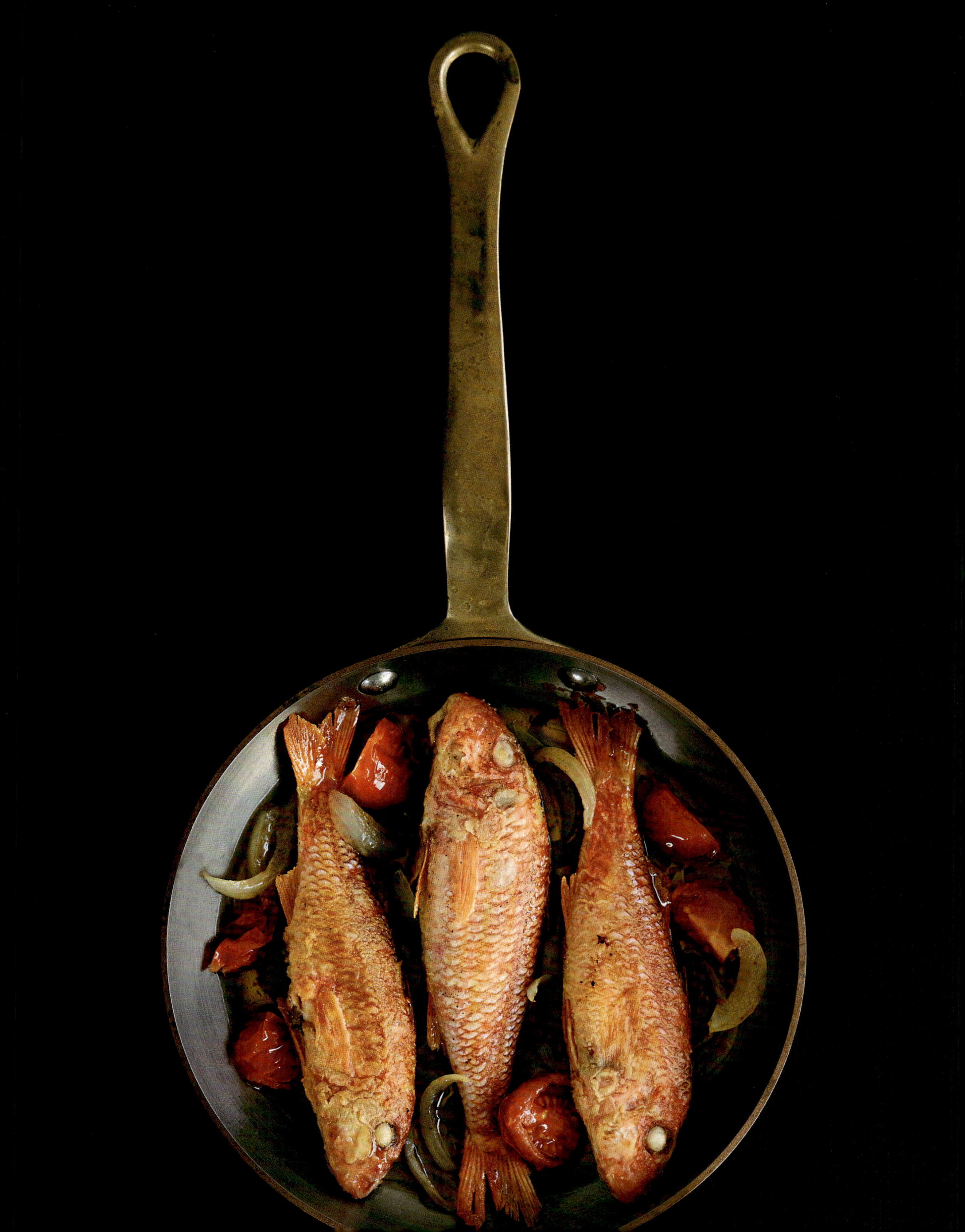

Red Mullet

serves 8

Creating this recipe, my tactic was to identify the essentials: red mullet and vegetables, add whatever I thought worked and finally eliminate unwanted components. As simple as that may sound, the journey was full of failures and setbacks trying a variety of red mullet dishes. But I wasn't alone. Luckily, I had a panel of volunteer judges who obediently gave their votes on each dish in my one-man cook-off. They inspired me with substantial advice: 'Add Martini to the pan, because Martini is always worth a glass.' 'Add vodka, because vodka is always worth a shot.' The only vehement protest arose when it came to the wine, clearly the judges' expert advice was that it worked best inside their glasses rather than inside the pan. The undisputed winner has finally surfaced, and it is beautiful. In fact the jury voted it to be one of my best recipes ever. They giggled audibly and I was sure I had created satisfied smiles on their faces, even though I could not see them behind so many empty bottles.

FOR THE RED MULLET

8	red mullets, whole and cleaned
	fine sea salt and freshly ground black pepper
	plain flour, for coating
	Greek olive oil, for frying
8	cherry tomatoes, quartered
½	white onion, thinly sliced
5	garlic cloves, crushed
1	sprig of fresh rosemary
3	sprigs of fresh thyme
	apple cider vinegar, for deglazing

1. Prepare the red mullets by generously sprinkling them with sea salt. Coat the fish in flour.

2. In a large sauté pan, heat olive oil over medium high heat. Once the oil is hot, add the fish and fry on one side for 3–4 minutes.

3. Before flipping the fish onto the other side, add the tomatoes, onion, crushed garlic cloves, rosemary and thyme. Give it a good stir, turn the fish and let the vegetables simmer alongside the fish for another 4 minutes.

4. Deglaze the pan with apple cider vinegar. Season to taste with salt and pepper and serve hot.

Lobster Moussaka

serves 6

Do you believe that you can do extraordinary things? I had a sky-high dream once of achieving something extraordinary: I wanted to climb Mount Kilimanjaro. But I failed. Another time I had a dream as deep as the ocean, where the freshest lobsters live, to create an extraordinary recipe: Lobster Moussaka. But, again, I failed. Extraordinariness, though, is not instant success. It is in stopping the climb of Mount Kilimanjaro, but not giving up climbing because I didn't reach the peak of the mountain upon the first attempt. Extraordinariness is to throw in the towel over the Lobster Moussaka, but then pick that same towel up again, wipe the sweat off my forehead and start over. Extraordinary results happen when you refuse to give up dreaming. I didn't and I was rewarded. Not yet with the view from the top of Mount Kilimanjaro, but with the taste of a stunning Lobster Moussaka recipe. With an ocean-deep failure becoming a sky-high triumph.

FOR THE LOBSTER BISQUE

	heads and shells of 3 lobsters
	Greek olive oil, for frying
1	stick celery, roughly chopped
1	white onion, roughly chopped
2	carrots, roughly chopped
50g	butter
	fresh thyme
30ml	cognac
60ml	dry white wine
1 tbsp	tomato purée
1.2l	chicken stock

1. Start with the lobster bisque. Put the lobster shells and heads into a large pan and fry in olive oil over high heat for 3 minutes. Use a potato masher to crush the pieces and stir briskly. Add the celery, onion, carrots, butter and thyme and continue to mash the ingredients while allowing the mixture to simmer for approximately 4 minutes, until all the cooking liquid has evaporated.

2. Deglaze the pan with the cognac and white wine. Add the tomato purée and boil for 5 minutes before pouring in the chicken stock. Reduce the heat to medium and simmer for 15 minutes.

3. Strain through a sieve into a clean pot and keep warm.

4. Preheat the oven to 180°C.

5. Continue with the aubergine and potato slices for the Moussaka. Sprinkle two baking trays with olive oil. On one, place the aubergine slices and allow them to cook in the oven for 35 minutes. On the second, place the potato slices. Season generously with salt on both sides and place them in the oven for 30 minutes.

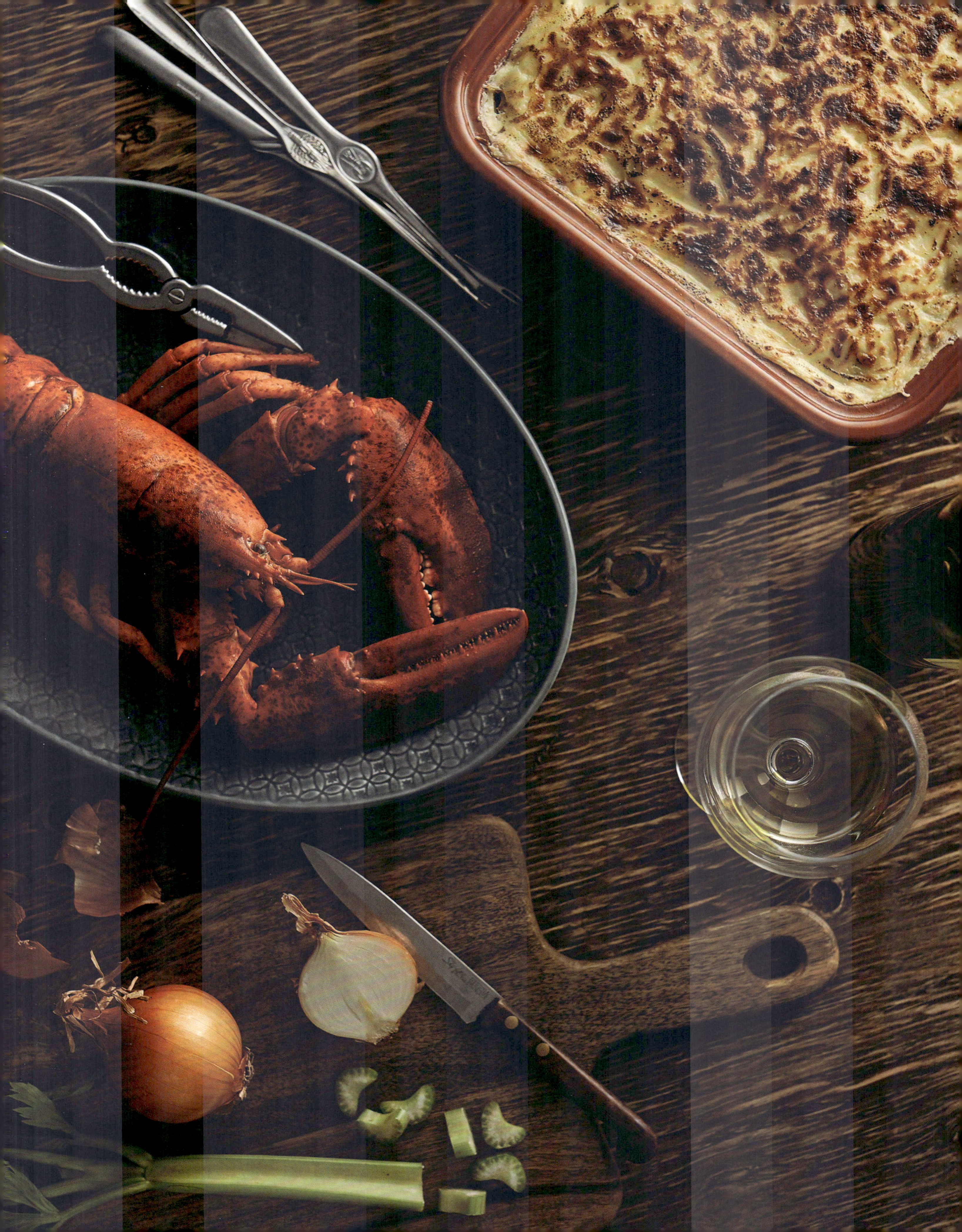

FOR THE MOUSSAKA

	Greek olive oil, for frying
3	aubergines, sliced
3	medium potatoes, peeled and sliced into finger-width pieces
	fine sea salt and freshly ground black pepper
	salted water
3	whole lobsters or 100g lobster meat
2	carrots, peeled and finely chopped
1	leek, finely chopped
1	celery stick, finely chopped
1	white onion, finely chopped
1	fennel bulb, finely chopped
1	garlic clove, finely chopped
2	sprigs of fresh thyme
1	sprig of fresh rosemary
3 tbsp	passata
1 tsp	tomato purée
	zest of 1 lemon
	juice of ½ lemon
1	pinch of fresh dill, finely chopped
4	leaves fresh basil, finely chopped
1	pinch of nutmeg
2 tbsp	breadcrumbs
50g	Parmesan cheese, grated

FOR THE BÉCHAMEL SAUCE

110g	unsalted butter
120g	plain flour
50g	Parmesan cheese
1	pinch of nutmeg
1 tsp	lemon juice
1	medium egg

6. Now begin with the lobster meat. Bring salted water to a boil and allow the meat to boil until tender for approximately 3 minutes. Drain the flesh and chop into fine pieces.

7. In a large sauté pan heat olive oil over medium heat to prepare the rest of the filling. Sauté the carrots, leek, celery, onion, fennel, garlic, thyme and rosemary and season with a pinch of salt. Sauté for 2 minutes, stirring constantly, before adding the lobster meat, passata and tomato purée. Lastly, add the lemon zest before adding 7 tbsp of the Lobster Bisque to the pan. Season to taste with salt and pepper and simmer for another 10 minutes over medium heat.

8. Switch off the heat. Remove the rosemary using tongs and stir in the lemon juice, dill and basil, then set aside.

9. Continue with the béchamel sauce. Heat the butter over high heat in a pan. Once melted, whisk in the flour and stir until thick. Now pour in 600ml of the Lobster Bisque and stir briskly for 6 minutes. Add the cheese and season with the nutmeg and lemon juice and continue to stir for approximately 3 minutes. Remove from the heat and stir in the egg. Set aside.

10. Meanwhile, the potato and aubergine slices should be soft. Remove from the oven and season to taste with salt, pepper and nutmeg. Increase the oven to 200°C.

11. Begin to layer the moussaka. Spread a layer of béchamel sauce, breadcrumbs and drops of olive oil over the base of a large baking dish. Add a layer of potato slices, then a layer of aubergine slices and spread 30g of the Parmesan cheese on top. Now proceed with layering the remaining lobster and vegetable mix. Cover with the remaining Béchamel Sauce and then the remaining Parmesan cheese. Place in the oven and bake for 30 minutes, until the cheese is golden brown.

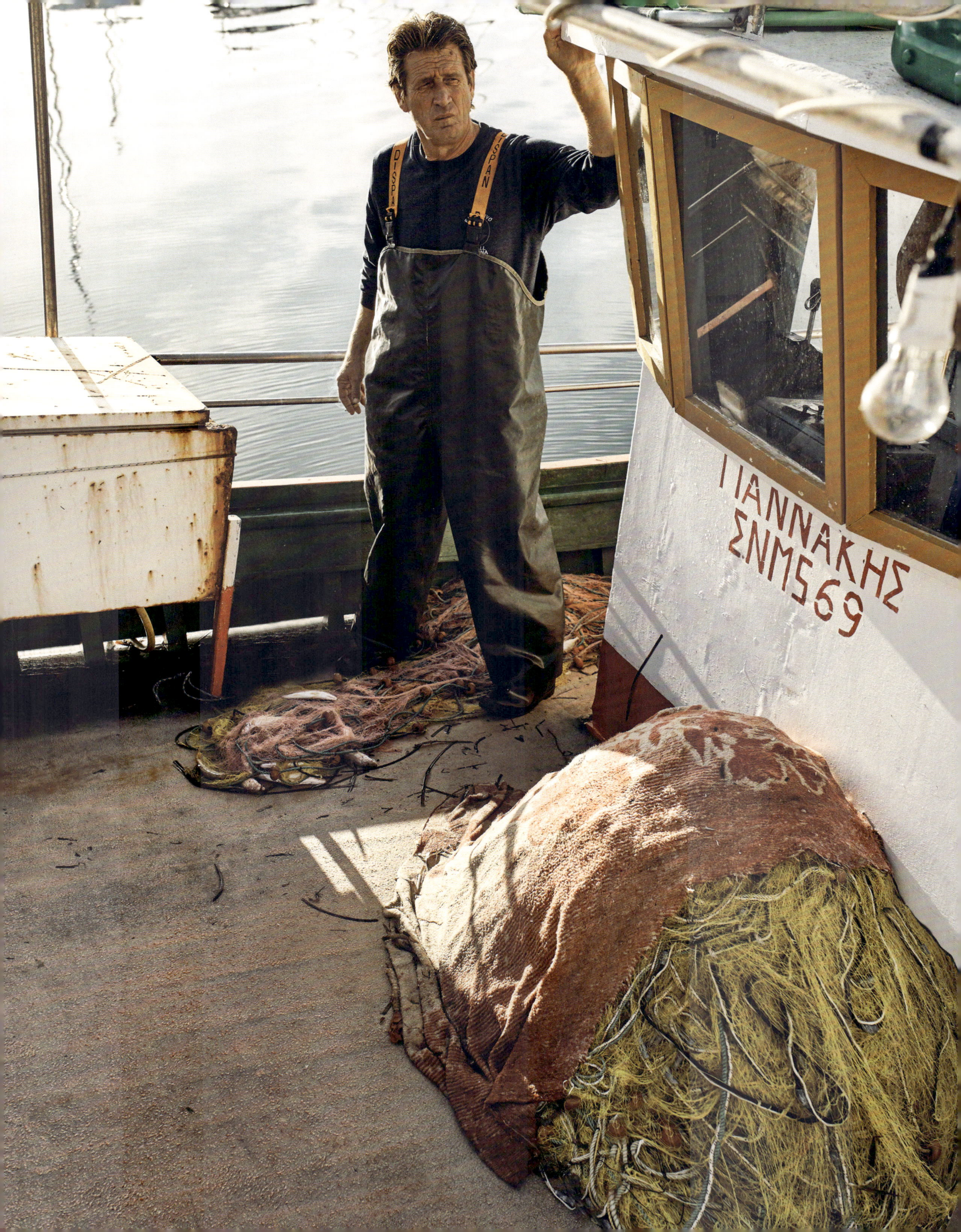
ΓΙΑΝΝΑΚΗΣ
ΣΝΜ569

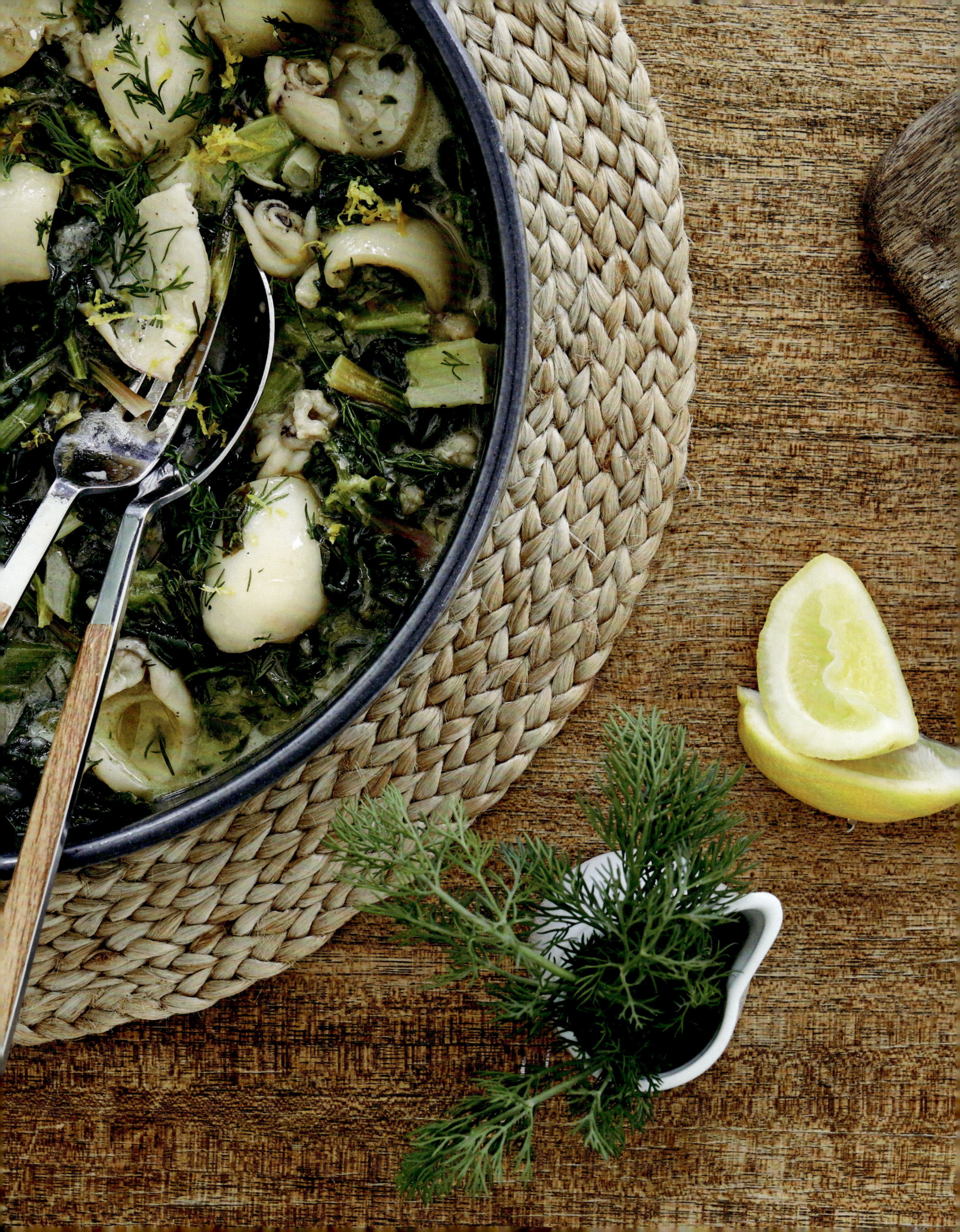

Calamari with Spinach

serves 2

My vision was blurred; I tried to fight my way through the crowds on wobbly legs, trying not to inhale the air which was thick with the fumes of fried meat. I used to have a hard time sticking to my fast before I discovered this fasting-friendly recipe of gorgeous calamari salad. During the traditional Orthodox fast, Greeks refrain from most animal products except for honey and seafood. The creation of this dish was the result of desperation in its purest form. I dare even to say that God was testing me one Sunday. My little niece Sophia came to pick me up from my house where I had barricaded myself from the outside world which was full of temptations. I could barely hear her voice since the monotone humming of my fridge sounded like a thunderstorm, but she somehow got me out of the door and right into a street market. As she led me through the flow of people I suddenly broke into a sweat when I smelled the smoke of a barbecue with juicy souvlaki meat crackling over the fire. I broke free from the smell only to almost collide with a chicken grill, each chicken starting to flirt with me. Sophia dragged me on to the fish section where I stumbled through the aroma of tempting foods that I could almost taste and all this while trying to soothe my coffee which started crying desperately because it missed its milk. I felt my body fade away when Sophia and I reached a gyros place. The last thing I heard before my world went black was little Sophia audibly chewing her gyros. 'Excuse me, my uncle collapsed! Could you please help me? Just drag him over to that ice cream parlour over there. Thank you.'

FOR THE CALAMARI

- 500g squid, cleaned
- Greek olive oil, for frying
- 1 white onion, finely chopped
- 2 garlic cloves, finely chopped
- juice and zest of 1 lemon
- 150ml white wine
- 300ml vegetable stock or water
- 500g spinach, cleaned
- 3 spring onions, finely chopped
- ½ bunch fresh dill, finely chopped
- ⅓ bunch of fresh mint, finely chopped
- fine sea salt and freshly ground black pepper

1. Cut the squid into 3–4cm chunks.

2. In a pan, heat olive oil over medium heat and sweat the onion and garlic until translucent. Toss in the squid and sauté for another 3–4 minutes until it has taken on colour. Season with the lemon zest before deglazing the pan with the white wine.

3. Once the white wine has evaporated, drizzle in the lemon juice and pour in the vegetable stock or water. Simmer for 35–40 minutes.

4. Stir the spinach into the pan before adding the spring onions and season with the dill and mint. Combine the ingredients with a wooden spoon and continue to simmer for another 5–6 minutes. Season to taste with more lemon juice, salt and pepper and serve hot.

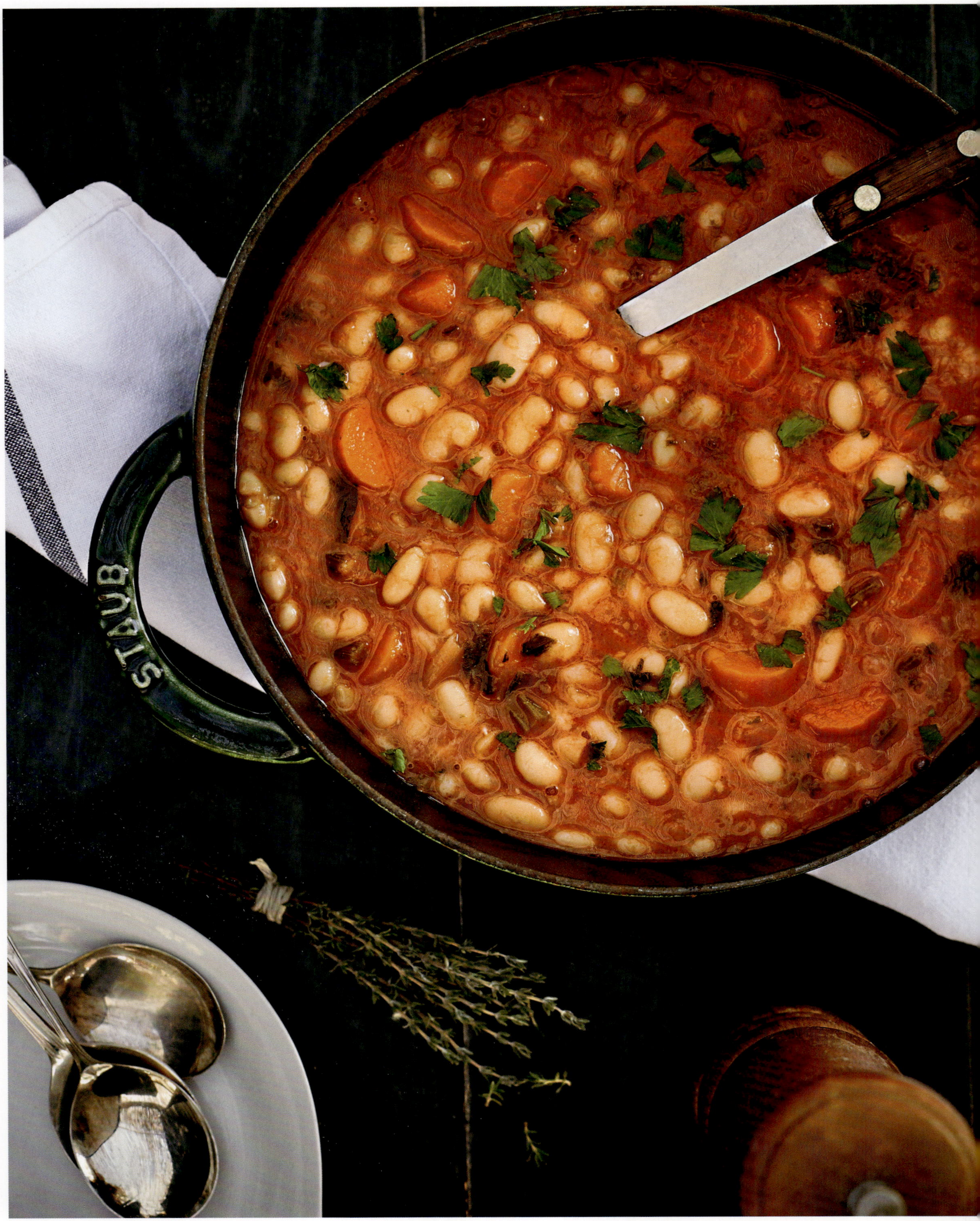
STAUB

Σούπες

SOUPS

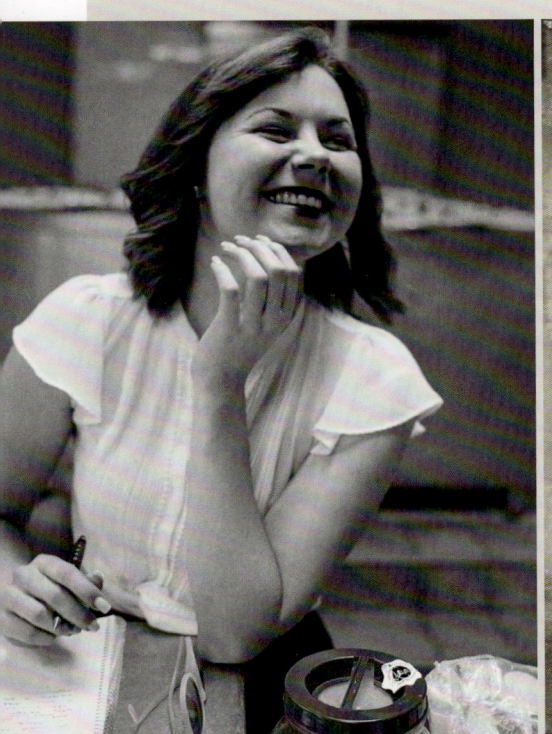

SOUPS

My cooking is not perfect. You can tell that from the apron I am wearing. It has quite a few loose threads these days and, once white, it now wears an array of colourful stains from all the dishes that I love to cook. Perhaps even one or two from the soup boiling in the pot behind me on the stove, which is surrounded by leftover vegetable peelings, or pieces of chicken, fish bones or some small beans that occasionally roll off the counter during food preparation. I shopped for these ingredients at the local market, which is as colourful a place as my apron. The market has a unique smell composed of the intense spices on display, the aroma of grilled snacks and of the freshest fish. I always meet people I know, but all conversation is drowned by the stall holders' cries offering their produce; the excited chatter of kids strolling hand in hand with their mothers; and by more loud greetings of other people meeting acquaintances. To me, all these sounds combined make the music of the market, an orchestra of Greek culture.

I take a sip of the soup, which creates a warm feeling in my stomach, and fling my old apron over the back of the chair. My country is like that apron. Greece is not perfect. It is splattered with all sorts of stains that cannot be washed out, a loose thread here and there, its former brightness perhaps faded. But I would never want to live any place else. I would never want a different apron. To me the stains do not diminish its beauty. Instead they are sprinkles of all the things I love. Stains like memories rooted in this country, colourful memories soaked into the fabric.

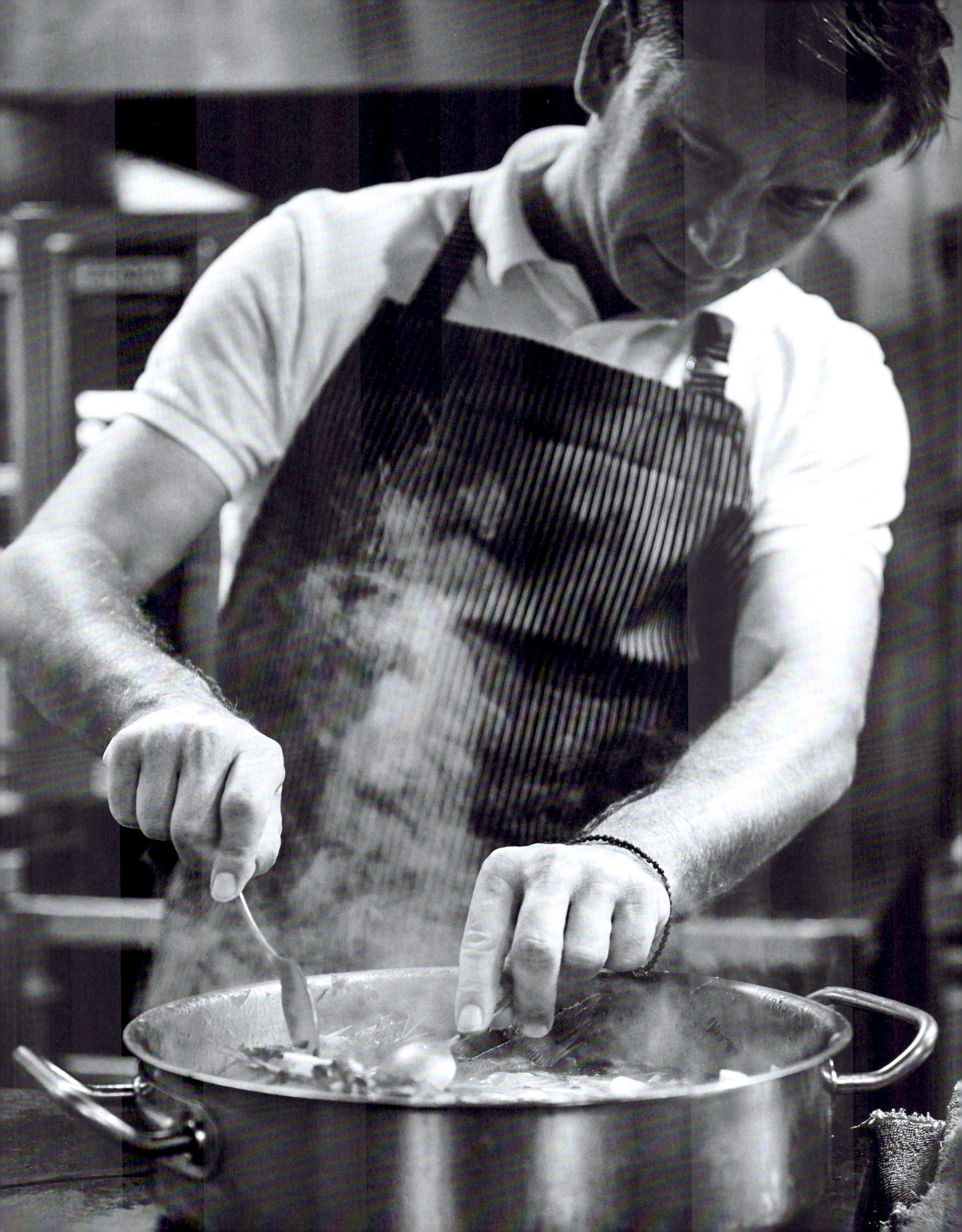

Giouvarlakia – Meatball Soup

serves 2

FOR THE MEATBALL SOUP

50g	Carolina rice, uncooked
500g	minced beef
1	egg
1	white onion, grated
50ml	Greek olive oil
1	handful fresh parsley, finely chopped
2	pinches of fresh dill, finely chopped
1.5l	salted water
	fine sea salt and freshly ground black pepper
1	carrot, diced, blanched and submerged in cold salted water
	Avgolemono Sauce (see page 227)

1. Soak the rice in water for 30 minutes so it starts to absorb moisture before making the meatballs.

2. Combine the softened rice with the minced beef, egg, onion, olive oil and parsley, one pinch of the dill, salt and pepper in a bowl and knead with your hands until you have a uniform mixture. Form into balls the size of small walnuts and coat each one with a thin layer of flour.

3. Heat salted water in a pot and bring to a boil. Toss in the meatballs and add in the carrot. Season with one pinch salt and pepper, give the soup a good stir and cover the pot with a lid. Cook for 30 minutes.

4. Meanwhile, make the Avgolemono Sauce.

5. Remove the pot from the heat. Use a wooden spoon to stir the Avgolemono Sauce into the soup. Add the remaining dill and serve immediately.

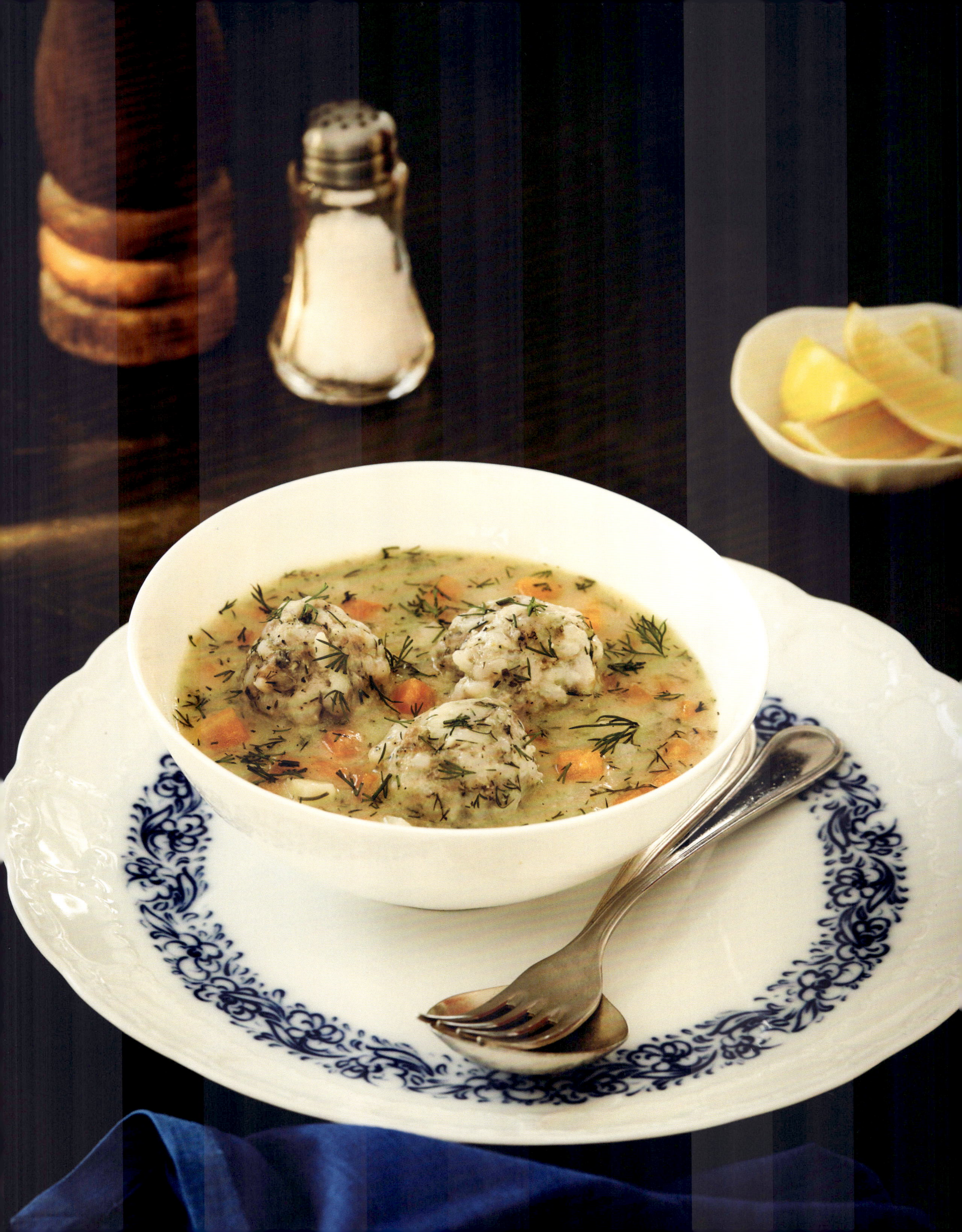

Fasolada – Classic Bean Soup

serves 4

FOR THE BEAN SOUP

500g	medium-sized dried white beans
1	white onion, finely chopped
80ml	Greek olive oil, plus extra to serve
2	garlic cloves, chopped
2	white onions, finely chopped
2	spring onions, chopped
2	carrots, chopped
2	sticks celery, chopped
50g	bacon, chopped
3	tomatoes, grated
2 tsp	tomato purée
2 tbsp	smoked paprika seasoning
1	pinch of sugar
3	sprigs of fresh thyme
2 tsp	fine sea salt
1 tsp	freshly ground black pepper
	celery leaves, chopped
	crumbled feta cheese (optional)

The day before you want to make the soup

1. Soak the beans in water overnight.

The following day

2. Fill a large pan with 1.8 l of cold water. Remove the soaked beans from the soaking water with a slotted spoon and transfer them to the pan. Now bring to the boil, add the chopped onion and cook over low heat.

3. Meanwhile continue with the soup. In a frying pan, heat the olive oil over medium heat and sweat the garlic, white and spring onions, carrots, celery and bacon. Reduce the heat to low and add the tomatoes, tomato purée, smoked paprika seasoning, sugar, thyme, salt, pepper and 100 ml water. Cook for 10–15 minutes. Add water if the mixture becomes too dry and stir frequently.

4. Transfer the contents of the frying pan to the pan of beans and cook over low heat for a minimum of 1½ hours, until the beans have softened.

5. When the beans are soft, and 3–4 minutes before you want to serve the soup, stir in the celery leaves and give the soup a final good stir. Serve in a soup bowl and garnish with olive oil and crumbled feta cheese, if desired.

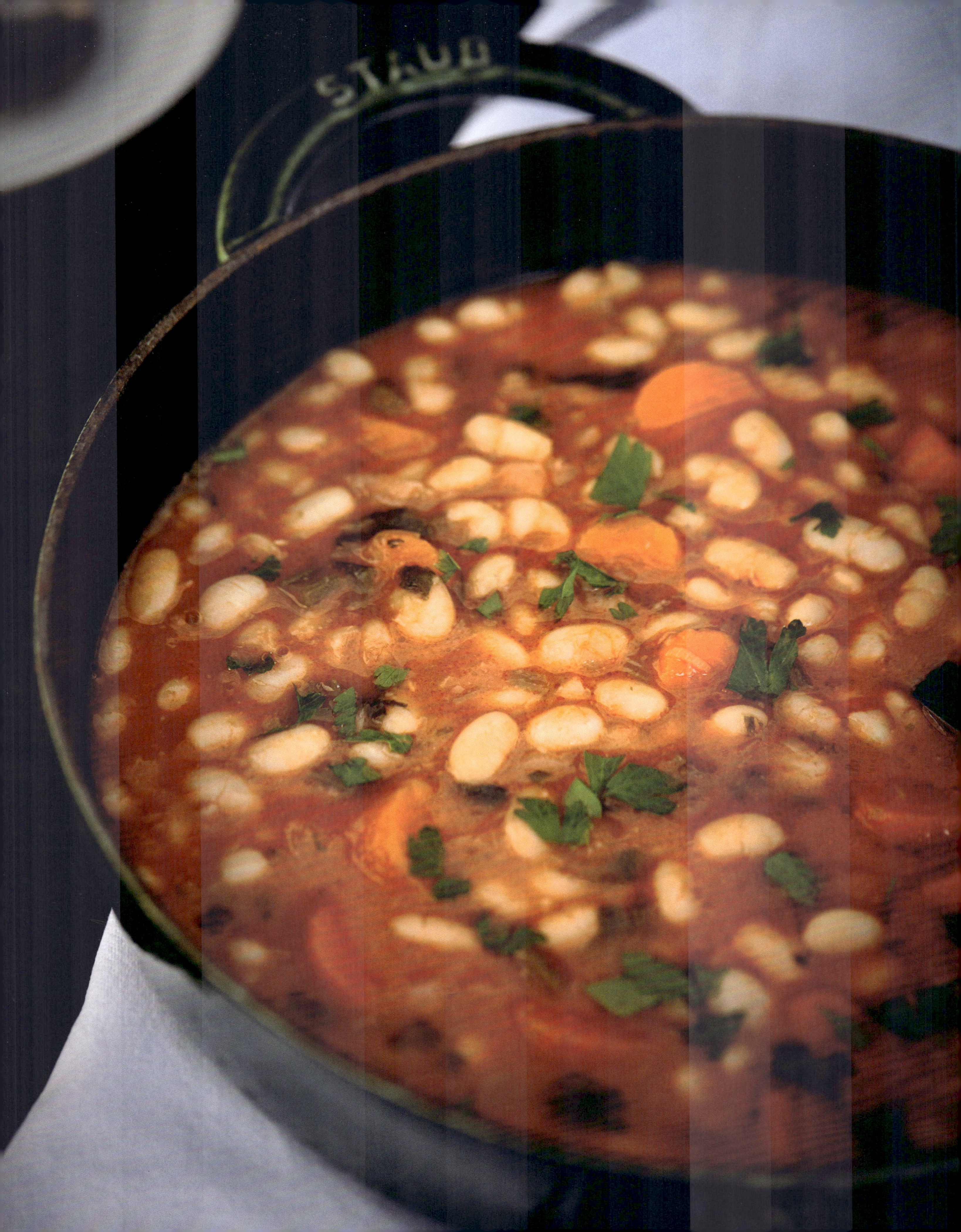
STAUB

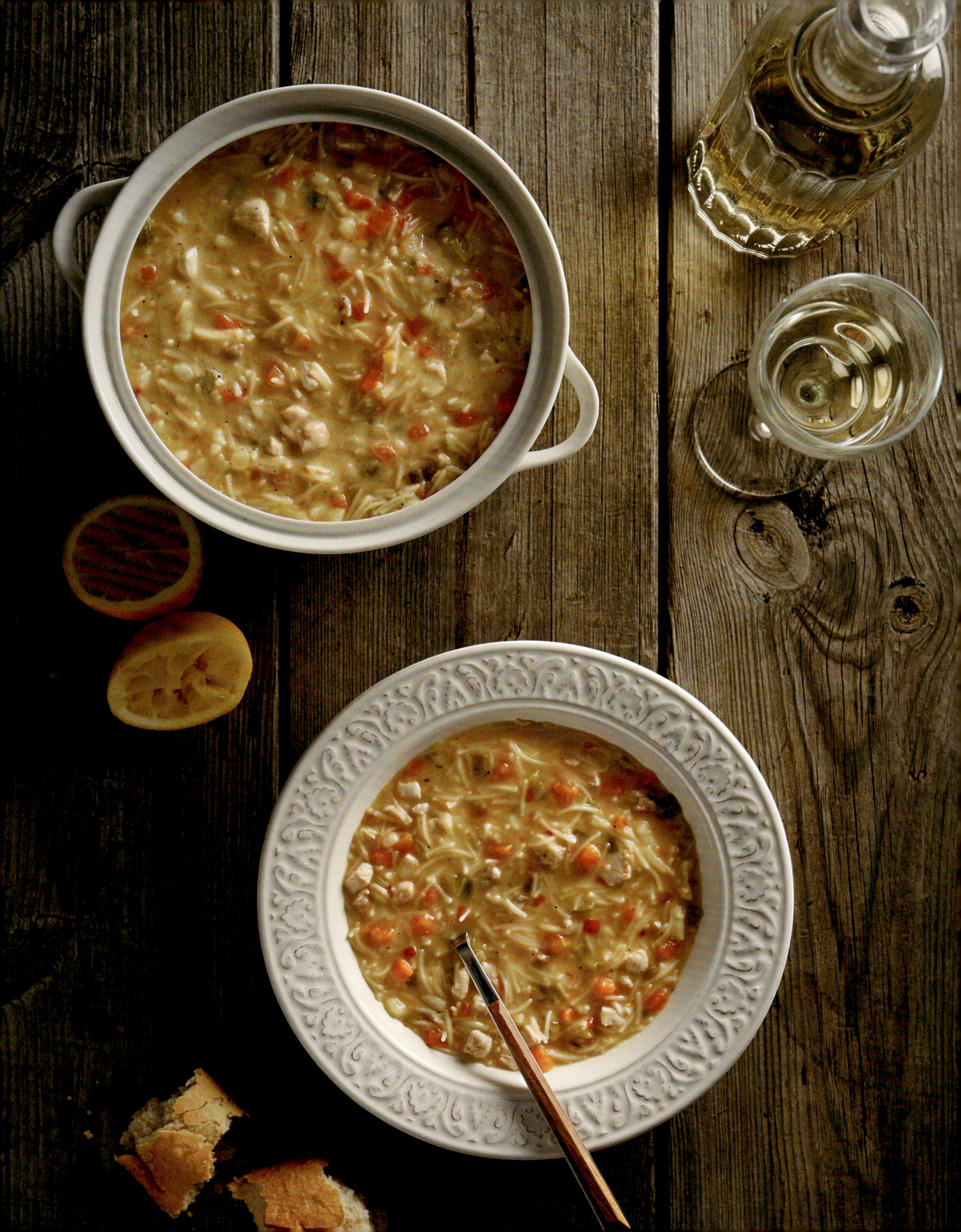

Chicken Soup

serves 4

FOR THE CHICKEN SOUP

	Greek olive oil
1	potato, finely chopped
2	carrots, finely chopped
	skin of 1 courgette, finely chopped
	fine sea salt and freshly ground black pepper
1	garlic clove, finely chopped
1	shallot, finely chopped
2	bay leaves
2	sprigs of fresh thyme
1.3l	chicken stock
250 g	chicken breast or thigh, chopped
50 g	vermicelli noodles
1 tbsp	fresh parsley, chopped
	juice of ½ lime
75g	unsalted butter

1. In a large pan, heat olive oil and toss in the potato. After 1 minute, stir in the carrots, courgette skin and a pinch of salt and pepper. Drizzle 2 teaspoons of olive oil over the contents of the pan before allowing them to sauté for about 2 minutes.

2. Now stir in the garlic and shallot. After 3 minutes, add the bay leaves and thyme.

3. Pour the chicken stock into the pan, season with 2 tsp salt and bring to the boil. Add the chicken and continue to cook for 10 minutes, stirring occasionally.

4. Lastly, add the noodles and let the soup boil for 1 minute. Remove the bay leaves, sprinkle in the parsley and add the lime juice. Toss in the butter and simmer for 1 minute. Ensure that the noodles are soft before serving the soup hot.

Cod & Vegetable Velouté

serves 4

FOR THE VEGETABLE SOUP

1	white onion, sliced
2	carrots, sliced
2	potatoes, roughly chopped
5	sticks celery, roughly chopped
700g	cod fillets
	juice of 1 lemon
	fine sea salt and freshly ground black pepper
	sprigs of fresh dill, to serve

1. Bring a large pan of water to the boil. Add the onion, carrots and potatoes. Cover with a lid and boil for 5 minutes over high heat.

2. Stir in the celery and then the cod. Reduce the heat to medium, cover with a lid and simmer for 12 minutes, turning the fish halfway through the cooking time.

3. Now remove the fish from the soup and set aside.

4. Transfer the soup and vegetables to a blender. Blend on high speed until smooth, then add the lemon juice and season to taste with salt and pepper. Blend once again on high speed.

5. Finally, add in the fish and serve hot, garnished with sprigs of dill.

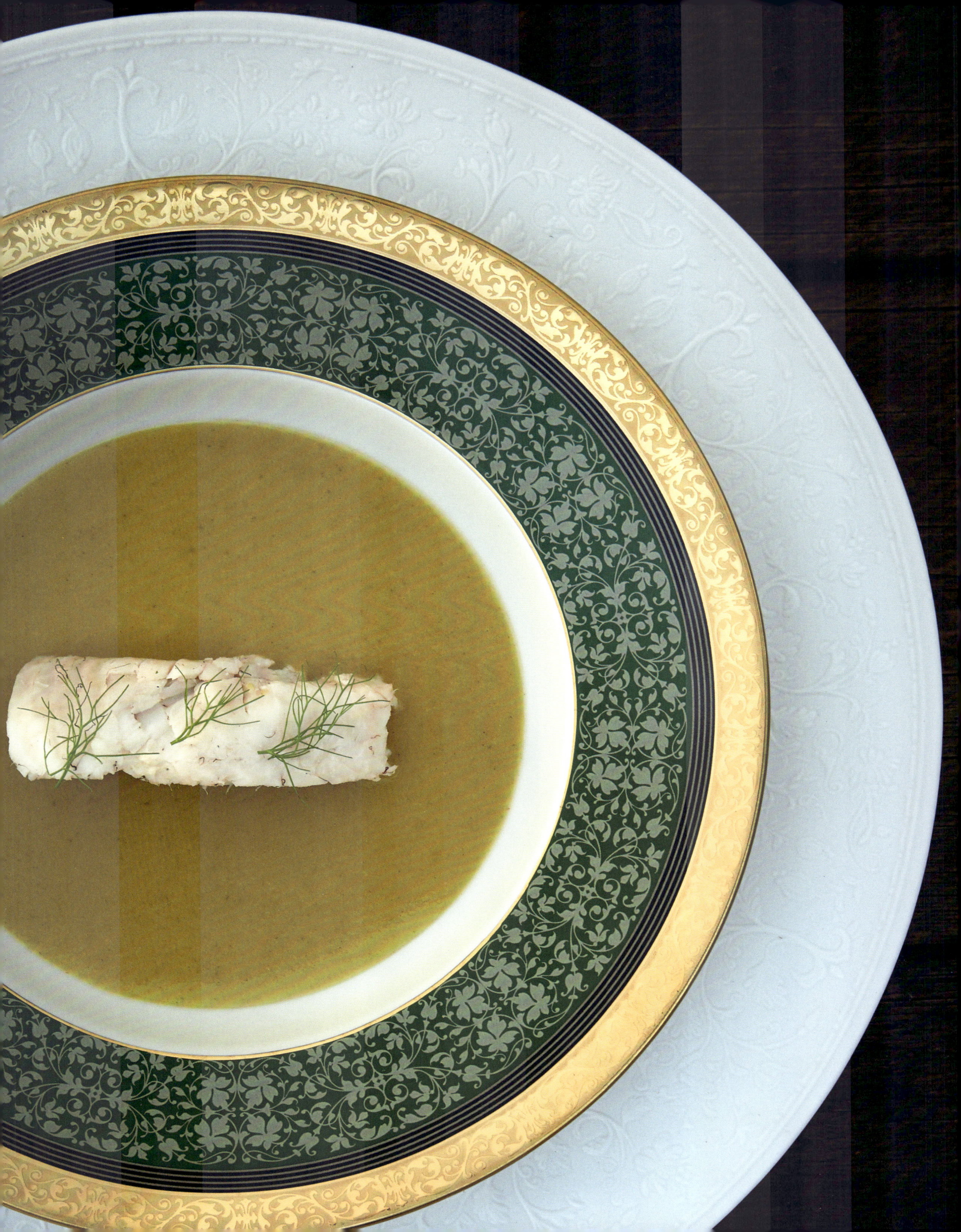

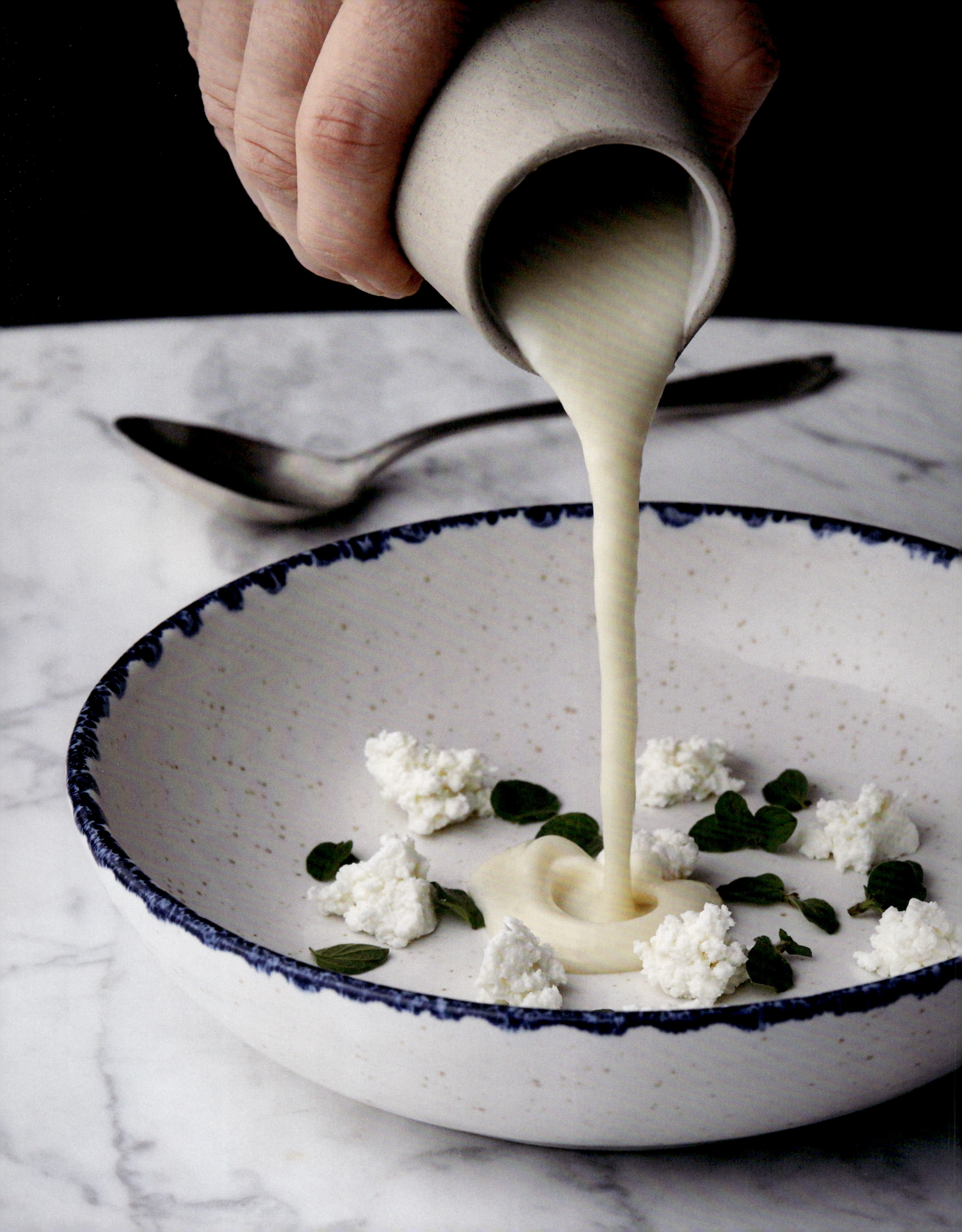

Celery Soup with Feta Cheese & Oregano

serves 4

FOR THE CELERY SOUP

1kg	celery, chopped
	juice and zest of 1 lemon
	Greek olive oil, for frying
2	onions, chopped
5	sprigs of fresh thyme
2	garlic cloves, crushed
45g	butter
1 tsp	fine sea salt, plus more to season
1.3l	chicken stock
500ml	full-fat milk
100g	cream
	white pepper
120g	feta cheese
	fresh oregano, chopped

1. Stir the celery into a bowl of water with half of the lemon juice and set aside.

2. Now, in a large pan, heat the olive oil over medium heat and sauté the onions, thyme and garlic. Add 30g of the butter to the pan and, when melted, simmer for 3 minutes.

3. Drain the celery and add to the pan. Add 1 tsp salt and the lemon zest. Sauté for 8 minutes, stirring frequently.

4. Now pour in 1l of the chicken stock, the milk and cream. Bring to the boil over medium heat and simmer for 30 minutes, stirring occasionally, until the celery has softened.

5. With a slotted spoon, remove the celery and place in a blender with 2 soup ladles of the soup. Blend on high speed until velvety, then return to the soup. If the soup is too thick, add the remaining chicken stock.

6. Strain the soup through a sieve and stir in the remaining butter. Season to taste with salt, white pepper and the remaining lemon juice.

7. To serve, place 30g of the feta cheese in each person's bowl, sprinkle with oregano, then pour over the soup.

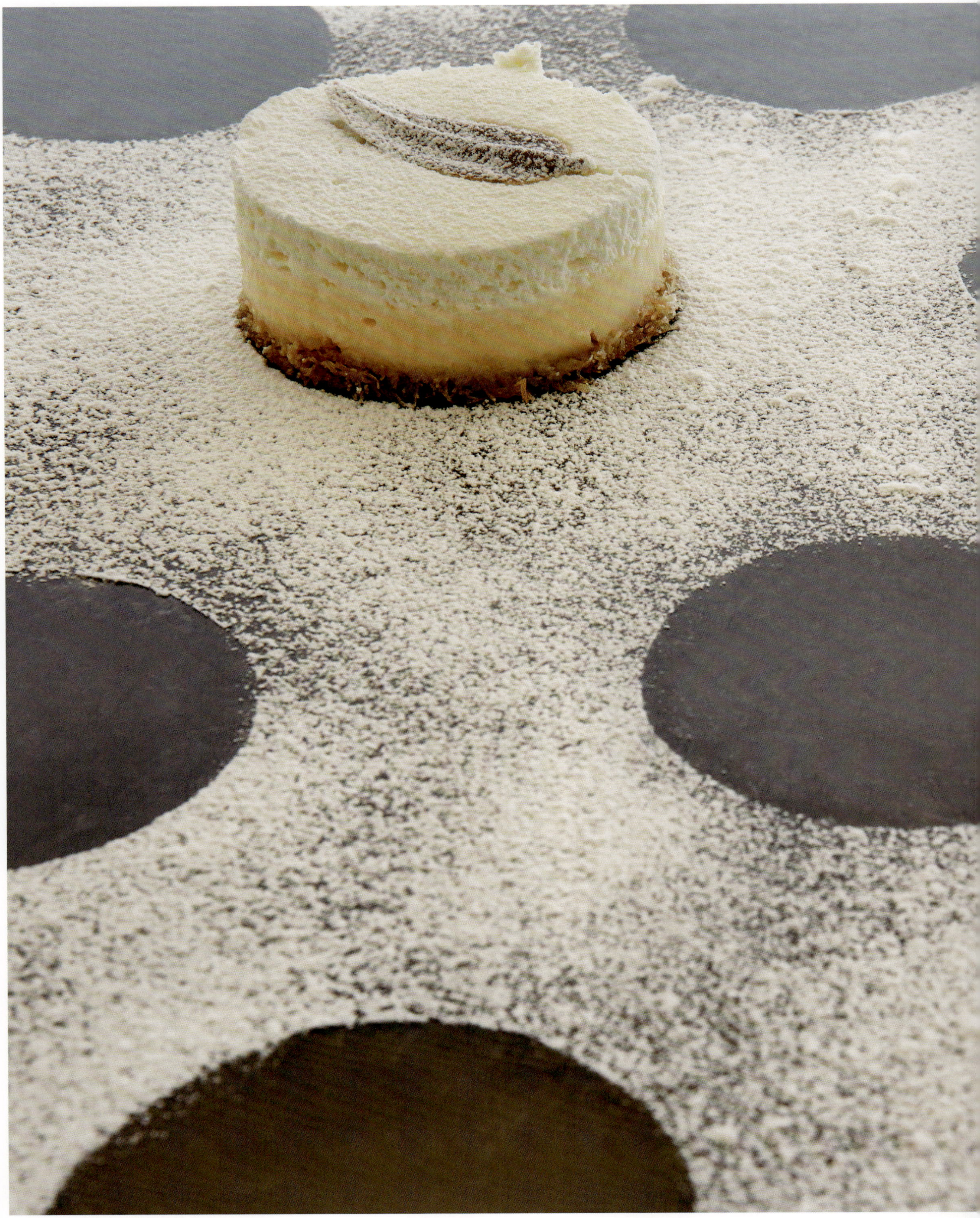

Γλυκά

DESSERTS

DESSERTS

There are wondrous things one can learn over a dessert. Every once in a while, I have the pleasure of spending an afternoon in the midst of a few elderly people from the nearby village. Year after year, it has been a long-kept tradition in our household to provide them a pleasant afternoon around our large round table on the white veranda under the shade of the pine trees. Every time we came together, I had grown a few centimetres in height, while they had grown a few more white hairs, but that never stopped us from having a merry time filled with Greek coffees, desserts, occasional quarrels, many discussions and a lot of laughter and pats on the cheek with advice for life.

I had just swallowed another piece of Orange Cake when I got one piece of advice from my left. 'You should never miss out on a dessert when there is some!' Thelma, one of my favourite old ladies winked at me and, of course, did not miss the opportunity to pet my cheek along with this piece of wisdom. 'Thelma', a deep voice sighed from the other end of the table: 'One should be modest with the desserts. You should practise moderation.' The elderly gentleman shook his head disapprovingly.

I looked down at my plate with my modest piece when, suddenly, my Orange Cake was joined by a chocolaty delight which slid down the cake fork held by Thelma's shaky hand. 'There. You deserve another piece! And so do I', she giggled and helped herself to some chocolate cake, too. 'Insatiable. You really should limit yourself!' another guest criticised. Thelma, though, happily ate her cake and nudged me whenever I stopped eating as an encouragement to continue.

All the plates were empty but, as usual, the table was still bending under the many desserts that remained. The conversation had turned into a joyful chatter and another round of Greek coffee was on its way. When we had the cups in front of us, Thelma started to eye the Ekmek pastry and admittedly, so was I. She looked at me and shrugged: 'One must treat oneself once in a while', and the cake fork dug into the white Ekmek to refill my plate and hers. I watched the other guests roll their eyes. 'Aren't you going to offer any to us, too?', one gentleman's rough voice demanded. Thelma seemed too busy with her piece of cake and enjoying each mouthful of whipped cream to pay him any attention. 'Thelma, you really should not be this greedy.' He eventually helped himself.

The afternoon went on, I brought over the tavli board, one of the most popular board games in Greece, and two of the gentlemen started to play, while the rest of us commented on and cheered the best moves. Finally I served some Loukoumades, fluffy dough balls drizzled with honey, and Thelma's face lit up. 'How can you still eat sweets, Thelma? This cannot be good for you.' The audience watched in silence when Thelma dug her fork into the first dough ball. She closed her eyes in enjoyment and turned to me. 'There is always space for more sweetness!' I laughed at her appetite and soon had a few Loukoumades myself. The sun set and the guests got up from their chairs. I kissed them goodbye and, when I said farewell to Thelma, I earnestly said: 'I could do this every day.' 'You could indeed. When you cannot find something sweet in every day just help yourself to a dessert. Enjoy each little bit of it. This is how I started and now I have at least one treat per day. There were too many days without, and looking back at it at this age, I never regret it. And when I want them all, I have them all.' She winked and walked away with small steps.

I stood there thinking about the wondrous words she had said me. I was deep in thought then yelled after her: 'But did you never care about what the people say? Their criticism? All day, they lectured you on being modest, not greedy, not having more …' I stopped in mid-sentence and looked after Thelma who kept walking with her small steps, not turning her face towards me. I smiled. I didn't recall her walking away this happily and satisfied in the past. At least not in the days when she could still hear.

Homemade Kaimaki & Loukoumi Ice Creams

serves 4

When you are unhappy in life, perhaps you should become the ice cream man. Here we don't have ice cream vans, those colourful painted vehicles bringing a scoop of joy right to your doorstep. How wonderful it must be to hear the playful jingle of the ice cream man announcing a cone filled with a sweet scoop for nothing but a handful of coins. How promising its melody must sound knowing that your portion of tasty happiness is just around the corner. Once everyone has had their cone and once all the money has gone into his pocket, the ice cream man watches the satisfied faces disappear in his rear window as he continues his round. The metallic jingle and the ice cream man's arrival are eagerly awaited by more attentive ears and sparkly eyes. More scoops to be served, more moments of satisfaction, more ice cream to be enjoyed while it lasts.

But what to do when it just melts right through your fingers? Lick it off or throw it away? Let me tell you: it does not really matter; the ice cream man will be back tomorrow. It's quite a simple piece of advice to remember when happiness slips through your fingers. Let go? Or hold on? It wouldn't matter if you knew that you could always make your own happiness tomorrow. If you were not waiting for it, assuming for it to come around the corner announced by a funny jingle. No waiting for it to be delivered to your doorstep. No more hoping for it to be served to you by someone else.

When you are unhappy in life, perhaps you should become the ice cream man.
I am waiting for nobody. I make my own ice cream. I am my own ice cream man.

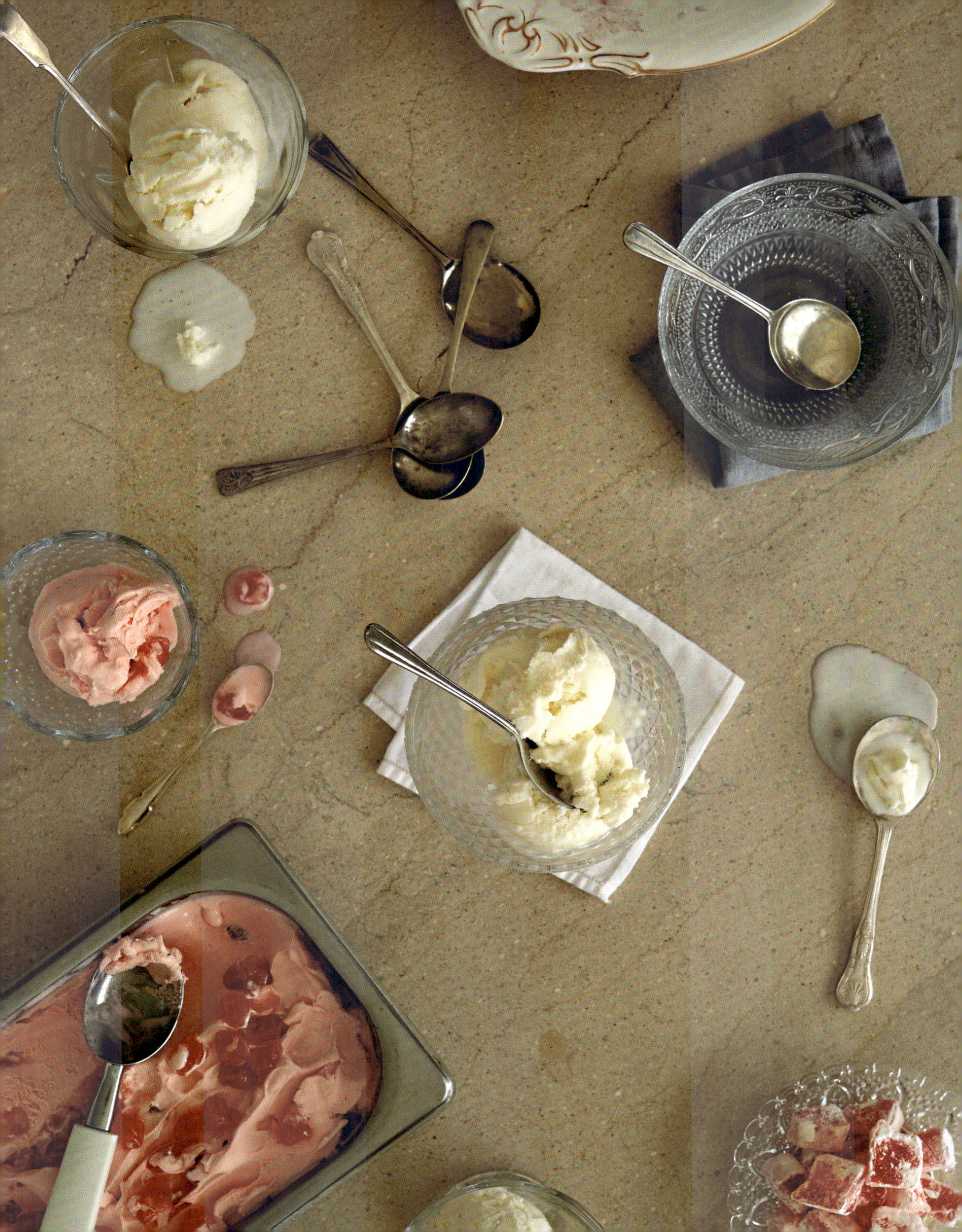

Homemade Kaimaki Ice Cream

serves 4

FOR THE ICE CREAM

- 3g gum mastic crystals, frozen solid
- 10 cinnamon sticks
- 1l full-fat cow's milk
- 260g cream
- 280g granulated sugar
- 5g salep

1. Place the mastic crystals and cinnamon sticks in a blender and process on high speed until powdery.

2. In a bowl, mix the milk, cream, sugar and salep. Use an electric whisk to mix the ingredients thoroughly on medium speed.

3. Transfer the liquid to a pan and cook until the temperature reaches 85°C. Stir frequently with a wooden spoon during this process. Once the recommended temperature has been reached, immediately remove the pan from the heat and set the liquid aside to cool.

4. Now pour the cooled liquid with the mastic and cinnamon powder into an ice cream maker to produce a sweet and spicy ice cream. Serve immediately or store in an airtight container in the freezer.

5. If you do not have access to an ice cream maker, pour the cooled liquid along with the mastic and cinnamon powder into an airtight container and freeze. Every 30 minutes give the liquid a good stir using a metal spoon. Repeat four to five times, until the ice cream has become solid.

Homemade Loukoumi Ice Cream

serves 4

FOR THE ICE CREAM

1l	full-fat cow's milk
260g	cream
280g	granulated sugar
5g	salep
80g	sweet biscuits, crushed
100g	loukoumi rose aroma

1. In a bowl, combine the milk, cream, sugar and salep. Use an electric whisk to mix the ingredients thoroughly on medium speed.

2. Transfer the liquid to a pan and cook until the temperature reaches 85°C. Stir frequently with a wooden spoon during this process. Once the recommended temperature has been reached, immediately remove the pan from heat and set the liquid aside to cool.

3. Combine the biscuit crumbs and loukoumi rose aroma in a blender and blend on high speed until powdery.

4. Now pour the cooled liquid into an ice cream maker with the biscuit crumbs to produce a creamy, loukoumi-flavoured ice cream. Serve immediately or store in an airtight container in the freezer.

5. If you do not have access to an ice cream maker, pour the cooled liquid along with the biscuit powder into an airtight container and freeze. Every 30 minutes, give the liquid a good stir using a metal spoon. Repeat four to five times, until the ice cream has become solid.

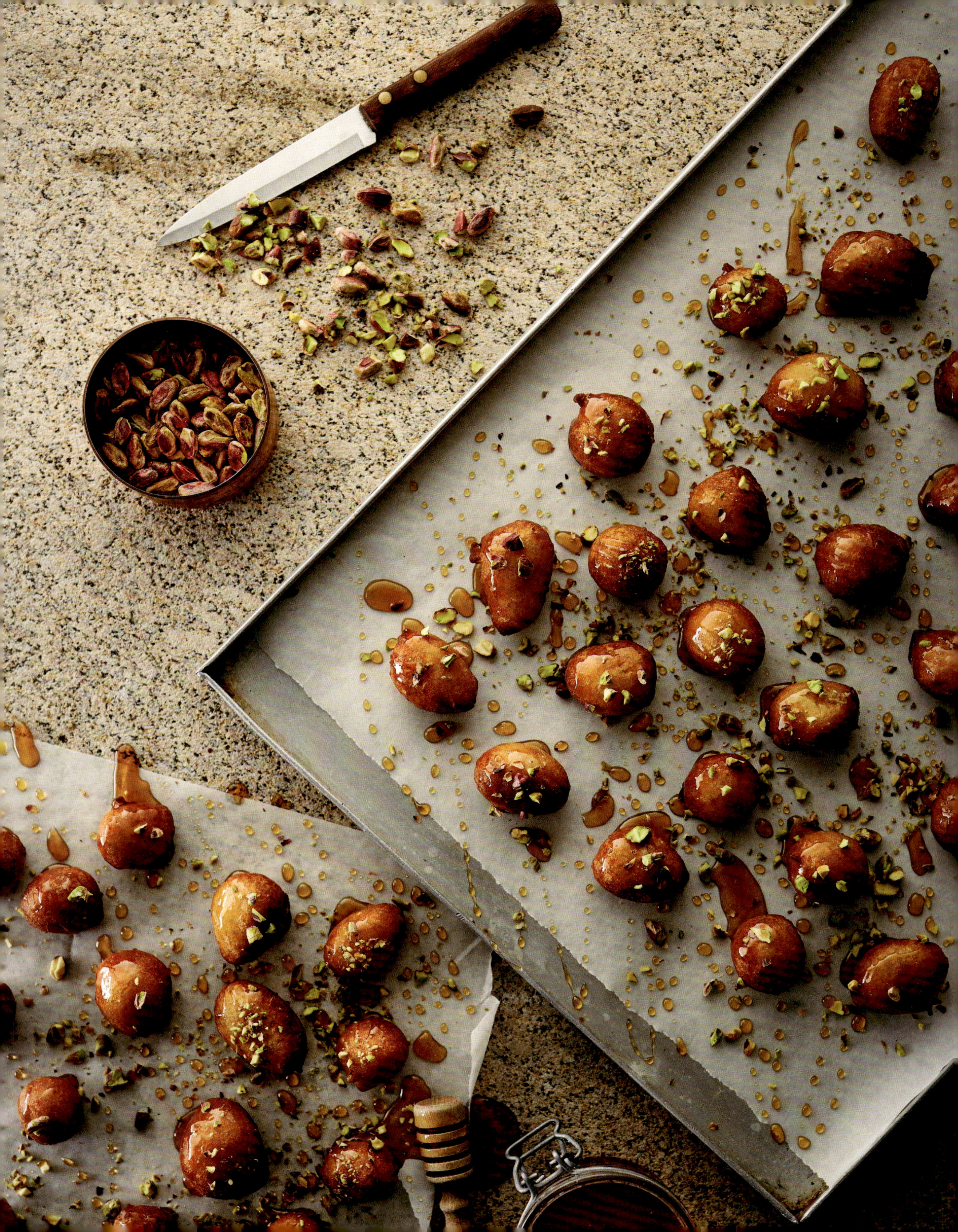

Loukoumades – Fluffy Yeast Balls Drizzled with Honey

serves 4

The most beautiful moment of the morning is just before sunrise when you step out onto your balcony and take a deep breath of the fresh air. When the morning mist is still lingering over the grass, when no street noises drown the chirping of the birds. Most people are still asleep, and you see only a few lights burning in the windows. I watch the sun's round silhouette slowly rising behind the rooftops painting the sky with shades of gold and saffron. Waiting for the sun to rise is just like waiting for my Loukoumades to finish frying when the kitchen already smells of the dough and cinnamon. The soft, fluffy balls are like little handfuls of sunshine with a golden colour, and they brighten my day every time. Sadly, the taste of Loukoumades as well as the beauty of the sunrise last only for a moment. But luckily, we can experience both over and over again.

FOR THE LOUKOUMADES

- 280ml lukewarm water
- 220g plain flour
- 45g cornflour
- 10g dried yeast
- 70g pistachios, chopped
- 1 tbsp honey
- 1 tsp salt
- sunflower oil, for deep-frying

TO SERVE

- honey
- ground cinnamon
- chopped pistachios

1. In a bowl combine the water, flour, cornflour, yeast, pistachios, honey and salt. Knead the ingredients together into a uniform dough.

2. Cover the bowl with cling film and allow the dough to prove in a warm environment for 30 minutes, until doubled in size.

3. Heat sunflower oil in a deep fat fryer to 180°C. Test if the oil is hot by dropping a small piece of dough into it. If it sizzles the oil is hot enough.

4. Use your hands to form the dough into balls the size of small walnuts. Use a wet spoon to transfer each ball to the deep fat fryer. Moisten the spoon with clean water from time to time to ensure it stays wet. Deep-fry the balls until brown all over. Use a slotted spoon to remove them from the oil and pat dry with paper towels.

5. Place the soft loukoumades balls on a serving plate. Drizzle generously with honey and sprinkle with cinnamon and chopped pistachios.

Tipsy Peaches

serves 2

I have a school friend called Sophia. When we were little kids she gave me a present: a small, green, unripe peach. I got home from school that day and left it in the fruit basket with other fruit presents from my school friends. I admit to having forgotten all about it, all about our friendship for almost 30 years. Then, one day, I felt like eating a piece of fruit and the only one still left in the fruit basket after all these years was Sophia's peach. The peach was no longer unripe and green, it had grown into a golden, scrumptious and soft peach; right at this point in time the peach was perfect. I called Sophia and we met and became closer friends than ever before. The other day we sat over a glass of Mastiha and she asked me whether I remembered the peach. I replied: 'The peach is still in the fruit basket. I put it there when it was green and tiny, I treasure it there now that it is golden and has ripened. And I hope that many, many years from now it will still be there where I can watch it become wrinkly and old. I don't keep it there for its taste. I never cared for its colour. I care about the stone.'

FOR THE SOUP

1 tbsp	brown sugar
4	ripe peaches, halved and pitted
3 tbsp	Greek mastic liqueur
3	fresh mint leaves, chopped
	vanilla ice cream, to serve

1. Heat the brown sugar in a hot pan over medium heat and stir with a wooden spoon until caramelised.

2. Toss in the peach halves and simmer until the fruits are soft.

3. Drizzle in the mastic liqueur and add the mint. Combine the ingredients for 2 minutes, turning the peach halves frequently to ensure they are fully coated with the sweet liquid.

4. Serve hot with vanilla ice cream on the side.

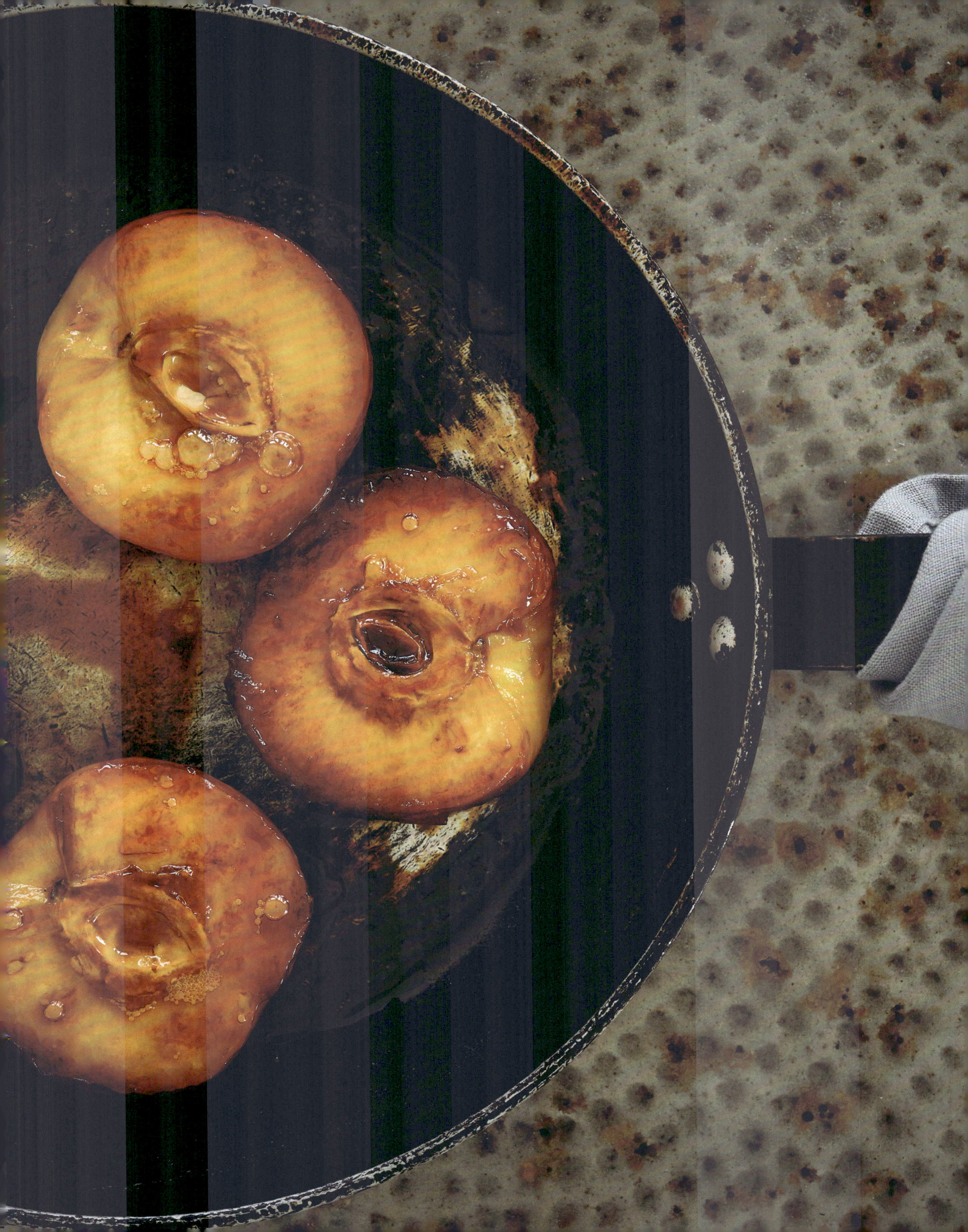

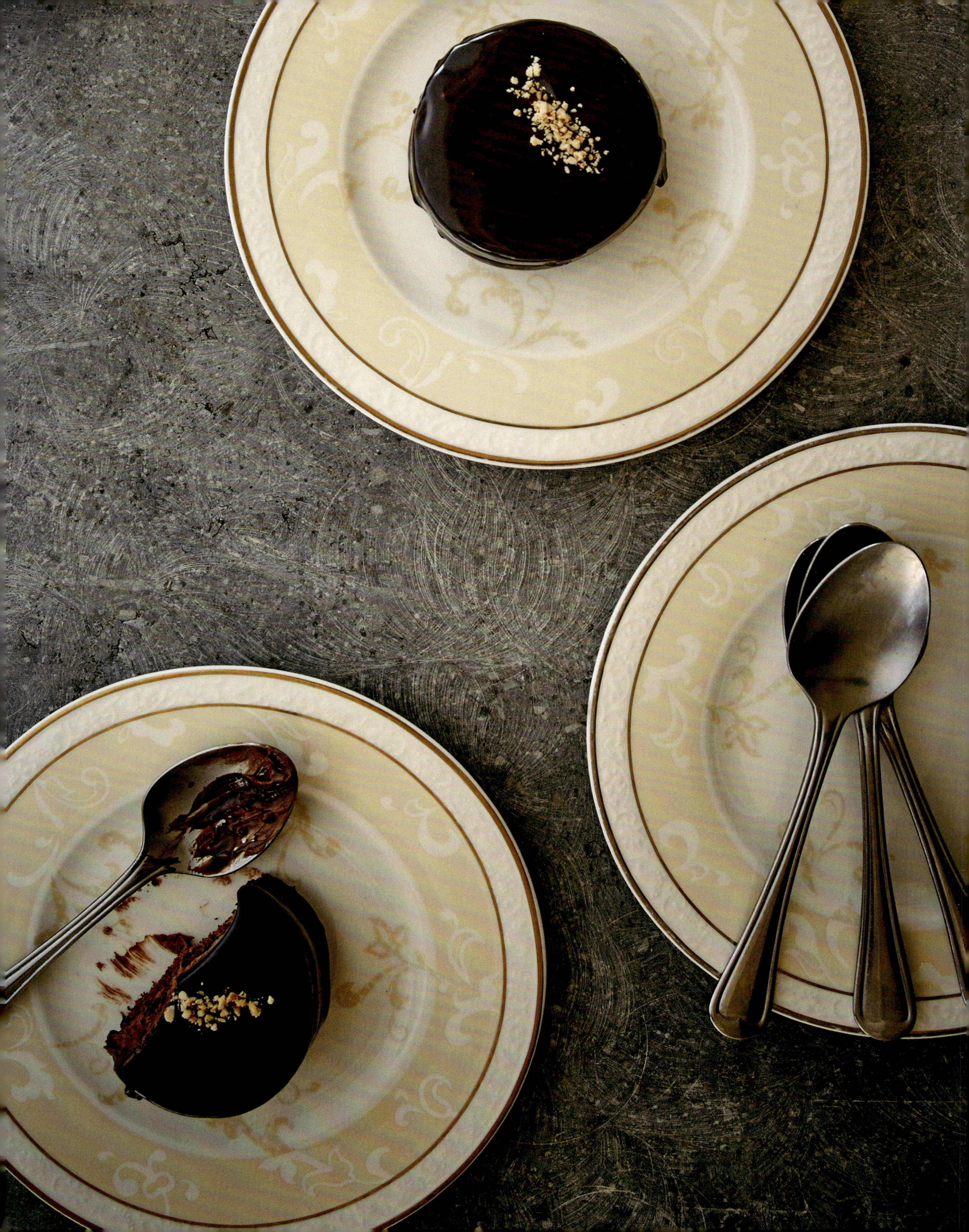

Rich Chocolate Cake

serves 4

There are more chocolate cake recipes out there than even the biggest chocolate lover could eat, but I wanted to include this one nevertheless. I challenged myself to create a special cake, one that would impress even the biggest of chocolate lovers. The recipe did turn out to be equally challenging, so some baking experience could be helpful. Unless you don't mind several attempts with lots of chocolatey leftovers, which technically makes this recipe suitable for everyone after all.

FOR THE SPONGE CAKE BASE

150g	ground almonds
200g	granulated sugar
150g	egg whites (about 4 medium egg whites)

FOR THE CHOCOLATE MIRROR GLAZE

200ml	water, luke warm
4	leaves of gelatine
340g	sugar
280ml	cream
120g	cocoa powder

FOR THE MOUSSE

90g	sugar
	water
1	whole egg
110g	egg yolks (about 6 medium egg yolks)
175g	dark chocolate containing 70% cocoa solids
300ml	cream

FOR THE DECORATION (OPTIONAL)

gold leaves

1. Begin with the sponge cake base. Preheat the oven to 180°C.

2. In a bowl mix the almonds and 150g of the sugar into a uniform powder by hand.

3. In a separate bowl whisk the egg whites on high speed for 3–4 minutes with an electric whisk until foamy. Add the remaining sugar and continue beating for another 4 minutes.

4. Use a silicone spatula to combine the almonds and sugar with the egg white mixture until you have a smooth batter.

5. Transfer the batter to a greased and lined baking pan to make a layer about 1.5cm deep. Bake in the oven for 10 minutes, until you have a sponge that springs back when touched. Remove from the oven and set aside to cool.

6. Continue with the chocolate mirror glaze by combining water and gelatine in a small bowl. Set aside once the gelatine has dissolved.

7. Combine the sugar and cream in a pan and bring the mixture to the boil over medium heat, stirring frequently with a wooden spoon. Once the boiling point is reached, instantly stir in the cocoa powder and continue simmering until the liquid reaches a temperature of 101°C.

8. Now remove the pan from the heat and add the gelatine mixture. Combine the ingredients and leave to cool while continuing with the mousse.

9. Proceed with the mousse filling. Toss the sugar into a small pan and drizzle with water to wet it. Now heat the pan over medium heat until the sugar reaches a temperature of 116°C and becomes syrupy.

10. While the sugar is heating, and not more than 5 minutes before the syrup reaches the indicated temperature, combine the egg and egg yolks in a separate bowl and whisk with an electric whisk on high speed until foamy.

11. Once the syrup is ready, add it to the bowl and continue beating for 15 minutes until the ingredients are thoroughly combined.

12. In the meantime, melt the chocolate using a bain marie and pour into a clean bowl. Pour in the egg mixture and use a silicone spatula to combine it with the melted chocolate.

13. Lastly, whisk the cream with an electric whisk. When the cream begins to stiffen add it to the bowl with the other ingredients and combine until the mousse is uniform and fluffy.

14. Proceed with layering the cake. Use mousse rings to cut out the sponge cake bases, top them with the fluffy mousse and transfer the cake rings to the freezer to set for 1 hour.

15. Place the cake rings on a cooling rack set over a baking tray. Carefully remove the mousse rings and cover the cakes with the chocolate glaze until fully coated with a shiny glaze. Return the cakes on the cooking rack and baking tray to the freezer and freeze until the cakes are solid. Optionally decorate with golden leaves.

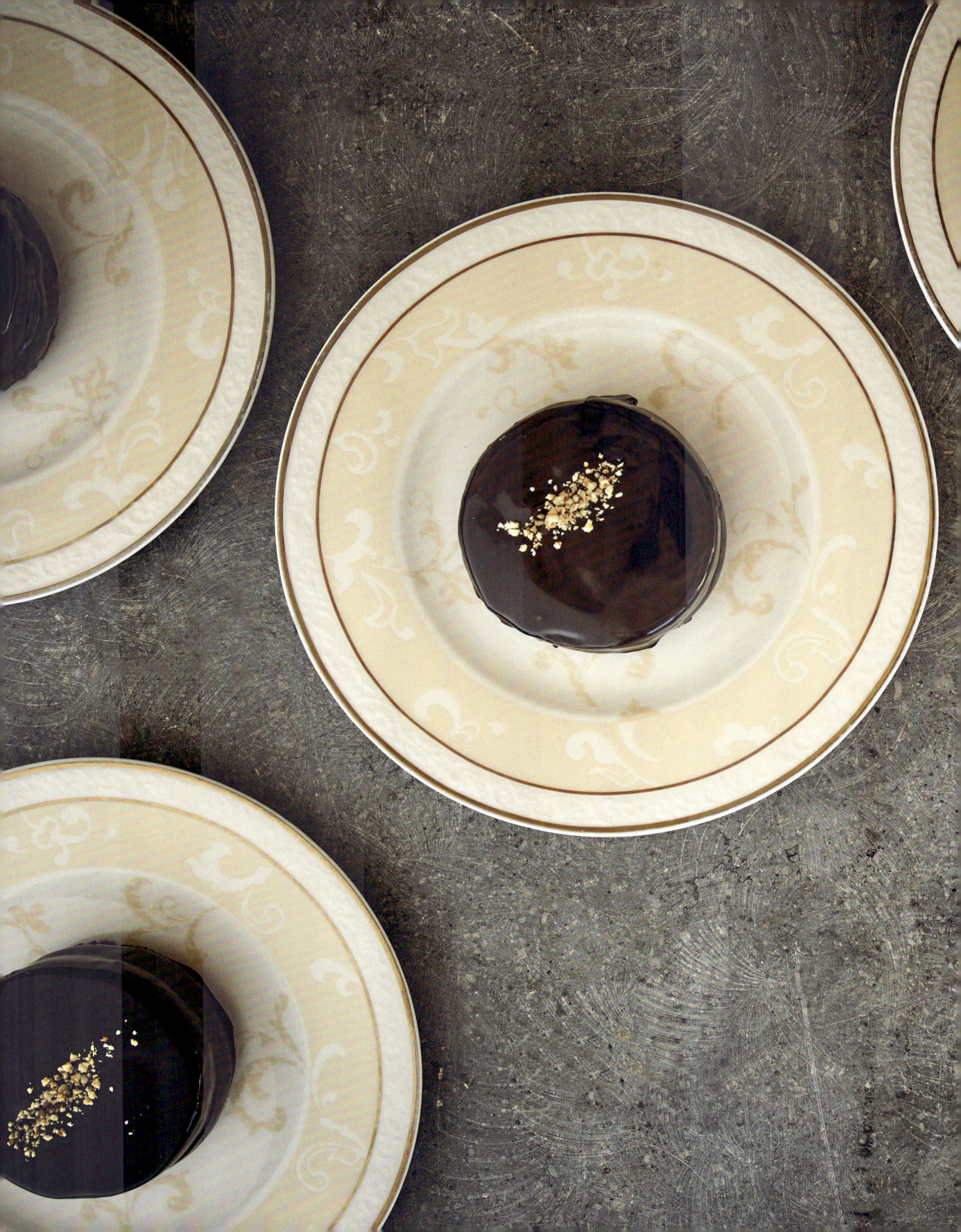

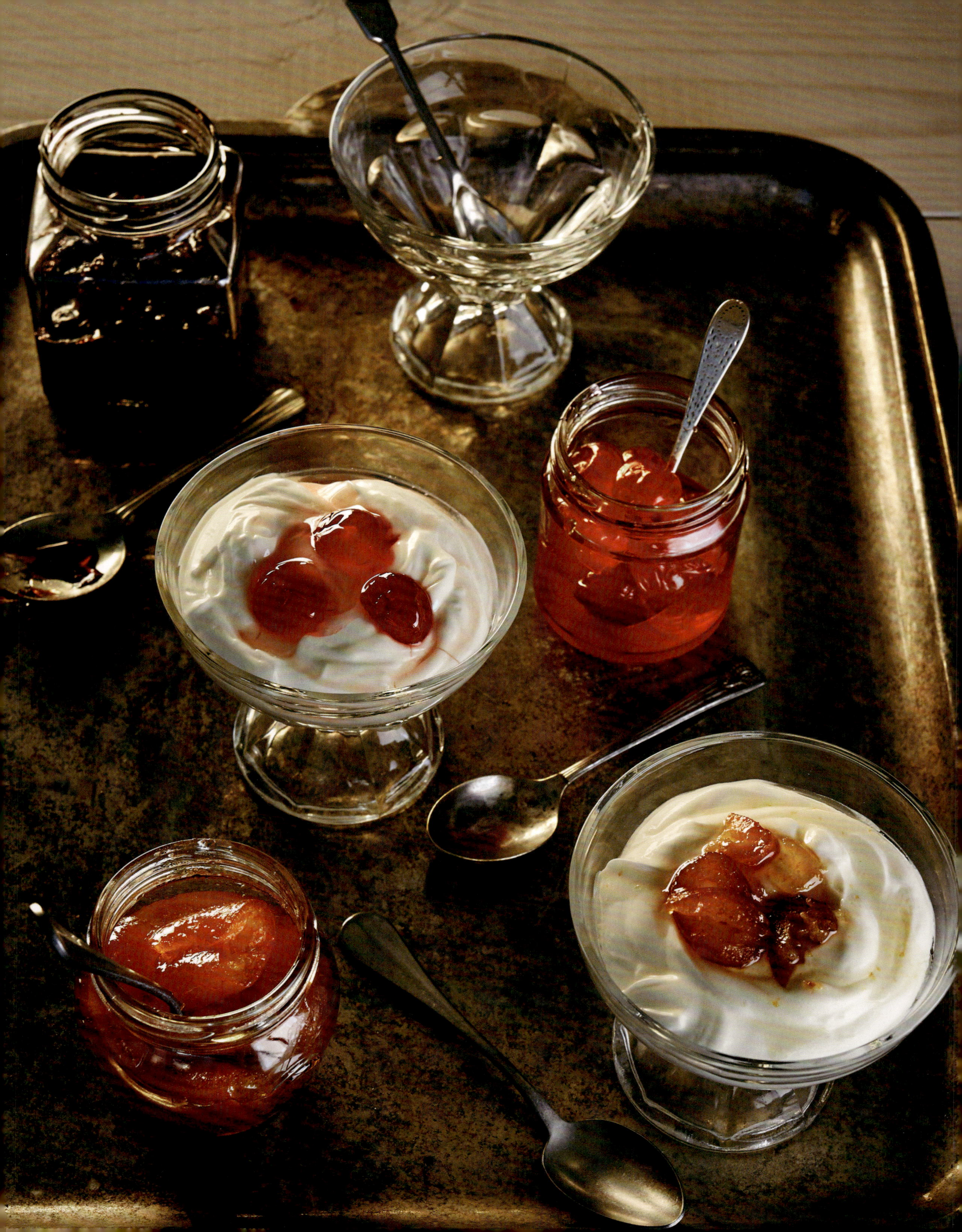

Glyko tou Koutaliou – A Spoonful of Sweetness

serves 4

A spoonful of sweetness, Glyko tou Koutaliou is a wonderfully light dessert – creamy Greek yoghurt with spoonfuls of sweet marmalade. Today I would describe this dish as a childhood treat, but as a child I would have described it as magic. Growing up, I learnt soon enough that life can be sour, even bitter, or lack flavour altogether. But as a little boy life was just sweet. I learnt soon enough that being an adult sometimes gets scarier than any monster under my bed could ever have been. But also, that life has more gifts to offer than Father Christmas could ever have carried. So eating this dessert, for a moment, feels just like a spoonful of childhood, a taste of how sweet life was, knowing nothing and believing in everything. Sounds almost like magic to me …

FOR THE SWEETNESS

- 300ml water
- 600g white sugar
- 50g liquid glucose
- 800g white grapes, halved and seeded
- Greek yoghurt, to serve

1. Combine the water, sugar and glucose in a small pan over medium heat. Bring to a boil, stirring constantly with a wooden spoon.

2. Toss in the grapes and reduce the heat to low. Allow the syrup to simmer for 45 minutes until thick, stirring frequently during this process.

3. Spoon the syrup into airtight jars and close them tightly with their lid. Place each jar upside down in a cool, dry place and allow the syrup to cool and set. Serve a spoonful with a bowl of Greek yoghurt as a light dessert.

4. Tip for the yoghurt: add a little cream to the Greek yoghurt and whip for 2 minutes for a finer texture.

Orange Cake

serves 9

FOR THE CAKE

1kg	ready-made puff pastry sheets
5	medium eggs
480ml	sunflower oil
480g	granulated sugar
300g	Greek yoghurt
	zest of 3 oranges
150ml	freshly squeezed orange juice
30g	baking powder
	butter, for greasing

FOR THE SYRUP

1.4kg	sugar
1l	water
600g	liquid glucose

FOR THE DECORATION

9	half-slices of orange
	thin strips of orange zest

The day before you want to make the cake

1. Unwrap the puff pastry. Unfold and carefully separate the layers. Spread them out individually in a dry, warm place and let them dry overnight until they take on a parchment-like texture.

The following day

2. Preheat the oven to 185°C. Crumble the crisp puff pastry into a bowl. In a second bowl, whisk together the eggs, oil and sugar. In a third bowl combine the yoghurt and the orange zest. Mix until smooth using an electric whisk.

3. Return to the crumbled puff pastry. Use your hands to mix the contents of the other two bowls into the crumble. Add the orange juice and baking powder and mix until all the ingredients are combined. Grease the baking pan with the butter and spoon in the batter. Bake in the oven for a minimum of 15 minutes.

4. Reduce the heat to 155°C and bake again for up to 20 minutes until the crust is crispy and browned. After 35 minutes of total baking time, ensure the centre is well-baked before removing and setting aside to chill.

5. Meanwhile, make the syrup. In a pan over high heat, bring the sugar, water and glucose to a simmer. Combine with a whisk for about 5 minutes until thick. Keep warm.

6. Once the cake has cooled, cut into 9 pieces while still inside the pan. Now soak with approximately 4 soup ladles of the warm syrup. Decorate each piece with a half-slice of orange and sprinkle with the orange zest. Allow to sit a few more minutes before serving.

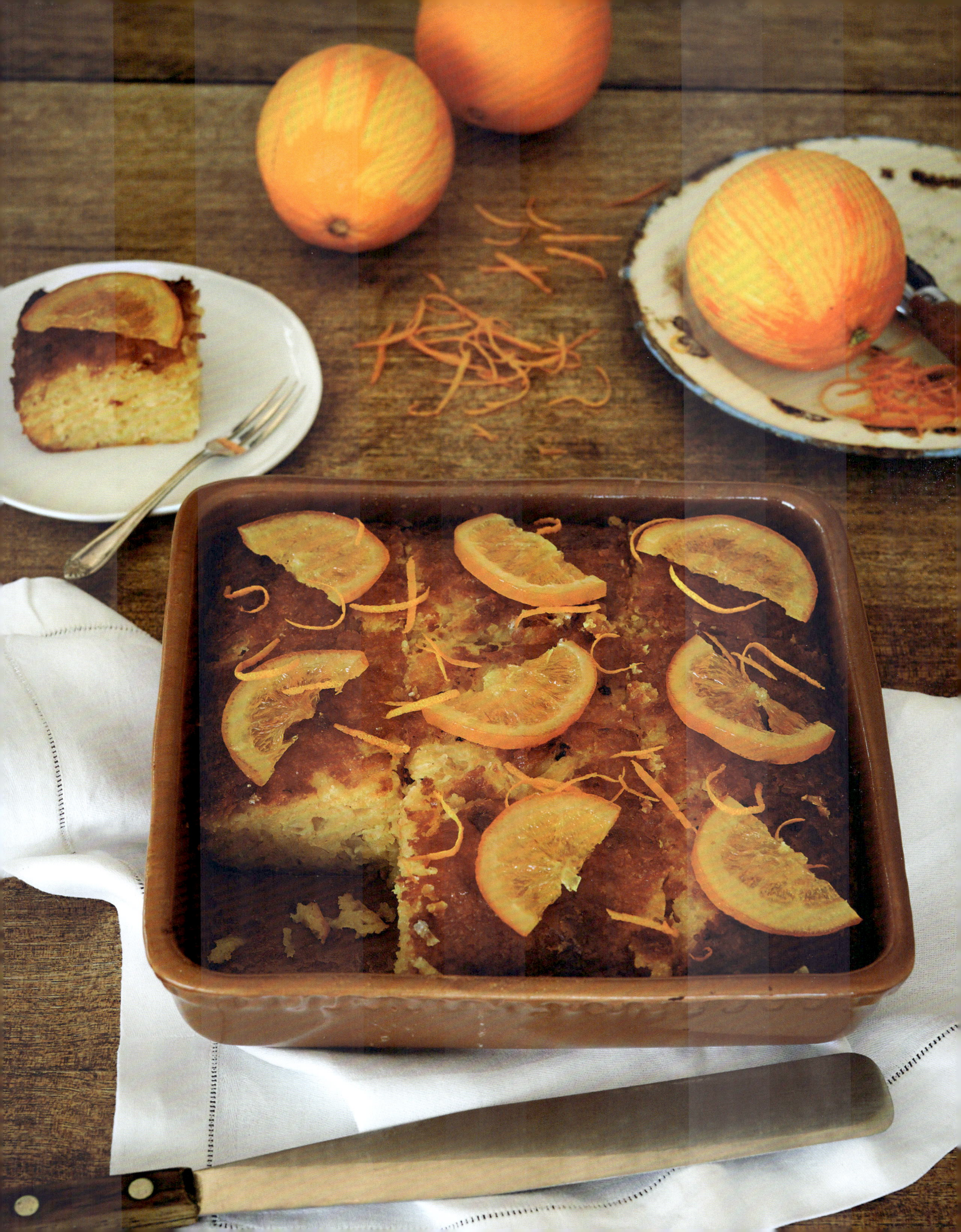

Ekmek

serves 12

The other day when I was casually walking through the city centre I spotted a blonde beauty inside a pastry shop. The vision alone made me feel instantly attracted, the just-perfect golden brown shade of the angel hair caused me to enter the pastry shop without hesitation and, on this lucky day, I did not leave alone. Truly this blonde was what attracted me initially, but as always I discovered again, that true beauty is found on the inside: a light, honey-sweetened whipped cream topped with crunchy pistachio nuts.

FOR THE SYRUP

- 1l water
- 1kg granulated sugar
- 250g liquid glucose
- 1 drop vanilla extract

Two days before you want to serve the dessert

1. Start with the syrup. In a pan over high heat, bring the water, sugar and glucose to a simmer. Combine with a whisk for about 5 minutes until thick and remove from the heat. Add the vanilla and leave to cool.

FOR THE BASE LAYER

340g	angel hair or kataifi pastry
60 ml	clarified butter
1l	cold syrup

FOR THE FILLING

1.5l	whole milk
600g	granulated sugar
100g	cornflour
5	medium eggs
1	drop vanilla extract
200ml	cream

FOR THE TOP LAYER

600ml	organic cream
1 tsp	vanilla extract
800ml	whipping cream

FOR THE DECORATION

icing sugar
(optional) chocolate decor

DISH

30 x 40 cm, deep baking pan

One day before you want to serve the dessert

2. Preheat the oven to 200°C. Start with the base layer. Loosen up the angel hair by gently tearing apart the delicate strands. Spread the angel hair over the base of the baking pan. Use a pastry brush to dab a generous amount of clarified butter onto the strands. Then transfer the pan to the oven for 7 minutes. Remove from the oven and turn the angel hair before returning it to the oven for 1–2 minutes, until crisp and golden. Pour over the cold syrup and set aside.

3. Continue with the filling. In a large pan, combine 1.2l of the milk and 500g of the sugar. Set aside. In a small pan, combine the remaining 300ml of the milk, 100g of the sugar, the cornflour and eggs. Mix until foamy.

4. Heat the pan over high heat. Add the vanilla and stir. At the point when it's about to start boiling, immediately add the mixture from the small pan. Stir for 2–3 minutes until bubbles form, then remove from the heat. Mix in the cream.

5. Pour the filling on top of the angel hair, level the surface until smooth and refrigerate overnight.

The day you want to serve the dessert

6. Prepare the top layer. In a bowl, combine the organic cream and vanilla and whisk with an electric hand mixer. When it begins to stiffen, add the whipping cream and whisk again until properly stiff.

7. Remove the pan from the refrigerator. Mark for 12 equal pieces using a spatula. Add the whipped cream as a third layer on top and level the surface until even.

8. Put into the refrigerator for another 30 minutes. Take out the pan and cut into 12 pieces, following the spatula outline. Optionally decorate with chocolate leaves. Serve on a plate dusted with icing sugar.

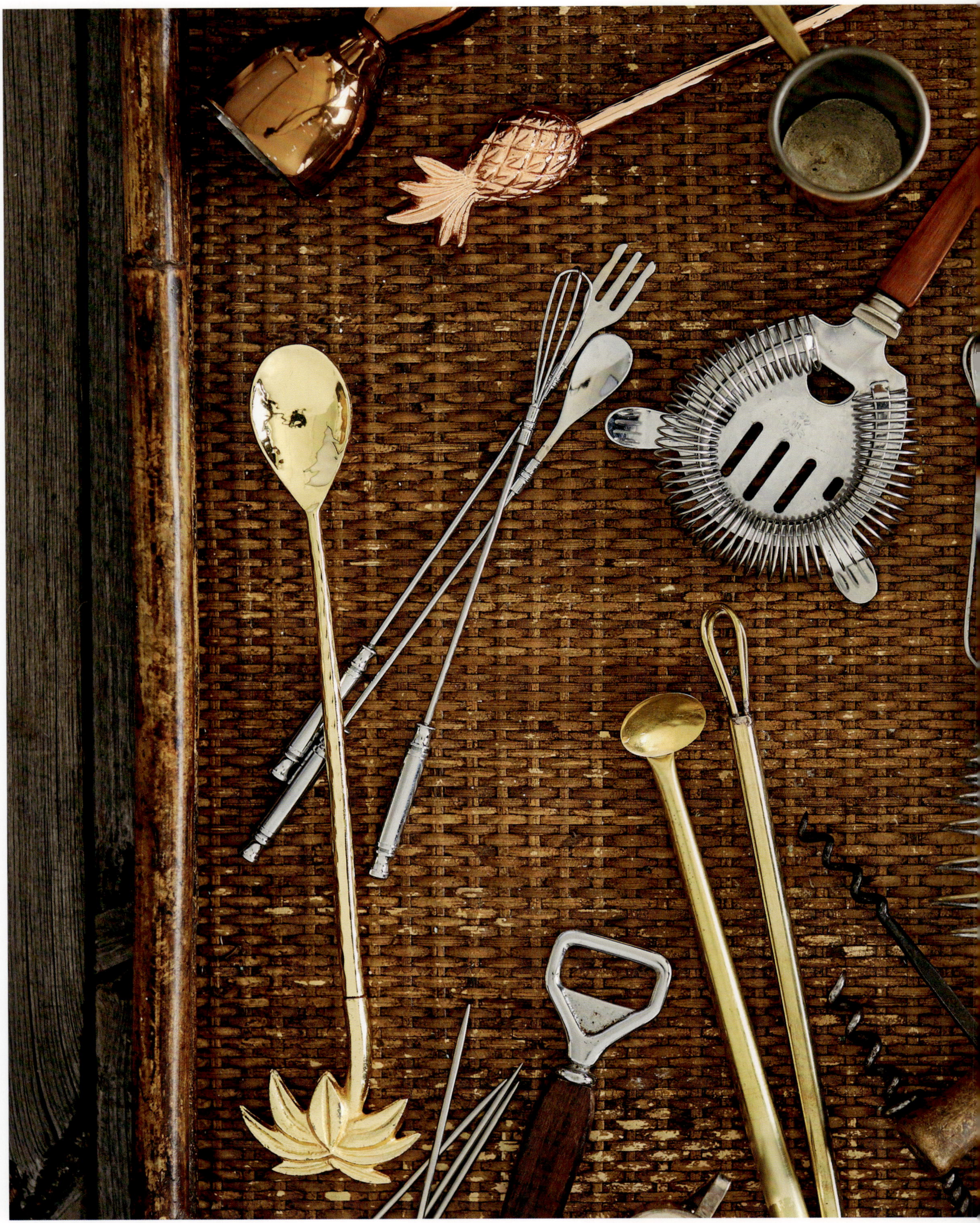

Koktéy

COCKTAILS

◆

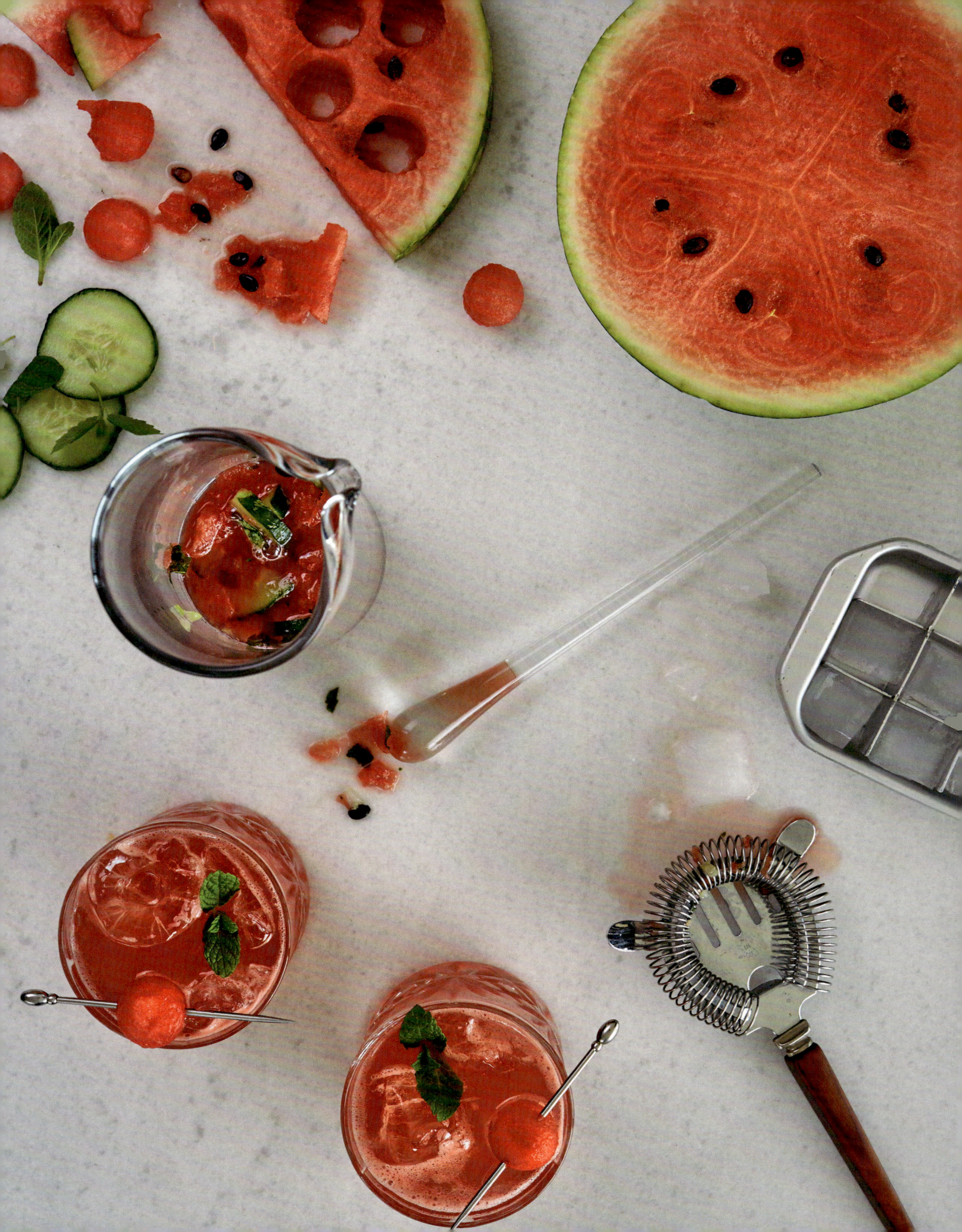

Minty Watermelon

FOR THE DRINK

60g	fresh watermelon, chopped
5	fresh mint leaves
5ml	cucumber syrup
5ml	watermelon syrup
40ml	cranberry juice
50ml	vodka
	ice

TO SERVE

2	fresh mint leaves
1	ball of fresh watermelon

1. Muddle the watermelon, mint leaves, cucumber and watermelon syrups in a Boston shaker mixing glass and shake to combine the ingredients.

2. Pour in the cranberry juice and vodka. Fill the shaker with ice and shake well.

3. Strain into a low old-fashioned glass over ice and garnish with the mint leaves and a watermelon ball.

Mastiha

FOR THE MASTIHA
100ml Mastiha liqueur
crushed ice
2–3 drops of lemon or tangerine juice

FOR THE GARNISH
2 mint leaves
strip of lemon zest

1. Pour the Mastiha into a chilled glass. Add the crushed ice.

2. Drizzle over the lemon or tangerine juice.

3. Garnish with mint leaves and a strip of lemon zest.

Metaxa Sour

FOR THE METAXA
50ml Metaxa
20ml sugar syrup
juice of ½ lime
3 drops Angostura bitters
ice

TO SERVE
1 cherry

1. Combine the Metaxa, sugar syrup, lime juice and Angostura bitters along with lots of ice in a Boston shaker mixing glass and shake well.

2. Fine-strain into an old-fashioned glass over ice and garnish with the cherry.

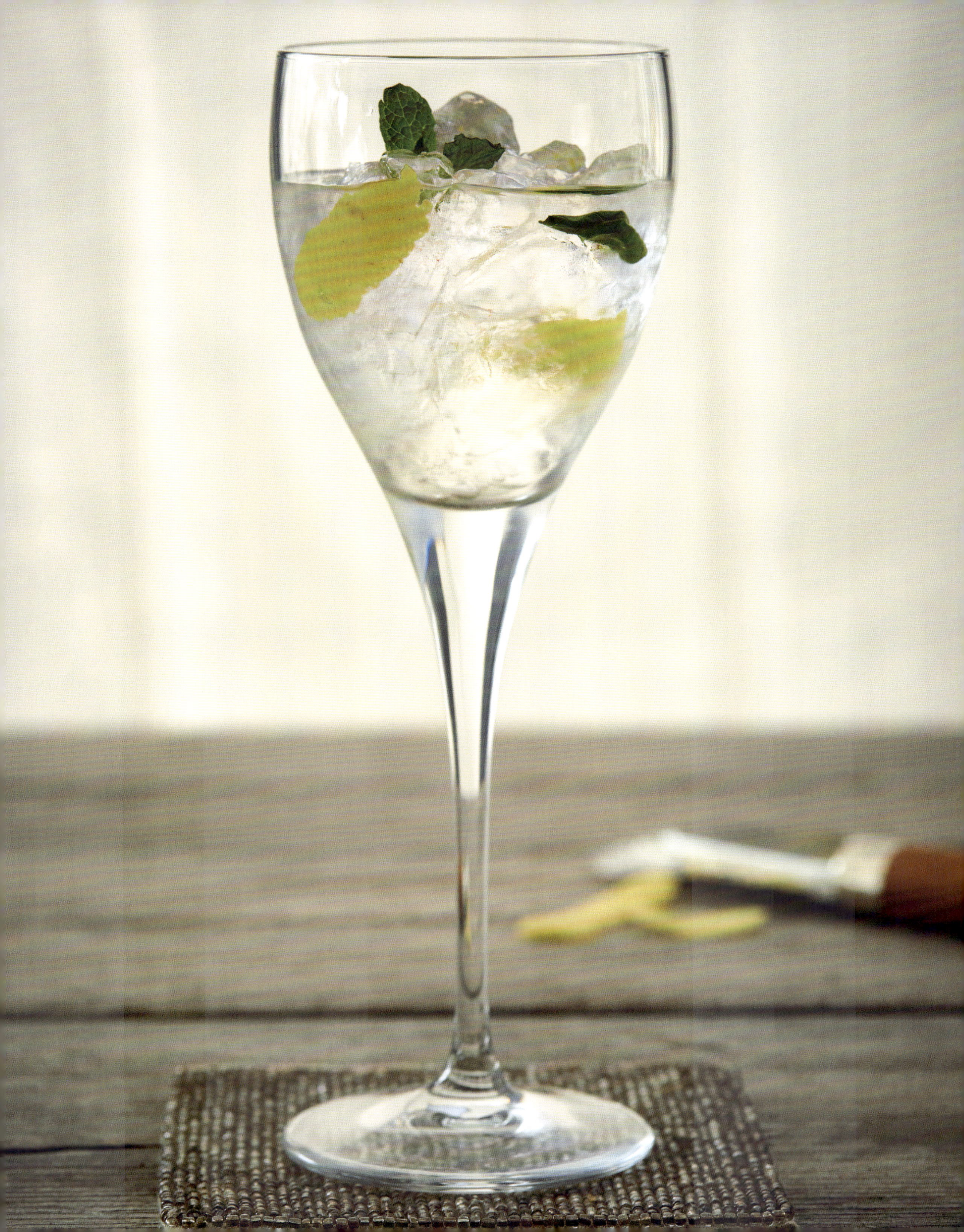

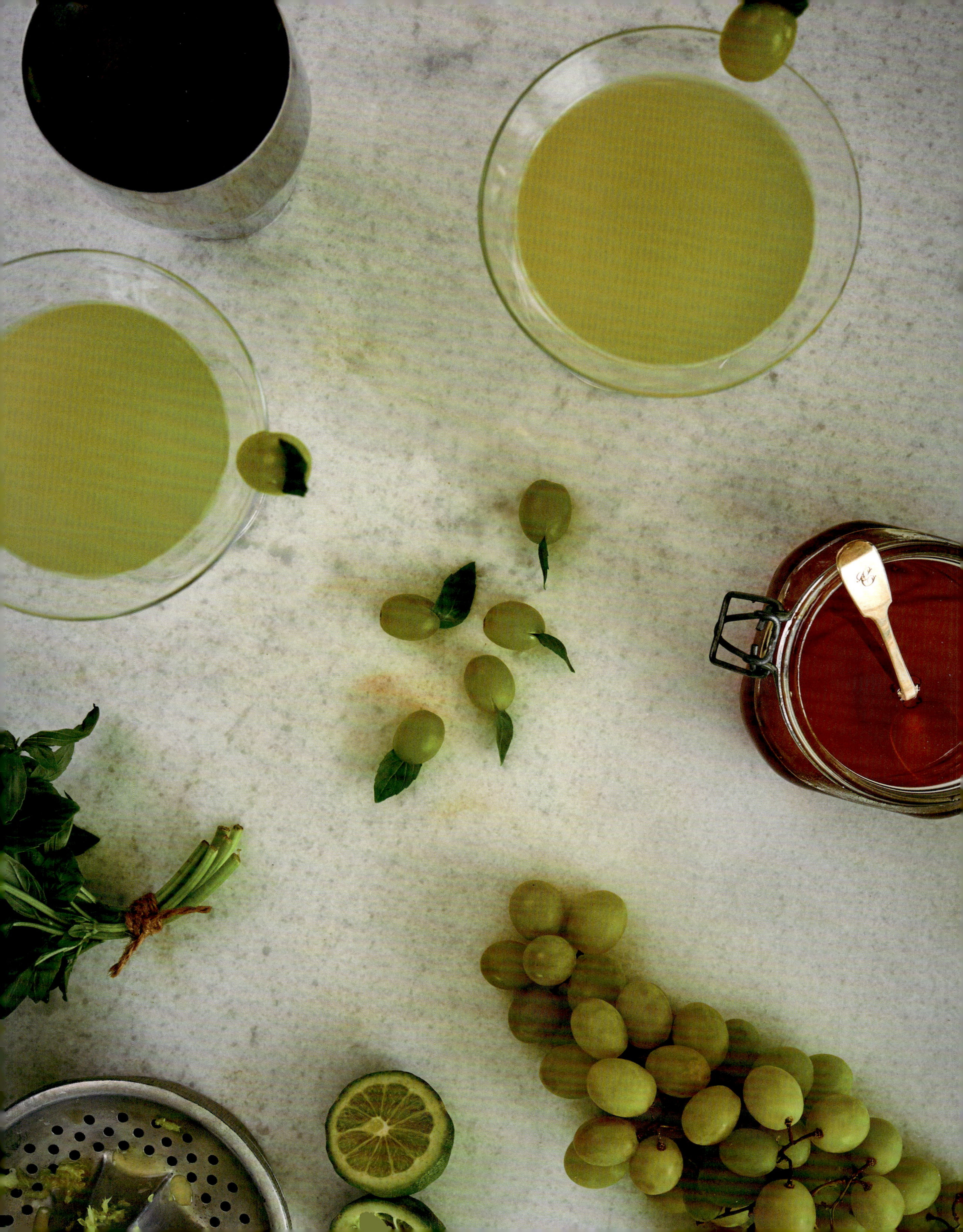

The Real Greek

FOR THE REAL GREEK

15	green grapes, halved and seeded
4 tsp	honey
	juice of ½ lime
	juice of ½ lemon
5	fresh basil leaves
25ml	tsipouro, without anise
25ml	Mastiha liqueur
	ice

TO SERVE

1	grape
1	basil leaf

1. Muddle the grapes in a Boston shaker mixing glass. Drizzle with honey, lime and lemon juices and, lastly, add the basil leaves. Shake well to combine the flavours.

2. Pour in the tsipouro and Mastiha liqueur. Fill with ice and shake.

3. Double-strain into a tall glass and garnish with the grape and basil leaf.

Pomegranate Liqueur

FOR THE VODKA
- 1 l vodka
- 250 ml Metaxa
- seeds of 5 pomegranates
- 1 tbsp freshly ground black pepper
- 1 handful lemon verbena
- 1 cinnamon stick

FOR THE SYRUP
- 1 l water
- 1 kg sugar

TO SERVE
- ice

For the vodka

1. Into a jar with a lid, pour the vodka and Metaxa. Then stir in the pomegranate seeds, pepper, lemon verbena and, lastly, the cinnamon stick.

2. Close the lid of the jar tightly and store the container in a cool, dry and dark place for 1 month. Once a week carefully shake the ingredients in order to combine them better.

3. Strain the liqueur before serving.

For the syrup

4. In a pan over high heat, bring the water and sugar to a simmer. Combine with a whisk for about 5 minutes until thick. Reserve 700 ml and set aside to cool.

5. Stir the syrup into the strained liqueur and enjoy as it is or over ice.

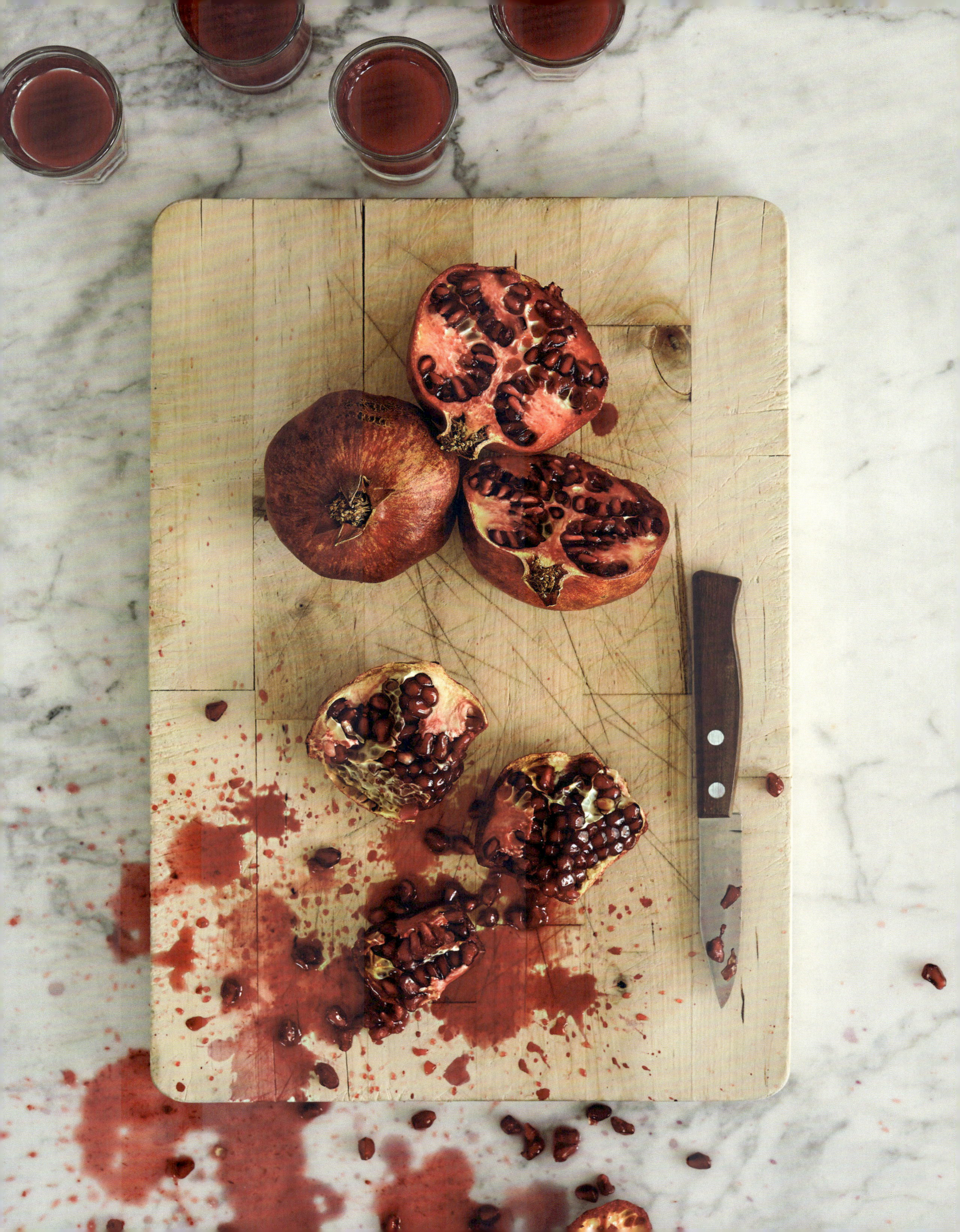

Rakomelo – Honey & Spice

FOR THE RAKOMELO

300ml	tsipouro, without anise
1½ tsp	honey
30ml	freshly squeezed orange juice
	zest of ½ orange cut into strips
3–4	cinnamon sticks
4	cloves

1. Combine the tsipouro, honey, orange juice and zest, cinnamon sticks and cloves in a small pan over low heat. Bring to a boil and stir until the honey has dissolved. Simmer for 6–7 minutes.

2. Remove from the heat and use tongs to pick out the cinnamon sticks and discard them. Strain the rakomelo through a sieve and serve warm in shot glasses.

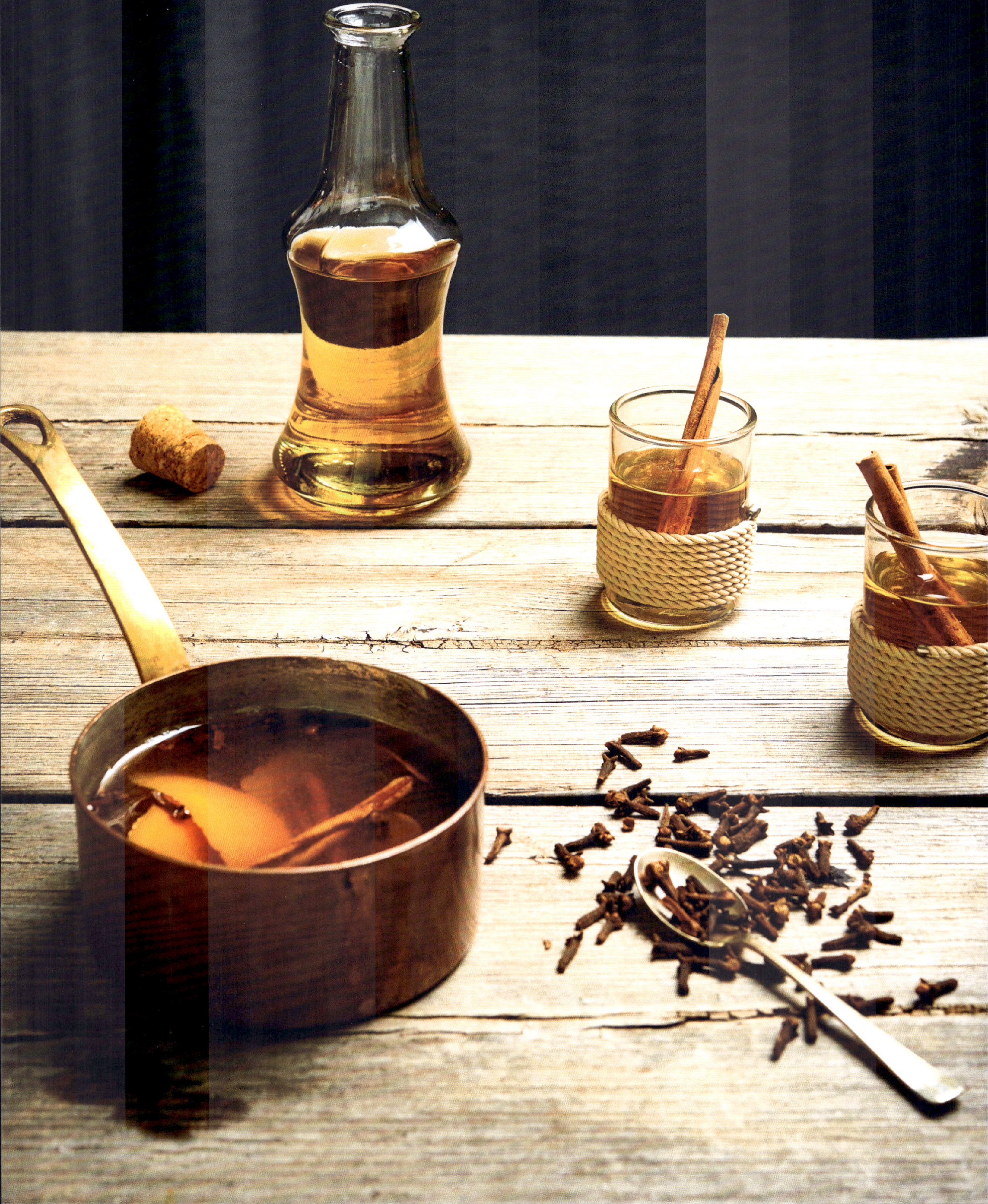

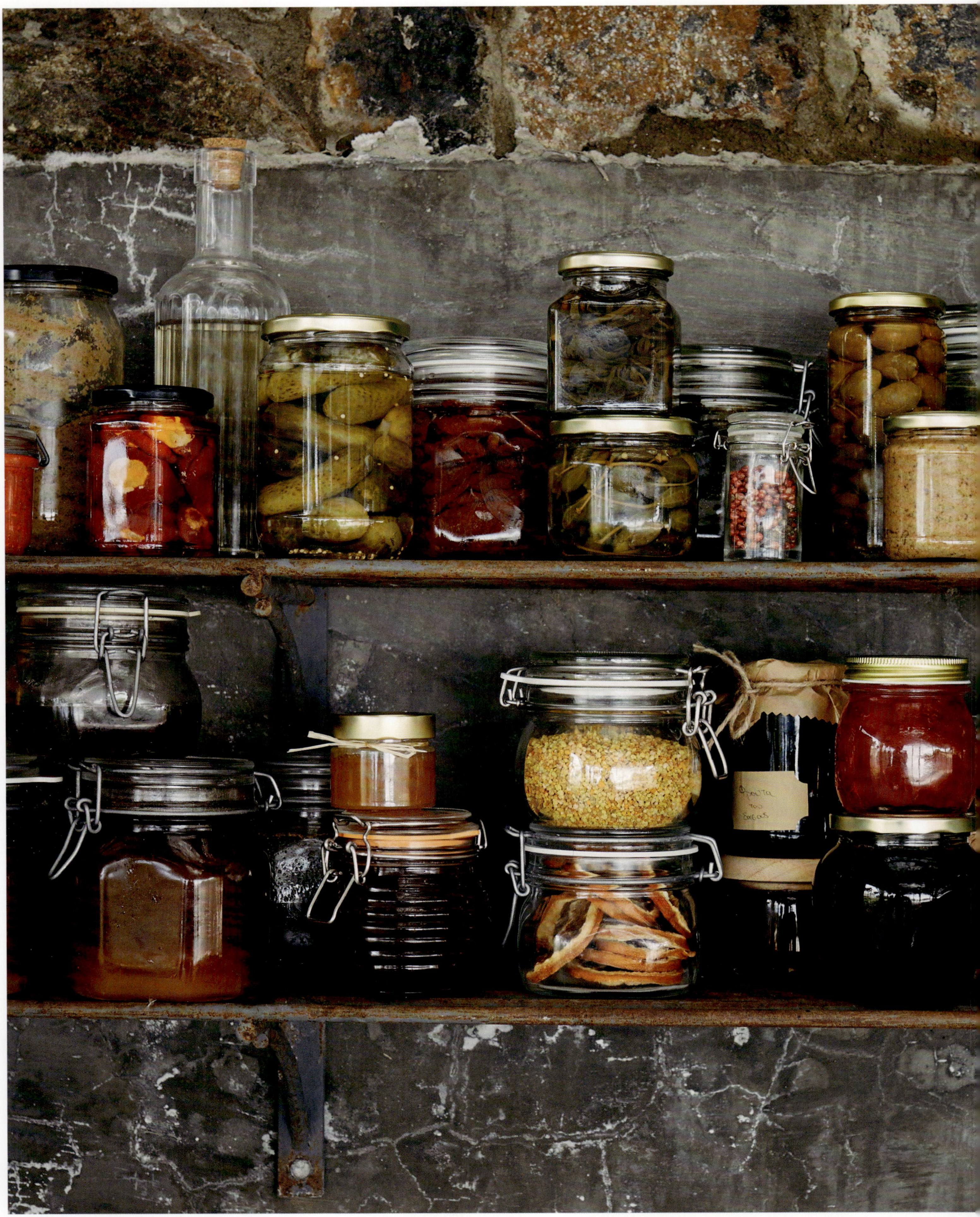

Κελάρι

THE LARDER

◆

'What is next? Now that you have said everything you wanted to say?'

———◆———

'Well, I hope that you will live in a larder, on a shelf between dried fruit, spicy sauces, oils, romance, tasteful jams and soft leather bindings, brittle pages and poetry. This is where you should be kept. To your left some jars to be your neighbours, a love story leaning against you, an adventure book to keep you company, olives in the corner. I would love you to have poems as friends, some pickled tomatoes perhaps. This is where you belong. You don't belong squeezed between other books, you cannot think next to an encyclopaedia. You cannot breathe trapped in a box. And if somebody was searching for you, my book, they would find you among food, love, adventure and poetry, like I did.
So I hope you will live in a larder and I will not forget you there. Even when dust will cover your jacket I will remember you there. I will miss you there.'

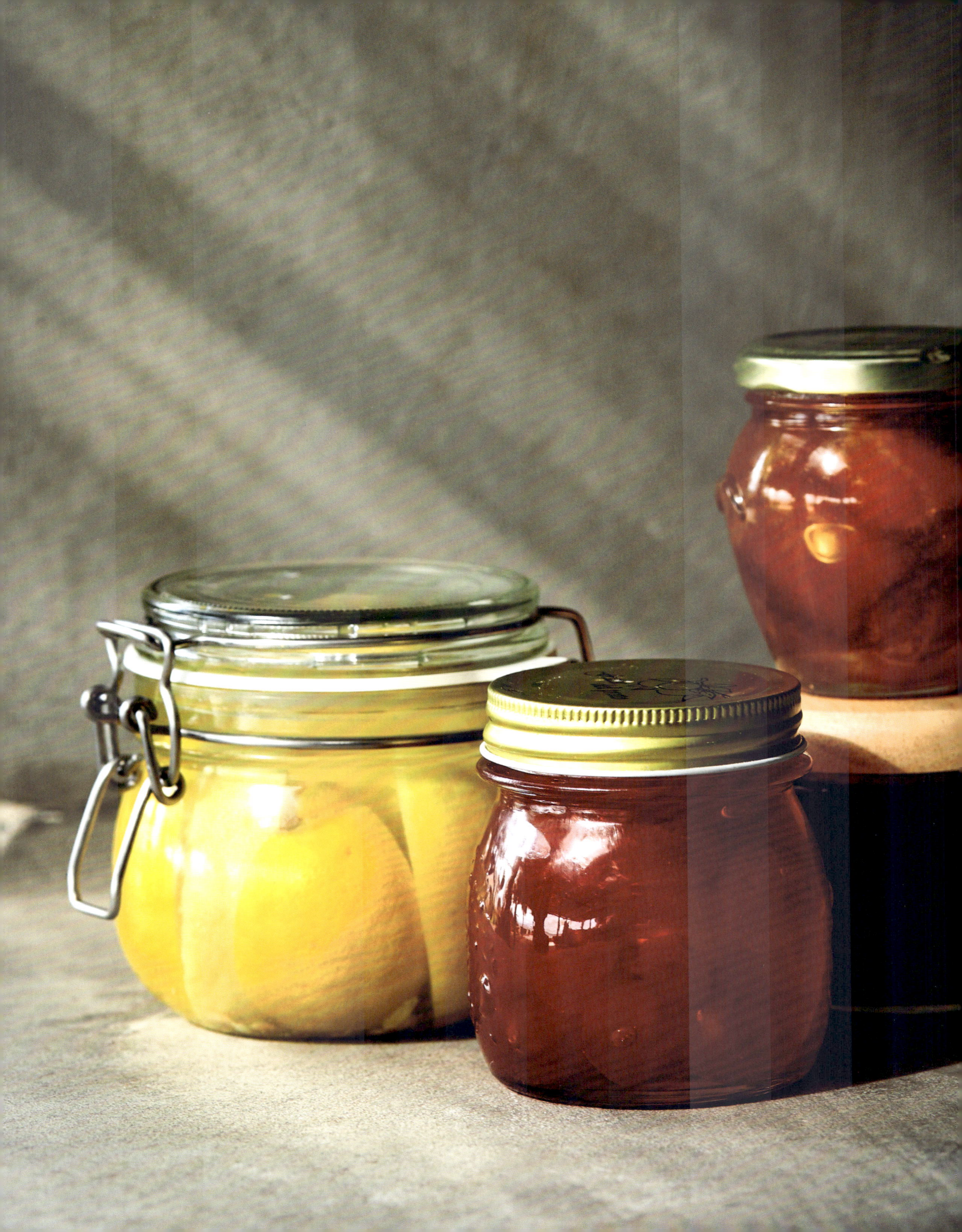

Ladolemono Sauce

FOR THE SAUCE

120ml	Greek olive oil
	juice of 2 lemons
1 tsp	fresh parsley, finely chopped

In a small bowl mix the olive oil, lemon juice and parsley. Use a whisk to combine the ingredients thoroughly.

Homemade Croutons

FOR THE HOMEMADE CROUTONS

1	loaf stale bread
1 or 2	garlic cloves, halved
2	pinches of fine sea salt
5	sprigs of fresh thyme
25ml	Greek olive oil

1. By hand, remove the interior of the stale bread and discard the crust. Tear the bread into bite-sized pieces and place them on a baking tray.

2. Add the garlic, salt and thyme and sprinkle with the olive oil. Cover with cling film and leave to marinate for 30 minutes.

3. Meanwhile, preheat the oven to 170°C.

4. Remove the cling film and bake the croutons for 15 minutes, until golden and crispy.

Avgolemono Sauce

FOR THE SAUCE

- 3 egg whites
- 2 egg yolks
- juice of 1 lemon
- 3–4 soup ladles of hot stock from the soup or sauce you are making

1. In a medium-sized mixing bowl, whisk the egg whites until creamy.

2. Gradually add the egg yolks and continue whisking to combine the ingredients. Drizzle with the lemon juice and continue whisking the ingredients briskly.

3. One after another, add in 3–4 soup ladles of hot broth from the cooking pan. Continue whisking the sauce between each ladle of stock. Make sure you add the hot broth a little bit at a time or the egg whites will curdle.

4. Remove the pan from the heat and add the sauce from the bowl. Use a wooden spoon to stir the sauce into the pan until fully combined with the stock shortly before serving for a rich-in-flavour enhancement to a soup or sauce.

BUTTER

What would bread be without butter? It would be like a man's world without women. Like a life without love. Our bread would be dry, our sweetest cakes non-existent and our meals tasteless, lacking our favourite sauces. I relish being able to enhance butter with different flavours. I like to experiment with all sorts of seasoning, curious to discover combinations matching this ingredient. Sometimes I would choose to mix butter with truffle oil to match an elegant dish, other times I would add lime and wild herbs. Or I would blend butter with authentic Greek classics such as yoghurt, olive oil, garlic and spices. I encourage you to embrace variations of butter as I encourage you to embrace the diversity of love. A woman's character is an exciting blend of elegance, free spirit and authenticity. Stay curious to discover all sides of her, try everything and you might happen to find new facets about your love that you can barely imagine to have lived without. Blend new flavours into your relationship. Experiment with the care of a lover, the imagination of a poet and the daring of a lunatic. A combination we all are when it comes to women, to love (and to cooking)!

Homemade Butter with Greek Yoghurt

—◆—

FOR THE YOGHURT BUTTER

2	garlic cloves, finely chopped
4 tsp	Greek olive oil
2 tsp	fine sea salt
1 tbsp	freshly ground red pepper
1 tbsp	freshly ground black pepper
600g	goat butter, softened
500g	Greek yoghurt

1. Combine the garlic, olive oil, salt, red and black pepper in a food processor and process on low speed.

2. Meanwhile, add the butter and yoghurt to the food processor. Blend all the ingredients until smooth.

3. Keep the aromatic butter refrigerated.

Homemade Truffle Butter

—◆—

FOR THE TRUFFLE BUTTER

250g	sheep's butter, softened
50ml	truffle oil

1. Combine the butter and truffle oil in a food processor and process on medium speed until smooth.

2. Transfer the butter into a freezer-proof container and freeze for approximately 2 hours before serving. Keep refrigerated.

Homemade Butter with Lemon and Aromatic Herbs

—◆—

FOR THE BUTTER WITH LEMON

250g	unsalted butter, softened
	zest of 1 lemon
½ tsp	fresh sage, chopped
½ tsp	fresh chamomile, chopped
1 tsp	fine sea salt
1 tsp	freshly ground pepper

1. Combine the butter, lemon zest, sage, chamomile, salt and pepper in a food processor and process on medium speed until smooth.

2. Wrap the aromatic butter in a sheet of baking parchment and freeze for approximately 2 hours before serving. Keep refrigerated.

Skordalia – Aromatic Garlic Dip

FOR THE SKORDALIA

800g	potatoes, peeled and chopped
	salted water
170ml	Greek olive oil, plus more to drizzle
5	garlic cloves, chopped
50g	coarse sea salt
	fine sea salt and freshly ground black pepper
40ml	white balsamic vinegar
1	spring onion, finely chopped
1	bunch fresh parsley, chopped

1. Heat a pan over medium heat and boil the potatoes in salted water until softened, for a minimum of 20 minutes.

2. Meanwhile, combine the olive oil, garlic, the coarse sea salt and a pinch of black pepper in a blender and blend on high speed until velvety.

3. Once the potatoes are cooked, drain them into a bowl and mash them until fine. Add the contents of the blender to the potatoes along with the balsamic vinegar and mix thoroughly. Season to taste with salt and pepper.

4. Lastly, add the spring onion and parsley, drizzle with more olive oil if desired, and give it a final good stir.

Greek Olives in Mandarin Marinade

FOR THE GREEK OLIVES

12 tbsp	Greek olive oil
2	garlic cloves, sliced
50g	sun-dried tomatoes
	zest of 2 mandarins, cut into strips
3	sprigs of fresh thyme
500g	whole black olives

1. Heat the olive oil in a pan over low heat. Stir in the garlic, sun-dried tomatoes, mandarin zest and thyme. Stir with a wooden spoon for 5 minutes before removing the pan from heat.

2. Lastly, add the olives and give the ingredients a gentle toss to mix. Cover the pan with a lid and allow the olives to marinate for at least 30 minutes.

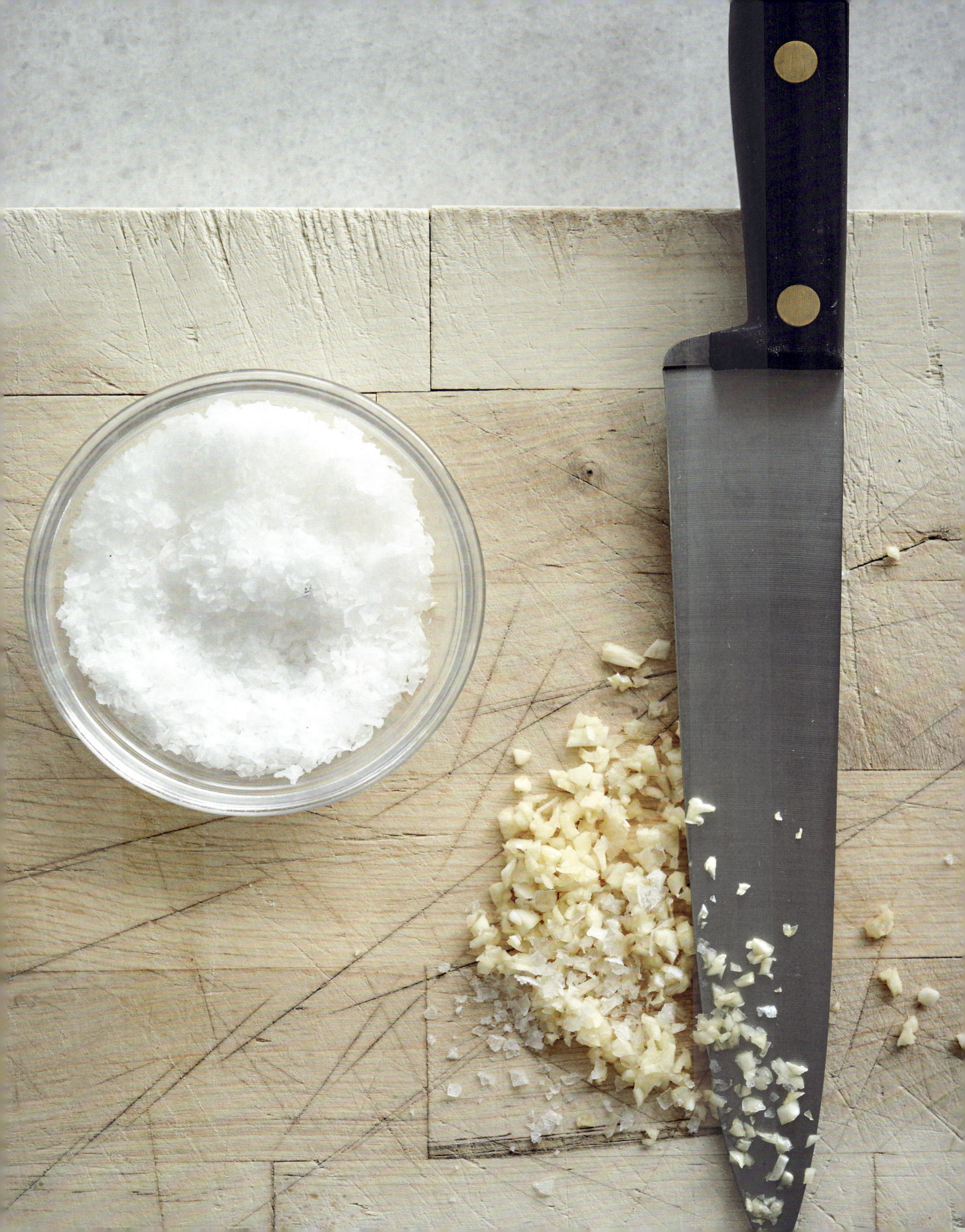

GOODBYE – BUT THIS IS NOT THE END

We've reached the point where all the pages have been turned and the time has come to close the book. It has been a beautiful journey working our way through the book, page by page, photo by photo and recipe by recipe. And now we have come to the last page. Do you ever walk through your neighbourhood, always following the same route? Every corner is familiar to you and most faces are, too. So, let's say you're walking along your route and there was a street, beyond which you have never explored your town. You start to wonder whether you would dare to cross that street, where familiarity ends and the unknown begins. To cross the border out of your familiar patch, out of your comfort zone. So, let's say my book has guided you through a new world of cooking and recipes, ingredients and assumptions. And now, on the last page, on the final step, the only thing that's between what you know and what's yet to be explored was this very street. Would you cross it? I lead you to this street but you won't need me to hold your hand to cross it. It's up to you now. Explore what's on the other side, with a new openness, full of curiosity. Start making quality time and fill it with a new wave of emotions. Find your own recipes. Make stories of your own; ones with a happy ending on the last pages. Because the happy ending will come, long after this book is closed. It will be on the other side of the street, in your new mindset, at the bottom of your pots, in the stack of dirty plates and inside your glasses when you toast one another. And I wish you the best of success in creating those happy endings. So, this is definitely not an end. This is only a last page. And even if this book ends now, your journey does not. So, I am saying goodbye. Without a happy ending. But with a happy beginning.

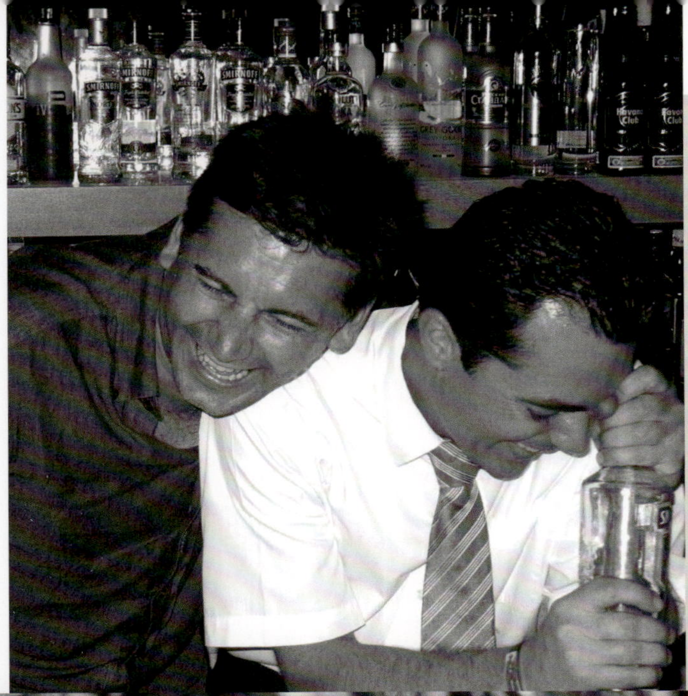
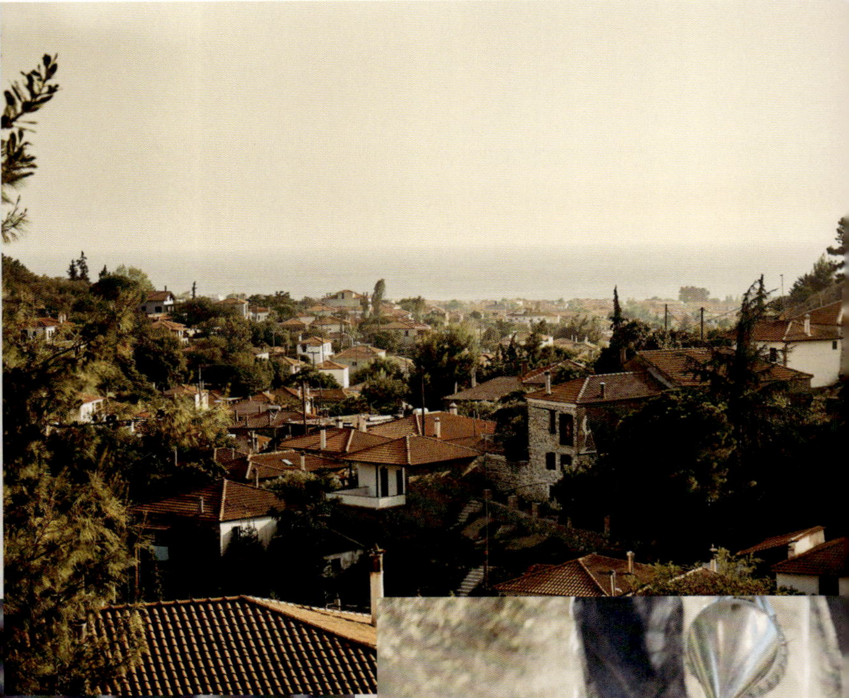
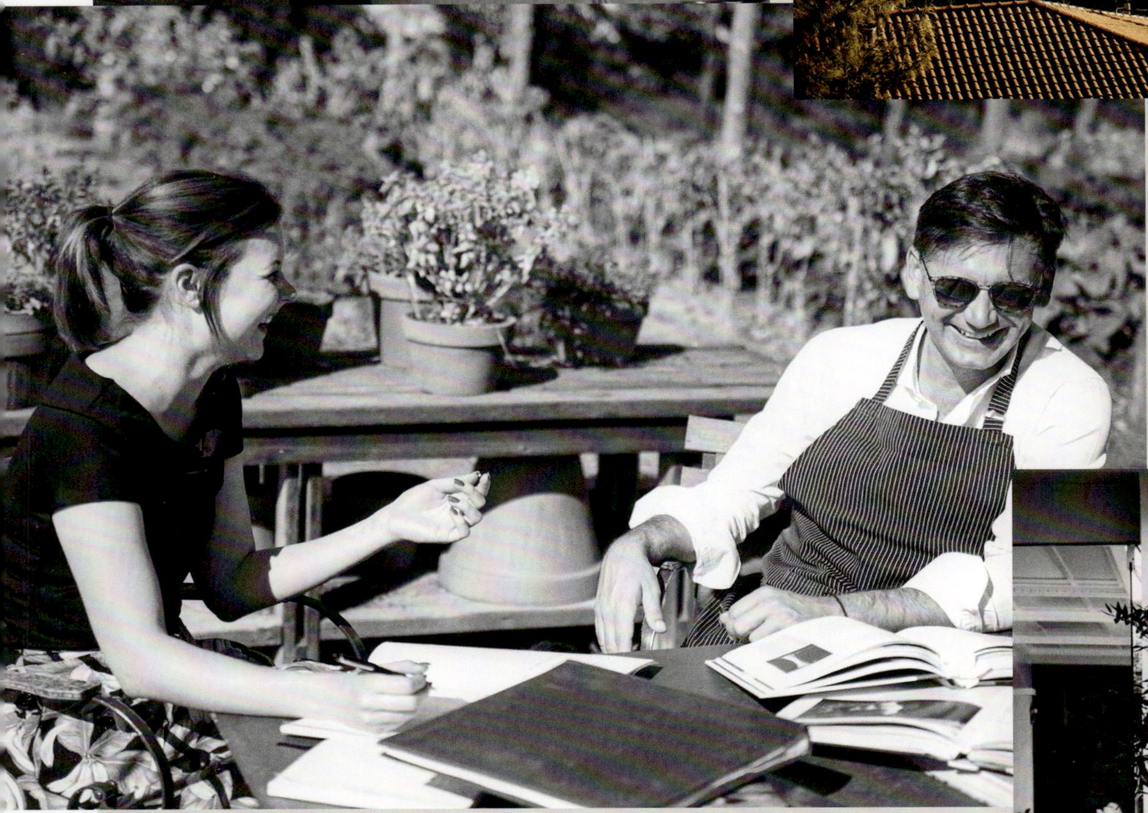
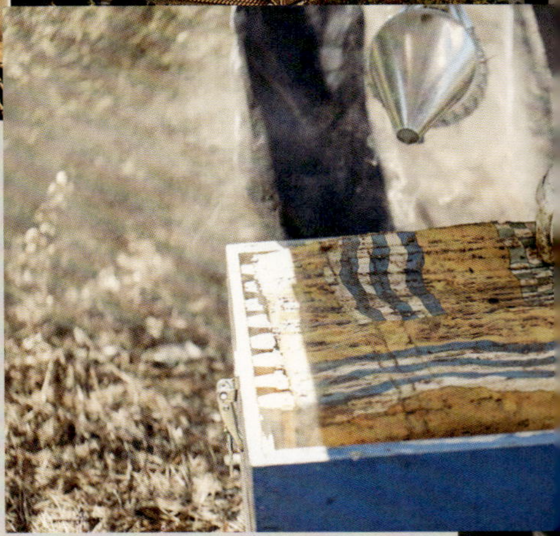
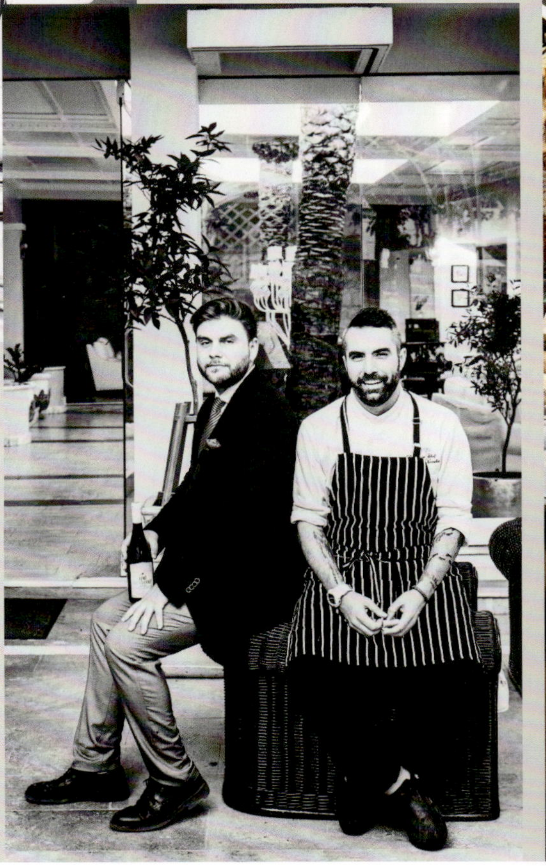
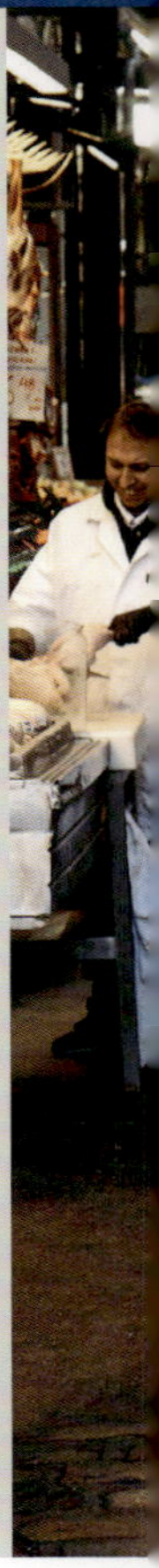
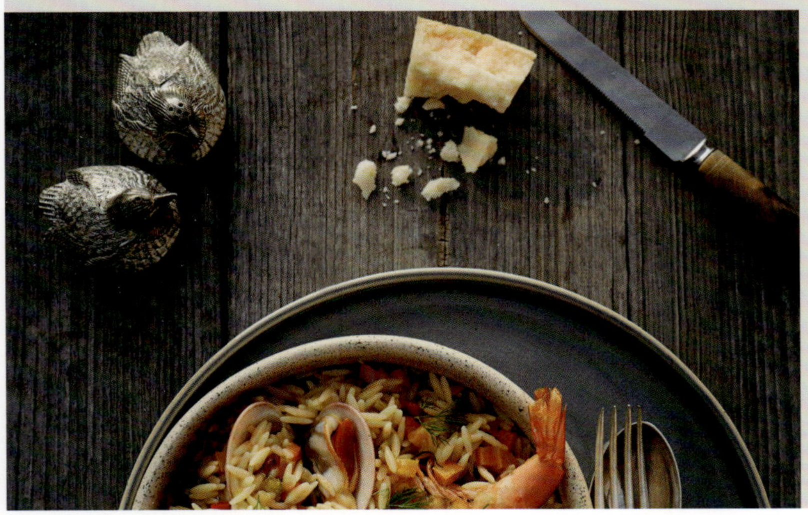

BEHIND THE SCENES

THANK YOU, MY TEAM

I had everything I needed in order to write this cookbook. And what I did not have, I borrowed: I borrowed one person's skilled hands, another's precise fingers and sharp eyes. I borrowed one person's positivity when my mood was low. Sometimes motivation when I lacked my own, or even complete recipes to fill my pages. With it, I got compliments and criticism, moments of laughter and all the help I could ask for before I even had the chance to ask for it. So eventually I had everything I needed in order to write this cookbook. I had you.

THE CREATIVE MINDS BEHIND THE STOVE
Vasilis Mouratidis
Kemal Canturk
Babis – Charalampos Pantazis
Petros Mouratidis
Afroditi Georgiadou
Dimitra Rafail
Antigoni Slamari
Aymeric Bredelle

THE MIXOLOGIST BEHIND THE BAR COUNTER
George Theodosas

THE SOMMELIER BEHIND THE BOTTLES
Apostolos Plahouras

THE EXPERT BEHIND THE CAMERA
Christopher Kennedy

THE CREATIVE BEHIND THE FOOD STYLING
Jayne Cross

THE ARTISTS BEHIND THE DESIGN
Niki Tabaki
Melina Maltsidou

THE WRITER BEHIND THE TEXT
Stella Dubrikow

INDEX

A
Aubergine & Pomegranate Dip 67
Augofetes – Greek Toast 18
Avgolemono Sauce 227

B
Beetroot Dip 68
Behind the Scenes 235
Bohemian Greek Salad 38
Bouyiourdi – Cheese Fondue 85
Breakfast 10–33
Butter 228

C
Calamari with Spinach 173
Celery Soup with Feta Cheese & Oregano 187
Chicken in Yoghurt Marinade 142
Chicken Soup 183
Chicken Tigania 82
Cocktails 210–221
Cod & Vegetable Velouté 184
Crispy Courgette Chips 57
Crispy Deep-fried Calamari 52

D
Desserts 188–209
Dorado with a Duo of Colourful Beetroot Purées 164
Dressing for Clams 99

E
Ekmek 208
Farm Egg 17

F
Fasolada – Classic Bean Soup 180
Fish & Seafood 144–173
Fish in Sea Salt Crust 148

G
Gastronomic Greek Salad 41
Giant Bean Dip 69
Giouvarlakia – Meatball Soup 178
Glyko tou Koutaliou – A Spoonful of Sweetness 205
Goat Cheese Coins with Sweet Tomato Marmalade 48
Goodbye – But This is Not The End 232
Greek Fava Bean Dip 74
Greek Olives in Mandarin Marinade 230
Greek Orzo with Seafood 112
Greek Salads 34–41
Greek Yoghurt with Honey, Nuts & Bee Pollen 14
Grilled Feta Cheese 70

H
Homemade Butter with Greek Yoghurt 229
Homemade Butter with Lemon and Aromatic Herbs 229
Homemade Croutons 226
Homemade Kaimaki & Loukoumi Ice Creams 192

Homemade Kaimaki Ice Cream 194
Homemade Loukoumi Ice Cream 195
Homemade Truffle Butter 229
Honey 30–34

J
Juicy Cherry Tomatoes with Goat Cheese and Fresh Herbs 61
Juicy Onion Wedges with Minced Meat Filling 94

K
Kalimera – Good Morning 12
Keftedes – Meatballs 128
Kleftiko – Savoury Parcels of Lamb & Vegetables 124

L
Ladolemono Sauce 226
Langoustines in Angel Hair with Strawberry Gazpacho 159
Lobster Moussaka 168
Loukoumades – Fluffy Yeast Balls Drizzled with Honey 197

M
Main Courses 116–173
Marble Cake 25
Marinated Anchovies 91
Mastiha 214

Meat 120–143
Metaxa Sour 214
Meze 42–99
Minty Watermelon 213
Mussel Pilaf 96

O
Olive Oil 100–101
One-Pan Sea Bream on a Bed of Mediterranean Vegetables 163
Orange Cake 206
Original Greek Tzatziki 46
Original Thessaloniki Koulouri 22

P
Pasta & Rice 102–115
Pomegranate Liqueur 218
Pork Shoulder with Leek & Celery 138
Pork Shoulder with Vegetables & Rice 134
Prawn Saganaki 156

R
Rack of Lamb 127
Rakomelo – Honey & Spice 220
Red Mullet 167
Red Pepper Paste 54
Rib Eye Steak with Marinated Cherry Tomatoes 140
Rich Chocolate Cake 201

S

Sea Bass with a Crunchy Bread Crust, Summery Tomatoes and Courgette Purée 152

Sea Urchin Salad 88

Skordalia – Aromatic Garlic Dip 230

Smoked Mackerel 58

Smoky Green Peppers 87

Soups 174–187

Spetsofai – Greek Farmer's Stew 50

Spicy Mediterranean Linguini 106

Spicy Scrambled Eggs with Feta Cheese 20

Stuffed Aubergine with Minced Meat and Feta Cheese 62

Stuffed Courgettes with Avgolemono Sauce 137

Stuffed Sardines 92

Stuffed Tomatoes & Peppers 110

T

Taramas – Fish Roe Dip 73

Tender Lamb with Lemon Potatoes 132

The Cockerel Recipe 104

The God of Wine 114–115

The Grapes 115

The Journey from Boat to Plate 144

The Langoustine Linguini 109

The Larder 222–231

The Real Greek 217

Three Dips 66

Tipsy Peaches 198

Traditional Greek Salad 37

Traditional Moussaka 122

Traditional Village Spinach & Cheese Pie 26

Trilogy of Cretan Dakos Toast 77

Trilogy of Cretan Dakos Toast for Fish Lovers 81

Tuna on a Bed of Quinoa & Lentils 154

THE AUTHOR

Kimon Riefenstahl invests as much passion and love into cooking as he invests into his family-owned Luxury Resort in Halkidiki, Northern Greece. There, the guests' culinary well-being is being looked after by a plethora of outstanding and prominent chefs who produce local, international and high-end gourmet delights at the hotel's three restaurants ranking amongst the best in the country. This is usually his chance to drop the cooking tools, switch off the lights in his office and call it a day as a managing director and hobby chef. He gets to pick up his saxophone, drink a chilled glass of wine among friends and lean back, while enjoying the fantastic view of the Mediterranean Sea.
www.danairesort.com

THE PHOTOGRAPHER

The evocative images of Mediterranean cuisine in this book were taken by the renowned London travel and food photographer Christopher Kennedy, whose atmospheric photographs skillfully capture the feeling of life in northern Greece.
www.christopher-kennedy.com

IMPRINT

© 2019 teNeues Media GmbH & Co. KG, Kempen
Photographs © 2019 Christopher Kennedy, except p. 36 centre, p. 234 top left and bottom centre:
© Kimon Riefenstahl. All rights reserved.

Food styling: Jayne Cross
Copy-editing by Julie Brooke
Proofreading by Sylvia Goulding
Design by Niki Tabaki and Melina Maltsidou
Editorial coordination and typesetting by bookwise Medienproduktion GmbH, Munich
Production by Sandra Jansen-Dorn
Color separation by Jens Grundei

ISBN 978-3-96171-201-4
Library of Congress Number: 2019909007

Printed in Slovakia by Polygraf Print

Picture and text rights reserved for all countries.
No part of this publication may be reproduced in any manner whatsoever.

While we strive for utmost precision in every detail, we cannot be held responsible for any inaccuracies, neither for any subsequent loss or damage arising.

Every effort has been made by the publisher to contact holders of copyright to obtain permission to reproduce copyrighted material. However, if any permissions have been inadvertently overlooked, teNeues Publishing Group will be pleased to make the necessary and reasonable arrangements at the first opportunity.

Bibliographic information published by the Deutsche Nationalbibliothek
The Deutsche Nationalbibliothek lists this publication in the Deutsche Nationalbibliografie; detailed bibliographic data are available on the Internet at http://dnb.dnb.de.

Published by teNeues Publishing Group

teNeues Media GmbH & Co. KG
Am Selder 37, 47906 Kempen, Germany
Phone: +49-(0)2152-916-0
Fax: +49-(0)2152-916-111
e-mail: books@teneues.com

Press department: Andrea Rehn
Phone: +49-(0)2152-916-202
e-mail: arehn@teneues.com

teNeues Media GmbH & Co. KG
Munich Office
Pilotystraße 4, 80538 Munich, Germany
Phone: +49-(0)89-443-8889-62
e-mail: bkellner@teneues.com

teNeues Media GmbH & Co. KG
Berlin Office
Mommsenstraße 43, 10629 Berlin, Germany
Phone: +49-(0)152-0851-1064
e-mail: ajasper@teneues.com

teNeues Publishing Company
350 7th Avenue, Suite 301, New York, NY 10001, USA
Phone: +1-212-627-9090
Fax: +1-212-627-9511

teNeues Publishing UK Ltd.
12 Ferndene Road, London SE24 0AQ, UK
Phone: +44-(0)20-3542-8997

teNeues France S.A.R.L.
39, rue des Billets, 18250 Henrichemont, France
Phone: +33-(0)2-4826-9348
Fax: +33-(0)1-7072-3482

www.teneues.com